Pro OpenGL ES for iOS

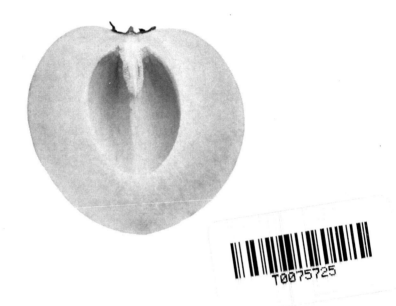

T0075725

Mike Smithwick

Apress®

Pro OpenGL ES for iOS

ISBN-13 (pbk): 978-1-4302-3840-9

ISBN-13 (electronic): 978-1-4302-3841-6

President and Publisher: Paul Manning
Lead Editor: Richard Carey
Technical Reviewer: Leila Muhtasib
Editorial Board: Steve Anglin, Mark Beckner, Ewan Buckingham, Gary Cornell, Morgan Ertel, Jonathan Gennick, Jonathan Hassell, Robert Hutchinson, Michelle Lowman, James Markham, Matthew Moodie, Jeff Olson, Jeffrey Pepper, Douglas Pundick, Ben Renow-Clarke, Dominic Shakeshaft, Gwenan Spearing Matt Wade, Tom Welsh
Coordinating Editor: Corbin Collins
Copy Editor: Kim Wimpsett
Production Support: Patrick Cunningham
Indexer: BIM Indexing & Proofreading Services
Artist: SPI Global
Cover Designer: Anna Ishchenko

Distributed to the book trade worldwide by Springer Science+Business Media New York, 233 Spring Street, 6th Floor, New York, NY 10013. Phone 1-800-SPRINGER, fax (201) 348-4505, e-mail orders-ny@springer-sbm.com, or visit www.springeronline.com.

For information on translations, please e-mail rights@apress.com, or visit www.apress.com.

Apress and friends of ED books may be purchased in bulk for academic, corporate, or promotional use. eBook versions and licenses are also available for most titles. For more information, reference our Special Bulk Sales–eBook Licensing web page at www.apress.com/bulk-sales.

Any source code or other supplementary materials referenced by the author in this text is available to readers at www.apress.com. For detailed information about how to locate your book's source code, go to www.apress.com/source-code.

To a couple of the greatest parents in the world, who always supported me, never flinching at my wacky requests such as sending me back to see an Apollo launch or buying a telescope.

Contents at a Glance

Contents

About the Author

Mike Smithwick's slow descent into programming computers began when he first got a little 3-bit plastic DigiComp 1 computer in 1963 (http://en.wikipedia.org/wiki/Digi-Comp_I). Not too long before that, he got interested in planetariums. Eventually he graduated to programming NASA flight simulator graphics through the 1980s. But what he really wanted to do was become a syndicated cartoonist (really!). Failing to get any syndication deals, he wrote and sold the popular Distant Suns planetarium program for the Commodore Amiga, old-school Mac, and Microsoft Windows while selling himself as a contract programmer on the side, working for Apple, 3DO, Sense-8, and Epyx. Eventually he landed a "real" job at Live365, working on client software Windows and Windows Mobile 6, TiVo, Symbian (ahhh...Symbian...), and iPhone. After 13 short years he decided to go back to the dark side of contracting, writing, and working on Distant Suns for the iPhone after it became modest success in the App Store. Sometimes late at night, he thinks he can hear his Woz-autographed Apple II sobbing for attention from the garage. He may be contacted via www.distantsuns.com, lazyastronomer on AIM, and @distantsuns or @lazyastronomer on Twitter.

About the Technical Reviewer

Leila Muhtasib has been passionate about programming since she wrote her first program on MS-DOS. Since then, she's graduated with a Computer Science degree from the University of Maryland, College Park. Fascinated by mobile technology and its increasing ubiquity, she has been programming iPhone applications since the first SDK was released. She is now a Senior Software Engineer and Tech Lead of a mobile development team at Cisco Systems.

Acknowledgments

Thanks to Corbin Collins and Richard Carey, my long-suffering editors, for putting up with a first-time author, someone who clearly needs to read *Writing iOS Books for Beginners*.

And to Leila Muhtasib, my tech editor, who was every bit as good as I thought she would be.

And to Matthew Moodie and Mark Beckner for approving the schedule slippage so I could add in iOS 5 content, ensuring that the book wasn't obsolete on its release day.

And, of course, to Steve Jobs for never compromising and for producing insanely great tools that make work fun and make fun "funner."

Introduction

In 1985 I brought home a new shiny Commodore Amiga 1000, about one week after they were released. Coming with a whopping 512K of memory, programmable colormaps, a Motorola 68K CPU, and a modern multitasking operating system, it had "awesome" writ all over it. Metaphorically speaking, of course. I thought it might make a good platform for an astronomy program, as I could now control the colors of those star-things instead of having to settle for a lame fixed color palette forced upon me from the likes of Hercules or the C64. So I coded up a 24-line basic routine to draw a random star field, turned out the lights, and thought, "Wow! I bet I could write a cool astronomy program for that thing!" Twenty-six years later I am still working on it (I'll get it right one of these days). Back then my dream device was something I could slip into my pocket, pull out when needed, and aim it as the sky to tell me what stars or constellations I was looking at.

It's called the iPhone.

I thought of it first.

As good as the iPhone is for playing music, making calls, or jumping Doodles, it really shines when you get to the 3D stuff. After all, 3D is all around us—unless you are a pirate and have taken to wearing an eye patch, in which case you'll have very limited depth perception. Arrrggghhh.

Plus 3D apps are fun to show off to people. They'll "get it." In fact, they'll get it much more than, say, that mulch buyer's guide app all the kids are talking about. (Unless they show off their mulch in 3D, but that would be a waste of a perfectly good dimension.)

So, 3D apps are fun to see, fun to interact with, and fun to program. Which brings me to this book. I am by no means a guru in this field. The real gurus are the ones who can knock out a couple of NVIDIA drivers before breakfast, 4-dimensional hypercube simulators by lunch, and port Halo to a TokyoFlash watch before the evening's *Firefly* marathon on SyFy. I can't do that. But I am a decent writer, have enough of a working knowledge of the subject to make me harmless, and know how to spell "3D." So here we are.

First and foremost this book is for experienced iOS programmers who want to at least learn a little of the language of 3D. At least enough to where at the next game programmer's cocktail party you too can laugh at the quaternion jokes with the best of them.

This book covers the basics in both theory of 3D and implementations using the industry standard OpenGL ES toolkit for small devices. While iOS supports both flavors—version 1.x for the easy way, and version 2.x for those who like to get where the nitty-is-gritty—I mainly cover the former, except in the final chapter which serves as an intro to the latter and the use of programmable shaders. And with the release of iOS 5, Apple has offered the 3D community a whole lotta lovin' with some significant additions to the graphics libraries.

Chapter 1 serves as an intro to OpenGL ES alongside the long and tortuous path of the history of computer graphics. Chapter 2 is the math behind basic 3D rendering, whereas Chapters 3 through 8 lead you gently through the various issues all graphics programmers eventually come across, such as how to cast shadows, render multiple OpenGL screens, add lens flare, and so on. Eventually this works its way into a simple (S-I-M-P-L-E!) solar-system model consisting of the sun, earth, and some stars—a traditional 3D exercise. Chapter 9 looks at best practices and development tools, and Chapter 10 serves as a brief overview of OpenGL ES 2 and the use of shaders.

So, have fun, send me some M&Ms, and while you're at it feel free to check out my own app in the Appstore: Distant Suns 3 for both the iPhone and the iPad. Yup, that's the same application that started out on a Commodore Amiga 1000 in 1985 as a 24-line basic program that drew a couple hundred random stars on the screen.

It's bigger now.

Chapter 1

Computer Graphics: From Then to Now

To predict the future and appreciate the present, you must understand the past.

—Probably said by someone sometime

Computer graphics have always been the darling of the software world. Laypeople can appreciate computer graphics more easily than, say, increasing the speed of a sort algorithm by 3 percent or adding automatic tint control to a spreadsheet program. You are likely to hear more people say "Cooooollllll!" at your nicely rendered image of Saturn on your iPad than at a Visual Basic script in Microsoft Word (unless, of course, a Visual Basic script in Microsoft Word can render Saturn, then that really would be cool). The cool factor goes up even more so when said renderings are on a device you can carry around in your back pocket. Let's face it—Steve Jobs has made the life of art directors on science-fiction films very difficult. After all, imagine how hard it must be to design a prop that looks more futuristic than an iPad. (Even before the iPhone was available for sale, the prop department at ABC's *LOST* borrowed some of Apple's screen iconography for use in a two-way radio carried by a helicopter pilot.)

If you are reading this book, chances are you have an iOS-based device or are considering getting one in the near future. If you have one, put it in your hand now and consider what a miracle it is of 21st-century engineering. Millions of man-hours, billions of dollars of research, centuries of overtime, plenty of all-nighters, and an abundance of Jolt-drinking, T-shirt–wearing, comic-book-loving engineers coding into the silence of the night have gone into making that little glass and plastic miracle-box so you could play DoodleJump when *Mythbusters* is in reruns.

Your First OpenGL ES Program

Some software how-to titles will carefully build up the case for their specific topic ("the boring stuff") only to get to the coding and examples ("the fun stuff") by around page 655. Others will jump immediately into some exercises to address your curiosity and save the boring stuff for a little later. This book will be of the latter category.

> **Note**   OpenGL ES is a 3D graphics standard based on the OpenGL library that emerged from the labs of Silicon Graphics in 1992. It is widely used across the industry in everything from pocketable machines running games up to supercomputers running fluid dynamics simulations for NASA (and playing really, really fast games). The ES variety stands for *Embedded Systems*, meaning small, portable, low-power devices. Unless otherwise noted, I'll use OpenGL and OpenGL ES interchangeably.

When developing any apps for iOS, it is customary to let Xcode do the heavy lifting at the beginning of any project via its various wizards. With Xcode (this book uses Xcode 4 as reference), you can easily create an example OpenGL ES project and then add on your own stuff to eventually arrive at something someone might want to buy from the App Store.

With Xcode 4 already running, go to **File ➤ New ➤ New Project**, and you should see something that looks like Figure 1-1.

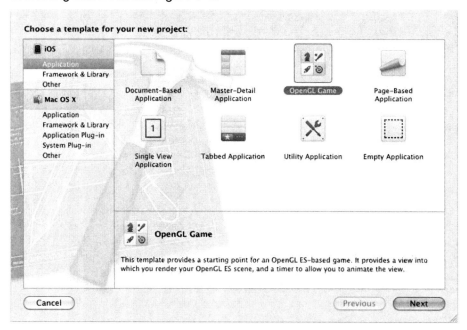

Figure 1-1. Xcode project wizard

Select the *OpenGL Game* template, and fill in the needed project data. It doesn't matter whether it is for the iPhone or iPad.

Now compile and run, making sure you have administrative privileges. If you didn't break anything by undue tinkering, you should see something like Figure 1-2.

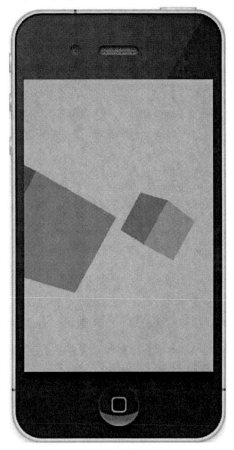

Figure 1-2. *Your first OpenGL ES project. Give yourself a high five.*

The code will be examined later. And don't worry, you'll build stuff fancier than a couple of rotating cubes. The main project will be to construct a simple solar-system simulator based on some of the code used in Distant Suns 3. But for now, it's time to get to the boring stuff: where computer graphics came from and where it is likely to go.

A Spotty History of Computer Graphics

To say that 3D is all the rage today is at best an understatement. Although forms of "3D" imagery go back to more than a century ago, it seems that it has finally come of age. First let's look at what 3D is and what it is not.

3D in Hollywood

In 1982 Disney released *Tron*, the first movie to widely use computer graphics depicting life inside a video game. Although the movie was a critical and financial flop (not unlike the big-budget sequel released in 2011), it would eventually join the ranks of cult favorites right up there with *Showgirls* and *The Rocky Horror Picture Show*. Hollywood had taken the bite out of the apple, and there was no turning back.

Stretching back to the 1800s, what we call "3D" today was more commonly referred to as *stereo vision*. Popular Victorian-era *stereopticons* would be found in many parlors of the day. Consider this technology an early Viewmaster. The user would hold the stereopticon up to their face with a stereo photograph slipped into the far end and see a view of some distant land, but in stereo rather than a flat 2D picture. Each eye would see only one half of the card, which carried two nearly identical photos taken only a couple of inches apart.

Stereovision is what gives us the notion of a depth component to our field of view. Our two eyes deliver two slightly different images to the brain that then interprets them in a way that we understand as depth perception. A single image will not have that effect. Eventually this moved to movies, with a brief and unsuccessful dalliance as far back as 1903 (the short *L'arrivée du Train* is said to have had viewers running from the theater to avoid the train that was clearly heading their way*)* and a resurgence in the early 1950s, with *Bwana Devil* being perhaps the best known.

The original form of 3D movies generally used the "anaglyph" technique that required the viewers to wear cheap plastic glasses with a red filter over one eye and a blue one over the other. Polarizing systems were incorporated in the early 1950s and permitted color movies to be seen in stereo, and they are still very much the same as today. Afraid that television would kill off the movie industry, Hollywood needed some gimmick that was impossible on television in order to keep selling tickets, but because both the cameras and the projectors required were much too impractical and costly, the form fell out of favor, and the movie industry struggled along just fine.

With the advent of digital projection systems in the 1990s and fully rendered films such as *Toy Story*, stereo movies and eventually television finally became both practical and affordable enough to move it beyond the gimmick stage. In particular, full-length animated features (*Toy Story* being the first) made it a no-brainer to convert to stereo. All one needed to do was simply rerender the entire film but from a slightly different viewpoint. This is where stereo and 3D computer graphics merge.

The Dawn of Computer Graphics

One of the fascinating things about the history of computer graphics, and computers in general, is that the technology is still so new that many of the giants still stride among us. It would be tough to track down whoever invented the buggy whip, but I'd know whom to call if you wanted to hear firsthand how to program the Apollo Lunar Module computers from the 1960s.

Computer graphics (frequently referred to as CG) come in three overall flavors: 2D for user interface, 3D in real time for flight or other forms of simulation as well as games, and 3D rendering where quality trumps speed for non-real-time use.

MIT

In 1961, an MIT engineering student named Ivan Sutherland created a system called Sketchpad for his PhD thesis using a vectorscope, a crude light pen, and a custom-made Lincoln TX-2 computer (a spin-off from the TX-2 group would become DEC). Sketchpad's revolutionary graphical user interface demonstrated many of the core principles of modern UI design, not to mention a big helping of object-oriented architecture tossed in for good measure.

> **Note**   For a video of Sketchpad in operation, go to YouTube and search for *Sketchpad* or *Ivan Sutherland*.

A fellow student of Sutherland's, Steve Russell, would invent perhaps one of the biggest time sinks ever made, the computer game. Russell created the legendary game of Spacewar in 1962, which ran on the PDP-1, as shown in Figure 1-3.

Figure 1-3. The 1962 game of Spacewar resurrected at the Computer History Museum in Mountain View, California, on a vintage PDP-1. Photo by Joi Itoh, licensed under the Creative Commons Attribution 2.0 Generic license (http://creativecommons.org/licenses/by/2.0/deed.en).

By 1965, IBM would release what is considered the first widely used commercial graphics terminal, the 2250. Paired with either the low-cost IBM-1130 computer or the IBM S/340, the terminal was meant largely for use in the scientific community.

Perhaps one of the earliest known examples of computer graphics on television was the use of a 2250 on the CBS news coverage of the joint Gemini 6 and Gemini 7 missions in December 1965 (IBM built the Gemini's onboard computer system). The terminal was used to demonstrate several phases of the mission on live television from liftoff to rendezvous. At a cost of about $100,000 in 1965, it was worth the equivalent of a very nice home. See Figure 1-4.

Figure 1-4. *IBM-2250 terminal from 1965. Courtesy NASA.*

University of Utah

Recruited by the University of Utah in 1968 to work in its computer science program, Sutherland naturally concentrated on graphics. Over the course of the next few years, many computer graphics visionaries in training would pass through the university's labs.

Ed Catmull, for example, loved classic animation but was frustrated by his inability to draw—a requirement for artists back in those days as it would appear. Sensing that computers might be a pathway to making movies, Catmull produced the first-ever computer animation, which was of his hand opening and closing. This clip would find its way into the 1976 film *Future World*.

During that time he would pioneer two major computer graphics innovations: texture mapping and bicubic surfaces. The former could be used to add complexity to simple forms by using images of texture instead of having to create texture and roughness using discrete points and surfaces, as shown in Figure 1-5. The latter is used to generate algorithmically curved surfaces that are much more efficient than the traditional polygon meshes.

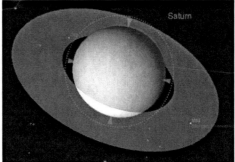

Figure 1-5. Saturn with and without texture

Catmull would eventually find his way to Lucasfilm and, later, Pixar and eventually serve as president of Disney Animation Studios where he could finally make the movies he wanted to see. Not a bad gig.

Many others of the top names in the industry would likewise pass through the gates of University of Utah and the influence of Sutherland:

- John Warnock, who would be instrumental in developing a device-independent means of displaying and printing graphics called PostScript and the Portable Document Format (PDF) and would be cofounder of Adobe.

- Jim Clark, founder of Silicon Graphics (SGI), which would supply Hollywood with some of the best graphics workstations of the day and create the 3D software development framework now known as OpenGL. After SGI, he co-founded Netscape Communications, which would lead us into the land of the World Wide Web.

- Jim Blinn, inventor of both bump mapping, which is an efficient way of adding true 3D texture to objects, and environment mapping, which is used to create really shiny things. Perhaps he would be best known creating the revolutionary animations for NASA's Voyager project, depicting their flybys of the outer planets, as shown in Figure 1-6 (compare that with Figure 1-7 using modern devices). Of Blinn, Sutherland would say, "There are about a dozen great computer graphics people, and Jim Blinn is six of them." Blinn would later lead the effort to create Microsoft's competitor to OpenGL, namely, Direct3D.

  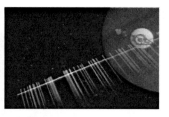

Figure 1-6. *Jim Blinn's depiction of Voyager II's encounter with Saturn in August of 1981. Notice the streaks formed of icy particles while crossing the ring plane. Courtesy NASA.*

Figure 1-7. *Compare Figure 1-6, using some of the best graphics computers and software at the time, with a similar view of Saturn from Distant Suns 3 running on a $500 iPad.*

Coming of Age in Hollywood

Computer graphics would really start to come into their own in the 1980s thanks both to Hollywood and to machines that were increasingly powerful while at the same time costing less. For example, the beloved Commodore Amiga that was introduced in 1985 cost less than $2,000, and it brought to the consumer market an advanced multitasking operating system and color graphics that had been previously the domain of workstations costing upwards of $100,000. See Figure 1-8.

Figure 1-8. *Amiga 1000, circa 1985. Photo by Kaivv, licensed under the Creative Commons Attribution 2.0 Generic license (*`http://creativecommons.org/licenses/by/2.0/deed.en`*).*

Compare this to the original black-and-white Mac that was released a scant 18 months earlier for about the same cost. Coming with a very primitive OS, flat file system, and 1-bit display, it was fertile territory for the "religious wars" that broke out between the various camps as to whose machine was better (wars that would also include the Atari ST).

> **Note**   One of the special graphics modes on the original Amiga could compress 4,096 colors into a system that would normally max out at 32. Called Hold and Modify (HAM mode), it was originally included on one of the main chips for experimental reasons by designer Jay Miner. Although he wanted to remove the admitted kludge that produced images with a lot of color distortion, the results would have left a big empty spot on the chip. Considering that unused chip landscape was something no self-respecting engineer could tolerate, he left it in, and to Miner's great surprise, people started using it.

A company in Kansas called NewTek pioneered the use of Amigas for rendering high-quality 3D graphics when coupled with its special hardware named the Video Toaster. Combined with a sophisticated 3D rendering software package called Lightwave 3D, NewTek opened up the realm of cheap, network-quality graphics to anyone who had a few thousand dollars to spend. This development opened the doors for elaborate science-fiction shows such as *Babylon 5* or *Seaquest* to be financially feasible considering their extensive special effects needs.

During the 1980s, many more techniques and innovations would work their way into common use in the CG community:

▓ Loren Carpenter developed a technique to generate highly detailed landscapes algorithmically using something called *fractals*. Carpenter was hired by Lucasfilm to create a rendering package for a new company named Pixar. The result was REYES, which stood for Render Everything You Ever Saw.

▓ Turner Whitted developed a technique called *ray tracing* that could produce highly realistic scenes (at a significant CPU cost), particularly when they included objects with various reflective and refractive properties. Glass items were common subjects in various early ray-tracing efforts, as shown in Figure 1-9.

▓ Frank Crow developed the first practical method of *anti-aliasing* in computer graphics. Aliasing is the phenomenon that generates jagged edges because of the relatively poor resolution of the display. Crow's method would smooth out everything from lines to text, producing far more natural and pleasing imagery. Note that one of Lucasfilm's early games was called *Rescue on Fractalus*. The bad guys were named *jaggies* (another term for anti-aliasing).

▓ *Star Trek II: The Wrath of Khan* brought with it the first entirely computer-generated sequence used to illustrate how a device called the Genesis Machine could generate life on a lifeless planet. That one simulation was called "the effect that wouldn't die" because of its groundbreaking techniques in flame and particle animation, along with the use of fractal landscapes.

Figure 1-9. *Sophisticated images such as this are within the range of hobbyists with programs such as the open source POV-Ray. Photo by Gilles Tran, 2006.*

The 1990s brought the T1000 "liquid metal" terminator in *Terminator 2: Judgment Day*, the first completely computer-generated full-length feature film of *Toy Story*, believable animated dinosaurs in *Jurassic Park*, and James Cameron's *Titanic*, all of which helped solidified CG as a common tool in the Hollywood director's arsenal.

By the decade's end, it would be hard to find any films that didn't have computer graphics as part of the production in either actual effects or in postproduction to help clean up various scenes. New techniques are still being developed and applied in ever more spectacular fashion, as in Disney's delightful *Up!* or James Cameron's beautiful *Avatar*.

Now, once again, take out your i-device and realize what a little technological marvel it is. Feel free to say "wow" in hushed, respectful tones.

Toolkits

All of the 3D wizardry referenced earlier would never have been possible without software. Many CG software programs are highly specialized, and others are more general purpose, such as OpenGL ES, the focus of this book. So, what follows are a few of the many toolkits available.

OpenGL

Open Graphics Library (OpenGL) came out of the pioneering efforts of SGI, the maker of high-end graphics workstations and mainframes. Its own proprietary graphics framework, IRIS-GL, had grown into a de-facto standard across the industry. To keep customers as competition increased, SGI opted to turn IRIS-GL into an open framework so as to strengthen their reputation as the industry leader. IRIS-GL was stripped of non-graphics-related functions and hardware-dependent features, renamed OpenGL, and released in early 1992. As of this writing, version 4.1 is the most current one available.

As small handheld devices became more common, OpenGL for Embedded Systems (OpenGL ES) was developed, which was a stripped-down version of the desktop version. It removed many of the more redundant API calls while simplifying other elements. making it run efficiently on lower-power CPUs. As a result, it has been widely adopted across many platforms, such as Android, iOS, Nintendo 3DS, and BlackBerry (OS 5.0 and newer).

There are two main flavors of OpenGL ES, 1.*x* and 2.*x*. Many devices support both. 1.*x* is the higher-level variant, based on the original OpenGL specification. Version 2.*x* (yes, I know it's confusing) is targeted toward more specialized rendering chores that can be handled by programmable graphics hardware.

Direct3D

Direct3D (D3D) is Microsoft's answer to OpenGL and is heavily oriented toward game developers. In 1995, Microsoft bought a small company called RenderMorphics that specialized in creating a 3D framework named RealityLab for writing games. RealityLab was turned into Direct3D and first released in the summer of 1996. Even though it was proprietary to Windows-based systems, it has a huge user base across all of Microsoft's platforms: Windows, Windows 7 Mobile, and even Xbox. There are constant ongoing debates between the OpenGL and Direct3D camps as to which is more powerful, flexible, and easier to use. Other factors include how quickly hardware manufacturers can update their drivers to support new features, ease of understanding (Direct3D uses Microsoft's COM interface that can be very confusing for newcomers), stability, and industry support.

The Other Guys

While OpenGL and Direct3D remain at the top of the heap when it comes to both adoption and features, the graphics landscape is littered with numerous other frameworks, many which are supported on today's devices.

In the computer graphics world, graphics libraries come in two very broad flavors: low-level rendering mechanisms represented by OpenGL and Direct3D and high-level systems typically found in game engines that concentrate on resource management with special extras that extend to common gameplay elements (sound, networking, scoring, and so on). The latter are usually built on top of one of the former for the 3D portion. And if done well, the higher-level systems might even be abstracted enough to make it possible to work with both GL and D3D.

QuickDraw 3D

An example of a higher-level general-purpose library is QuickDraw 3D (QD3D). A 3D sibling to Apple's 2D QuickDraw (used in pre-OS-X days), QD3D had an elegant means of generating and linking objects in an easy-to-understand hierarchical fashion (*a scene-graph*). It likewise had its own file format for loading 3D models and a standard viewer and was platform independent. The higher-level part of QD3D would calculate the scene and determine how each object and, in turn, each piece of each object would be shown on a 2D drawing surface. Underneath QD3D there was a very thin layer called RAVE that would handle device-specific rendering of these bits.

Users could go with the standard version of RAVE, which would render the scene as expected. But more ambitious users could write their own that would display the scene in a more artistic fashion. For example, one company generated the RAVE output so as to look like their objects were hand-painted on the side of a cave. It was very cool when you could take this modern version of a cave drawing and spin it around. The plug-in architecture also made QD3D highly portable to other machines. When potential users balked at using QD3D since it had no hardware solution on PCs, a version of RAVE was produced that would use the hardware acceleration available for Direct3D by actually using its competitor as its rasterizer. Sadly, QD3D was almost immediately killed on the second coming of Steve Jobs, who determined that OpenGL should be the 3D standard for Macs in the future. This was an odd statement because QD3D was not a competitor to the other but an add-on that made the lives of programmers much easier. After Jobs refused requests to make QD3D open source, the Quesa project was formed to re-create as much as possible the original library, which is still being supported at the time of this writing. And to nobody's surprise, Quesa uses OpenGL as its rendering engine.

A disclaimer here: I wrote the RAVE/Direct3D layer of QD3D only to have the project canceled a few days after going "gold master" (ready to ship).

OGRE

Another scene-graph system is Object-oriented Rendering Engine (OGRE). First released in 2005, OGRE can use both OpenGL and Direct3D as the low-level rasterizing solution, while offering users a stable and free toolkit used in many commercial products. The size of the user community is impressive. A quick peek at the forums shows more than 6,500 topics in the General Discussion section alone at the time of this writing.

OpenSceneGraph

Recently released for iOS devices, OpenSceneGraph does roughly what QuickDraw 3D did, by providing a means of creating your objects on a higher level, linking them together, and performing scene management duties and extra effects above the OpenGL layer. Other features include importing multiple file formats, text support, particle effects (used for sparks, flames, or clouds), and the ability to display video content in your 3D applications. Knowledge of OpenGL is highly recommended, because many of the OSG functions are merely thin wrappers to their OpenGL counterparts.

Unity3D

Unlike OGRE, QD3D, or OpenSceneGraph, Unity3D is a full-fledged game engine. The difference lies in the scope of the product. Whereas the first two concentrated on creating a more abstract wrapper around OpenGL, game engines go several steps further, supplying most if not all of the other supporting functionality that games would typically need such as sound, scripting, networked extensions, physics, user interface, and score-keeping modules. In addition, a good engine will likely have tools to help generate the assets and be platform independent.

Unity3D has all of these so would be overkill for many smaller projects. Also, being a commercial product, the source is not available, and it is not free to use, costing a modest amount (compared to other products in the past that could charge $100,000 or more).

And Still Others

Let's not ignore A6, Adventure Game Studio, C4, Cinder, Cocos3d, Crystal Space, VTK, Coin3D, SDL, QT, Delta3D, Glint3D, Esenthel, FlatRedBall, Horde3D, Irrlicht,

Leadwerks3D, Lightfeather, Raydium, Panda3D (from Disney Studios and CMU), Torque (available for iOS), and many others. Although they're powerful, one drawback of using game engines is that more often than not, your world is executed in their environment. So if you need a specific subtle behavior that is unavailable, you may be out of luck. That brings me back to the topic of this book.

Back to the Waltz of the Two Cubes

Up through iOS4, Apple saw OpenGL as more of a general-purpose framework. But starting with iOS5, they wanted to emphasize it as a perfect environment for game development. That is why, for example, the project icon in the wizard is titled "OpenGL Game," where previously it was "OpenGL ES Application." That also explains why the example exercise pushes the better performing—but considerably more cumbersome—OpenGL ES 2 environment, while ignoring the easier version that is the subject of this book.

> **Note**   Also starting with iOS5, Apple has added a number of special helper-objects in their new GLKit framework that take over some of the common duties developers had to do themselves early on. These tasks include image loading, 3D-oriented math operations, creating a special OpenGL view, and managing special effects.

With that in mind, I'll step into 2.0-land every once in a while, such as via the example app described below, because that's all we have for now. Detailed discussions of 2.0 will be reserved for the last chapter, because it really is a fairly advanced topic for the scope of this book.

A Closer Look

The wizard produces six main files not including those of the plist and storyboards. Of these, there are the two for the view controller, two for the application delegate, and two mysterious looking things called shader.fsh and shader.vsh.

The shader files are unique to OpenGL ES 2.0 and are used to fine-tune the look of your scenes. They serve as small and very fast programs that execute on the graphics card itself, using their own unique language that resembles C. They give you the power to specify exactly how light and texture should show up in the final image. Unfortunately, OpenGL ES 2.0 requires shaders and hence a somewhat steeper learning curve, while the easier and more heavily used version 1.1 doesn't use shaders, settling for a few standard lighting and shading effects (called a "fixed function" pipeline). The shader-based applications are most likely going to be games where a visually rich experience is as important as anything else, while the easier 1.1 framework is just right for simple games, business graphics, educational titles, or any other apps that don't need to have perfect atmospheric modeling.

The application delegate has no active code in it, so we can ignore it. The real action takes place in the viewController via three main sections. The first initializes things using some of the standard view controller methods we all know and love, the second serves to render and animate the image, and the third section manages these shader things. Don't worry if you don't get it completely, because this example is merely intended to give you a general overview of what a basic OpenGL ES program looks like.

> **Note** All of these exercises are available on the Apress site, including additional bonus exercises that may not be in the book.

You will notice that throughout all of the listings, various parts of the code are marked with a numbered comment. The numbers correspond to the descriptions following the listing and that highlight various parts of the code.

Listing 1-1. *The initialization of the wizard-generated view controller.*

```
#import "TwoCubesViewController.h"

#define BUFFER_OFFSET(i) ((char *)NULL + (i))

// Uniform index.
Enum                                                            //1
{
    UNIFORM_MODELVIEWPROJECTION_MATRIX,
    UNIFORM_NORMAL_MATRIX,
    NUM_UNIFORMS
};
GLint uniforms[NUM_UNIFORMS];

// Attribute index.
enum
{
    ATTRIB_VERTEX,
    ATTRIB_NORMAL,
    NUM_ATTRIBUTES
};

GLfloat gCubeVertexData[216] =                                  //2
{
    // Data layout for each line below is:
    // positionX, positionY, positionZ,     normalX, normalY, normalZ,
    0.5f, -0.5f, -0.5f,         1.0f, 0.0f, 0.0f,
    0.5f, 0.5f, -0.5f,          1.0f, 0.0f, 0.0f,
    0.5f, -0.5f, 0.5f,          1.0f, 0.0f, 0.0f,
    0.5f, -0.5f, 0.5f,          1.0f, 0.0f, 0.0f,
    0.5f, 0.5f, 0.5f,           1.0f, 0.0f, 0.0f,
    0.5f, 0.5f, -0.5f,          1.0f, 0.0f, 0.0f,

    0.5f, 0.5f, -0.5f,          0.0f, 1.0f, 0.0f,
    -0.5f, 0.5f, -0.5f,         0.0f, 1.0f, 0.0f,
    0.5f, 0.5f, 0.5f,           0.0f, 1.0f, 0.0f,
    0.5f, 0.5f, 0.5f,           0.0f, 1.0f, 0.0f,
```

```
        -0.5f, 0.5f, -0.5f,        0.0f, 1.0f, 0.0f,
        -0.5f, 0.5f, 0.5f,         0.0f, 1.0f, 0.0f,

        -0.5f, 0.5f, -0.5f,        -1.0f, 0.0f, 0.0f,
        -0.5f, -0.5f, -0.5f,       -1.0f, 0.0f, 0.0f,
        -0.5f, 0.5f, 0.5f,         -1.0f, 0.0f, 0.0f,
        -0.5f, 0.5f, 0.5f,         -1.0f, 0.0f, 0.0f,
        -0.5f, -0.5f, -0.5f,       -1.0f, 0.0f, 0.0f,
        -0.5f, -0.5f, 0.5f,        -1.0f, 0.0f, 0.0f,

        -0.5f, -0.5f, -0.5f,       0.0f, -1.0f, 0.0f,
        0.5f, -0.5f, -0.5f,        0.0f, -1.0f, 0.0f,
        -0.5f, -0.5f, 0.5f,        0.0f, -1.0f, 0.0f,
        -0.5f, -0.5f, 0.5f,        0.0f, -1.0f, 0.0f,
        0.5f, -0.5f, -0.5f,        0.0f, -1.0f, 0.0f,
        0.5f, -0.5f, 0.5f,         0.0f, -1.0f, 0.0f,

        0.5f, 0.5f, 0.5f,          0.0f, 0.0f, 1.0f,
        -0.5f, 0.5f, 0.5f,         0.0f, 0.0f, 1.0f,
        0.5f, -0.5f, 0.5f,         0.0f, 0.0f, 1.0f,
        0.5f, -0.5f, 0.5f,         0.0f, 0.0f, 1.0f,
        -0.5f, 0.5f, 0.5f,         0.0f, 0.0f, 1.0f,
        -0.5f, -0.5f, 0.5f,        0.0f, 0.0f, 1.0f,

        0.5f, -0.5f, -0.5f,        0.0f, 0.0f, -1.0f,
        -0.5f, -0.5f, -0.5f,       0.0f, 0.0f, -1.0f,
        0.5f, 0.5f, -0.5f,         0.0f, 0.0f, -1.0f,
        0.5f, 0.5f, -0.5f,         0.0f, 0.0f, -1.0f,
        -0.5f, -0.5f, -0.5f,       0.0f, 0.0f, -1.0f,
        -0.5f, 0.5f, -0.5f,        0.0f, 0.0f, -1.0f
};

@interface TwoCubesViewController () {
    GLuint _program;

    GLKMatrix4 _modelViewProjectionMatrix;            //3
    GLKMatrix3 _normalMatrix;
    float _rotation;

    GLuint _vertexArray;
    GLuint _vertexBuffer;
}
@property (strong, nonatomic) EAGLContext *context;
@property (strong, nonatomic) GLKBaseEffect *effect;

- (void)setupGL;
- (void)tearDownGL;

- (BOOL)loadShaders;
- (BOOL)compileShader:(GLuint *)shader type:(GLenum)type file:(NSString *)file;
- (BOOL)linkProgram:(GLuint)prog;
- (BOOL)validateProgram:(GLuint)prog;
@end
```

```objc
@implementation TwoCubesViewController

@synthesize context = _context;
@synthesize effect = _effect;

- (void)viewDidLoad
{
    [super viewDidLoad];

    self.context = [[EAGLContext alloc] initWithAPI:kEAGLRenderingAPIOpenGLES2];    //4

    if (!self.context) {
        NSLog(@"Failed to create ES context");
    }

    GLKView *view = (GLKView *)self.view;                                           //5
    view.context = self.context;
    view.drawableDepthFormat = GLKViewDrawableDepthFormat24;                        //6

    [self setupGL];
}

- (void)viewDidUnload
{
    [super viewDidUnload];

    [self tearDownGL];

    if ([EAGLContext currentContext] == self.context) {
        [EAGLContext setCurrentContext:nil];
    }
        self.context = nil;
}

- (void)didReceiveMemoryWarning
{
    [super didReceiveMemoryWarning];
    // Release any cached data, images, etc. that aren't in use.
}

-
(BOOL)shouldAutorotateToInterfaceOrientation:(UIInterfaceOrientation)interfaceOrientatio
n
{
    // Return YES for supported orientations.
    if ([[UIDevice currentDevice] userInterfaceIdiom] == UIUserInterfaceIdiomPhone) {
        return (interfaceOrientation != UIInterfaceOrientationPortraitUpsideDown);
    } else {
        return YES;
    }
}
```

```
- (void)setupGL
{
    [EAGLContext setCurrentContext:self.context];                    //7

    [self loadShaders];

    self.effect = [[GLKBaseEffect alloc] init];                      //8
    self.effect.light0.enabled = GL_TRUE;                            //9
    self.effect.light0.diffuseColor = GLKVector4Make(1.0f, 0.4f, 0.4f, 1.0f);  //10

    glEnable(GL_DEPTH_TEST);                                         //11

    glGenVertexArraysOES(1, &_vertexArray);                         //12
    glBindVertexArrayOES(_vertexArray);

    glGenBuffers(1, &_vertexBuffer);                                //13
    glBindBuffer(GL_ARRAY_BUFFER, _vertexBuffer);
    glBufferData(GL_ARRAY_BUFFER,
sizeof(gCubeVertexData), gCubeVertexData, GL_STATIC_DRAW); //14

    glEnableVertexAttribArray(GLKVertexAttribPosition);             //15
    glVertexAttribPointer(GLKVertexAttribPosition, 3, GL_FLOAT, GL_FALSE, 24,
BUFFER_OFFSET(0));
    glEnableVertexAttribArray(GLKVertexAttribNormal);
    glVertexAttribPointer(GLKVertexAttribNormal, 3, GL_FLOAT, GL_FALSE, 24,
BUFFER_OFFSET(12));

    glBindVertexArrayOES(0);                                        //16
}

- (void)tearDownGL                                                  //17
{
    [EAGLContext setCurrentContext:self.context];

    glDeleteBuffers(1, &_vertexBuffer);
    glDeleteVertexArraysOES(1, &_vertexArray);

    self.effect = nil;

    if (_program) {
        glDeleteProgram(_program);
        _program = 0;
    }
}
```

So, what is happening here?

- In lines 1ff (the *ff* means "and the lines following"), some funky-looking enums are defined. These hold "locations" of various parameters in the shader code. We'll get to this later in the book.

- Lines 2ff actually define the data used to describe the two cubes. You will rarely have to define anything in code like this. Usually, primitive shapes (spheres, cubes, and cones, for example) are generated on the fly, while more complicated objects are loaded in from a file generated by a 3D authoring tool.

  Both cubes actually use the same dataset but just operate on it in a slightly different fashion. There are six sections of data, one for each face, with each line defining a vertex or corner of the face. The first three numbers are the x, y and z values in space, and the second three have the normal of the face (the normal being a line that specifies the direction the face is aiming and that is used to calculate how the face is illuminated). If the normal is facing a light source, it will be lit; if away, it would be in shadow.

  You will notice that the cube's vertices are either 0.5 or -0.5. There is nothing magical about this, merely defining the cube's size as being 1.0 unit on a side.

  The faces are actually made up of two triangles. The big-brother of OpenGL ES can render four-sided faces, but not this version, which can do only three sides. So we have to fake it. That is why there are six vertices defined here: three for each triangle. Notice that two of the points are repeated. That is not really necessary, because only four unique vertices will do just fine.

- Lines 3ff specify the *matrices* that are used to rotate and translate (move) our objects. In this use, a matrix is a compact form of trigonometric expressions that describe various transformations for each object and how their geometry in 3 dimensions is eventually mapped to a two-dimensional surface of our screens. In OpenGL ES 1.1, we rarely have to refer to the actual matrices directly because the system keeps them hidden from us, while under 2.0, we see all of the inner workings of the system and must handle the various transformations ourselves. And it is not a pretty sight at times.

- Line 4 allocates an OpenGL context. This is used to keep track of all of our specific states, commands, and resources needed to actually render something on the screen. This line actually allocates a context for OpenGL ES 2, as specified via the parameter passed via initWithAPI. Most of the time we'll be using *kEAGLRenderingAPIOpenGLES1*.

▓ In line 5, we grab the view object of this controller. What makes this different is the use of a GLKView object, as opposed to the more common UIView that you are probably familiar with. New to iOS5, the GLKView takes the place of the much messier EAGLView. With the former, it takes only a couple of lines of code to create a GLKView and specify various properties, whereas in those dark and unforgiving days before iOS5, it could take dozens of lines of code to do only basic stuff. Besides making things easier to set up, the GLKView also handles the duties of calling your update and refresh routines and adds a handy snapshot feature to get screen grabs of your scene.

▓ Line 6 states that we want our view to support full 24-bit colors.

▓ Line 7 features the first 2.0-only call. As mentioned above, shaders are little C-like programs designed to execute on the graphics hardware. They exist in either a separate file, as in this exercise, or as some people prefer, embedded in text strings in the main body of the code.

▓ Line 8 illustrates another new feature in the GLKit: effect objects. The effect objects are designed to hold some date and presentation information, such as lighting, materials, images, and geometry that are needed to create a special effect. On iOS5's initial release, only two effects were available, one to do reflections in objects and the other to provide full panoramic images: Both are commonly used in graphics, so they are welcomed by developers who would otherwise have to code their own. I expect libraries of effects to eventually become available, both from Apple and from third parties.

In this case, the example is using the "base effect" to render one of the two cubes. You'd likely never use an effect class to draw just basic geometry like this, but it demonstrates how the effect encapsulates a miniature version of OpenGL ES 1.1. That is, it has a lot of the missing functionality, mainly in lights and materials, that you'd otherwise have to reimplement when porting 1.1 code over to 2.0.

▓ Also a part of the setup of the effect, line 9 shows us how to turn on the lights, followed by line 10, which actually specifies the color of the light by using a four-component vector. The fields are ordered as red, green, blue, and alpha. The colors are normalized between 0 and 1, so here red is the main color, with green and blue both at only 40%. If you guessed this is the color of the reddish cube, you'd be right. The fourth component is alpha, which is used to specify transparency, with 1.0 being completely opaque.

- Depth-testing is another important part of 3D worlds. It is used in line 11, in what is otherwise a very nasty topic, for occluding or blocking stuff that is hidden behind other stuff. What depth-testing does is to render each object on your screen with a depth component. Called a z-buffer, this lets the system know, as it renders an object, whether something is in front of that object. If so, the object (or pieces of it) is not rendered. In earlier days, z-buffering was so slow and took up so much extra memory that it was invoked only when absolutely necessary, but nowadays there is rarely any reason not to use it, except for some special rendering effects.

- Lines 12f (the single *f* meaning "the line following") sets the system up for something called Vertex Array Objects (VAOs). VAOs enable you to cache your models and their attributes in the GPU itself, cutting down a lot of overhead otherwise incurred by copying the data across the bus for each frame. Up until iOS4, VAOs were available only on OpenGL ES 2 implementations, but now both versions can use them.

  Seen here, we first get a "name" (actually just a unique handle) used to identify our array of data to the system. Afterwards, we take that and "bind" it, which merely makes it the currently available array for any calls that need one. It can be unbound, either by binding a new array handle or by using 0. This process of naming and binding objects is a common one used across all of OpenGL.

- In lines 13ff, the same process is repeated, but this time on a vertex buffer. The difference is that a vertex buffer is the actual data, and in this case, it points to the statically defined data for the cube at the very top of this file.

- Line 14 supplies the cube's data to the system now, specifying both the size and the location of the data, which is then sent up to the graphics subsystem.

- Remember how both the 3D xyz coordinates of each corner were embedded with the normals of the faces (the things that say where a face is pointing)? You can actually embed almost any data in these arrays, as long as the data format doesn't change. Lines 15f tell the system which data is which. The first line says that we're using `GLKVertexAttribPosition` data made up of three floating point values (the x, y, and z components), offset by 0 bytes from the start of the data supplied in line 14, and a total of 24 bytes long for each structure. That means when it comes time to draw this cube, it will grab three numbers from the very start of the buffer, jump 24 bytes, grab the next three, and so on.

  The normals are treated almost identical, except they are called *GLKVertexAttribNormal*, and start at an offset of 12 bytes, or immediately after the xyz data.

- Line 16 "closes" the vertex array object. Now, whenever we want to draw one of these cubes, we can just bind this specific VAO and give a draw command without having to supply the format and offset information again.

- Finally, in line 17, the buffers are deleted.

If your head hurts, it's understandable. This is a lot of fussing around to draw a couple of cubes. But a visual world is a rich one, and needs a lot of stuff to define it. And we're far from done yet. But the principles remain the same.

Showing the Scene

In Listing 1-2, we can now actually draw the data to the screen and see some pretty pictures. This uses two different approaches to display things. The first hides everything under the new GLKit available from iOS5 and beyond. It hides all of the shaders and other stuff that OpenGL ES 2 normally exposes, and does so under the new GLKBaseEffect class. The second way is just straight 2.0 stuff. Together, the both of them show how the two different approaches can be part of the same rendering loop. But remember, using the effects classes to render a simple cube is overkill, sort of like hopping in the car to drive 6 feet to the mailbox.

> **Note**   Apple has pitched the use of GLKBaseEffect as a means to get 1.1 users to port their
> code to 2.0, because it has lights, materials, and other features that 2.0 doesn't have. But it
> really doesn't work well for a simple migration because it has far too many limitations to host
> the entire 1.1 environment of most OpenGL apps.

Listing 1-2. Rendering the scene to the display.

```
- (void)update                                                              //1
{
                                                                            //2
    float aspect = fabsf(self.view.bounds.size.width / self.view.bounds.size.height);
    GLKMatrix4 projectionMatrix =
GLKMatrix4MakePerspective(GLKMathDegreesToRadians(65.0f), aspect, 0.1f, 100.0f);

    self.effect.transform.projectionMatrix = projectionMatrix;              //3


    GLKMatrix4 baseModelViewMatrix =                                        //4
                GLKMatrix4MakeTranslation(0.0f, 0.0f, -4.0f);
    baseModelViewMatrix =                                                   //5
                GLKMatrix4Rotate(baseModelViewMatrix, _rotation, 0.0f, 1.0f, 0.0f);

    // Compute the model view matrix for the object rendered with GLKit.
```

```
    GLKMatrix4 modelViewMatrix =                                       //6
                GLKMatrix4MakeTranslation(0.0f, 0.0f, -1.5f);

    modelViewMatrix =                                                  //7
                GLKMatrix4Rotate(modelViewMatrix, _rotation, 1.0f, 1.0f, 1.0f);

    modelViewMatrix =                                                  //8
                GLKMatrix4Multiply(baseModelViewMatrix, modelViewMatrix);

    self.effect.transform.modelviewMatrix = modelViewMatrix;           //9

    // Compute the model view matrix for the object rendered with ES2.

    modelViewMatrix =
                GLKMatrix4MakeTranslation(0.0f, 0.0f, 1.5f);           //10
    modelViewMatrix =
                GLKMatrix4Rotate(modelViewMatrix, _rotation, 1.0f, 1.0f, 1.0f);
    modelViewMatrix =
                GLKMatrix4Multiply(baseModelViewMatrix, modelViewMatrix);

    _normalMatrix =                                                    //11
                GLKMatrix3InvertAndTranspose(GLKMatrix4GetMatrix3(modelViewMatrix),
NULL);

                                                                       //12
    _modelViewProjectionMatrix = GLKMatrix4Multiply(projectionMatrix, modelViewMatrix);

    _rotation += self.timeSinceLastUpdate * 0.5f;                      //13
}

- (void)glkView:(GLKView *)view drawInRect:(CGRect)rect
{
    glClearColor(0.65f, 0.65f, 0.65f, 1.0f);                           //14
    glClear(GL_COLOR_BUFFER_BIT | GL_DEPTH_BUFFER_BIT);

    glBindVertexArrayOES(_vertexArray);                                //15

    // Render the object with GLKit.

    [self.effect prepareToDraw];                                       //16

    glDrawArrays(GL_TRIANGLES, 0, 36);                                 //17

    // Render the object again with ES2.

    glUseProgram(_program);                                            //18

    glUniformMatrix4fv(uniforms[UNIFORM_MODELVIEWPROJECTION_MATRIX], 1, 0,
_modelViewProjectionMatrix.m);
    glUniformMatrix3fv(uniforms[UNIFORM_NORMAL_MATRIX], 1, 0, _normalMatrix.m);

    glDrawArrays(GL_TRIANGLES, 0, 36);                                 //19
}
```

Let's take a look at what's going on here:

- Line 1, the start of the update method, is actually one of the delegate calls from the new GLKViewController object. This supports frame-rate hints, as in, "I'd love to have my new game Dangerous Poodles update at 100 fps, if you can do so please." It will also let you know what its real frame rate is, the number of frames since starting the session, and it handles pause and resume functions.

- In line 2, besides defining the objects to show, we need to define the *viewing frustum.* This simply specifies how big of a swath of area you want to see in your world. Think of it as a camera's zoom lens, where you can zoom in or out. This then gets converted into a projection-matrix, similar to a transformation matrix that we saw earlier. This encapsulates the information to project your object up against you device's display.

  Note that the first value supplied to GLKMatrix4MakePerspective is 65, meaning that we want our "lens" to have a 65 degree field-of-view.

  This is generated using one of the many new math library calls that also form a part of the GLKit. The calls include support for vectors, matrices, and quaternions (covered later), exclusively for 3D scene manipulation.

- The GLKBaseEffect used to contain one of the cubes needs to be told to use this matrix in line 3.

- Line 4 generates a *translation* matrix. This describes how to move, or translate, your object through space. In this case, the -4 value moves it away from our eyepoint by 4 units. By default, the OpenGL coordinate system has the X-axis, left and right, the Y-axis up and down, and the Z-axis, forward and back. We are looking towards –Z.

  The matrix, baseModelViewMatrix, gets its name from OpenGL's "ModelView" matrix, which the one invoked more frequently than any others.

  By applying it first, we are actually moving our entire world away by 4 units. Below we add separate motions to the individual cubes.

- Now we want to rotate the cube. Line 5 shows that transformations can be concatenated by multiplying them together. Here we reuse the baseModelView matrix from the previous line.

- "What?" you are no doubt asking, "another one of these silly matrix things?" Even seemingly simple motions sometimes require a convoluted assortment of rotations and translations. Here in line 6 the cube is moved -1.5 units away from its own origin. That's why neither is actually centered in the screen but orbit around an invisible something.

▩ Line 7 applies a rotation to each axis of the cube's world. The rotation value is updated each time through this loop.

▩ Line 8 applies the baseModelViewMatrix done earlier to this one moving it away from our eyepoint. This combined matrix is then assigned to the GLKBaseEffect object along with the projection matrix in line 9.

▩ In line 10, much of the same is repeated for the OpenGL ES 2-only code block that draws the blue cube. Lines 10ff, are exactly like lines 6, 7, and 8, except the translation is in a positive direction, not a negative one.

▩ Now, in line 11, we need another matrix, this one for the face normals described earlier. Normals are generally at their happiest when exactly 1 unit in length, otherwise known as being "normalized." This counteracts any distortions the previous transformation matrices might otherwise introduce.

▩   Line 12 combines the model view matrix with the projection matrix done earlier.

▩ In line 13, the rotational value is bumped up a bit. Multiplying it against the value timeSinceLastUpdate ensures that the rotation rates are smooth.

▩ The second method, drawInRect(), is the one that actually renders the objects. Lines 14f clear the screen's background. Here glClearColor() is set to display 65% values of all three colors, to give the light gray you see. glClear() actually performs the clearing operation but only on buffers you specify—in this case, the "color buffer," which is the main one, and the depth buffer, which holds the z-values for hidden surface removal.

▩ In line 15, we can finally use the VAO created way back in the day. Binding it to the system means to use the collection of stuff previously uploaded to the GPU.

▩ The first cube rendered is the one managed by the GLKBaseEffect object. Line 16 tells it to prepare to render, and line 17 actually commands it to do so.

▩ Now in lines 18ff, we start using the shader stuff for the other cube. glUseProgram() tells it to use the two mysterious shader files, Shader.fsh and Shader.vsh, which had previously been loaded, while the two glUniform calls hand off the model view and the projection matrices to them.

▩ Now a second call to glDrawArrays() in line 19, and that does it!

The only other section is that which handles the loading and using of the shaders. This process is to load them first in memory, compile, and then link them. If all works as planned, they can be turned on with the call to glUseProgram() above.

One of the files, Shader.vsh, intercepts the vertices as the hardware starts processing them, while the other, Shader.fsh, in effect lets you play with each individual pixel before it's sent to the display hardware.

Tweak and Tweak Some More

Whenever I learn some new technology, I start tweaking the values to see what happens. If it happens the way I expect, I feel as if I've just acquired a new super-power. So, let's play here.

Let's tweak a couple of the values just for kicks. First, go to the gCubeVertexData a few pages up, and change the very first value from 0.0 to 1.0. What do you think you'll see? How about Figure 1-10?

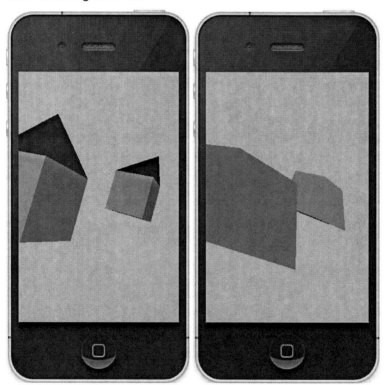

Figure 1-10. *With one vertex moved out.*

What About the Shaders?

Here is not the place to get into a detailed breakdown of shader design and the language, but let's remove a little of the mystery by playing with those as well. Listing 1-3 is the vertex shader.

Listing 1-3. Shader.vsh that preprocesses the vertices.

```
attribute vec4 position;
attribute vec3 normal;

varying lowp vec4 colorVarying;

uniform mat4 modelViewProjectionMatrix;
uniform mat3 normalMatrix;

void main()
{
    vec3 eyeNormal = normalize(normalMatrix * normal);
    vec3 lightPosition = vec3(0.0, 0.0, 1.0);                        //1
    vec4 diffuseColor = vec4(0.4, 0.4, 1.0, 1.0);

    float nDotVP = max(0.0, dot(eyeNormal, normalize(lightPosition)));

    colorVarying = diffuseColor * nDotVP;

    gl_Position = modelViewProjectionMatrix * position;             //2
}
```

Here in the vertex shader is where the light is hidden for this particular cube; the values are the x, y, and z values. Change the middle value to 5.0, which will move it way above the scene but will affect only the blue cube.

In line 2, gl_Position is predefined object that carries the position of the current vertex. Add in the following line to the end: gl_Position.x*=.5;. Figure 1-11a shows the result.

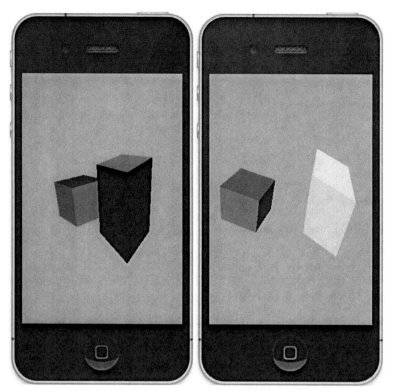

Figure 1-11a,b. Changing the vertical scaling in the vertex shader on the left, and coloring in the fragment shader on the right.

Now for a quick look at the fragment shader, in Listing 1-3. This does absolutely nothing and is merely a pass-through shader. However, it is here where you can intercept the calls to each of the "fragments," something like pixels at this level. Add the line gl_FragColor.g=1.0; at the end. This will add green to every pixel in the image, looking something like Figure 1-11b. See? That wasn't so hard was it? Now you can proudly go out and tell your friends that you've been programming shaders all day and watch the garlands pile up around your feet.

Listing 1-3. The fragment shader.

```
varying lowp vec4 colorVarying;

void main()
{
    gl_FragColor = colorVarying;
}
```

Finally, we are done with the very first example. Yes, for the 3D newcomers out there, it was likely too much information too soon. But I have a theory that if the first thing you do in the morning is to eat a cold frog, the rest of the day is bound to be much better. Consider this first example a cold frog, at least until Chapter 7 that is.

OpenGL Architecture

Now since we've analyzed to death a "simple" OpenGL program, let's take a brief look at what goes on under the hood at the graphics pipeline.

The term *pipeline* is commonly used to illustrate how a tightly bound sequence of events relate to each other, as illustrated in Figure 1-12. In the case of OpenGL ES, the process accepts a bunch of numbers in one end and outputs something really cool-looking at the other end, be it an image of the planet Saturn or the results of an MRI.

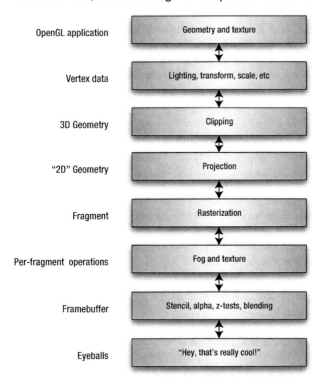

Figure 1-12. Basic overview of the OpenGL ES 1.x pipeline

▨ The first step is to take the data that describes some geometry along with information on how to handle lighting, colors, materials, and textures and send it into the pipeline.

▨ Next the data is moved and rotated, after which lighting on each object is calculated and stored. The scene—say, a solar-system model—must then be moved, rotated, and scaled based on the viewpoint you have set up. The viewpoint takes the form of a frustrum, a rectangular cone of sorts, which limits the scene to, ideally, a manageable level.

Next the scene is clipped, meaning that only stuff that is likely to be visible is actually processed. All of the other stuff is culled out as early as possible and discarded. Much of the history of real-time graphics development has to do with object culling techniques, some of which are very complex.

Let's get back to the example of a solar system. If you are looking at the Earth and the Moon is behind your viewpoint, there is no need whatsoever to process the Moon data. The clipping level does just this, both on an object level on one end and on a vertex level on the other. Of course, if you can pre-cull objects on your own before submitting to the pipeline, so much the better. Perhaps the easiest is to simply tell whether an object is behind you, making it completely skippable. Culling can also take place if the object is just too far away to see or is completely obscured by other objects.

▨ The remaining objects are now *projected* against the "viewport," a virtual display of sorts.

▨ At this point is where *rasterization* takes place. Rasterization breaks apart the image into *fragments* that are in effect single pixels. Fragments are pixels bundled with additional information such as texture and fog, in preparation for the next step.

▨ Now the fragments can have texture and fog effects applied to them. Additional culling can likewise take place if the fog might obscure the more distant fragments, for example.

▨ The final phase is where the surviving fragments are written to the frame buffer, but only if they satisfy some last-minute operations. Here is where the fragment's alpha values are applied for translucency, along with depth tests to ensure that the closest fragments are drawn in front of further ones and stencil tests used to render to nonrectangular viewports.

Now to compare things, Figure 1-13 shows the pipeline for OpenGL ES 2. Somewhat simpler in design, but it can be considerably more cumbersome to code for.

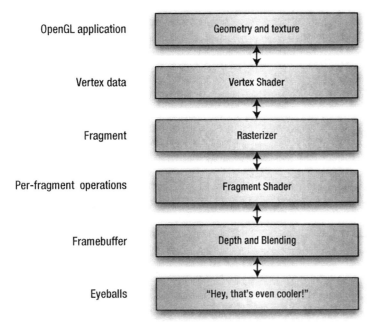

OpenGL application — Geometry and texture

Vertex data — Vertex Shader

Fragment — Rasterizer

Per-fragment operations — Fragment Shader

Framebuffer — Depth and Blending

Eyeballs — "Hey, that's even cooler!"

Figure 1-13. *Basic overview of the OpenGL ES 2.x pipeline*

When this is done, and all the rasters have been rasterized, the vertices shaded, and the colors blended, you might actually see something that looks like that teapot shown in Figure 1-14.

> **Note**   The more you delve into computer graphics, the more you'll see a little teapot popping up here and there in examples in books all the way to television and movies (*The Simpsons*, *Toy Story*). The legend of the teapot, sometimes called the Utah Teapot (everything can be traced back to Utah), began with a PhD student named Martin Newell in 1975. He needed a challenging shape but one that was otherwise a common object for his doctoral work. His wife suggested their white teapot, at which point Newell laboriously digitized it by hand. When he released the data into the public domain, it quickly achieved the status of being the "Hello World!" of graphics programming. Even one of the early OpenGL ES examples from Apple's developer web site had a teapot demo. The original teapot now resides at the Computer History Museum in Mountain View, California, just a few blocks from Google. See the upper left image of Figure 1-14.

Figure 1-14. Upper left, the actual teapot used by Newell, currently on display at the Computer History Museum in Mountain View, California. Photo by Steve Baker. An example OpenGL application from Apple's developer site on the right. The green teapot at the lower left is by Hay Kranen.

Summary

In this chapter, we covered a little bit of computer graphics history, a basic example program, and, most importantly, the Utah Teapot. Next up is a deep and no doubt overly detailed look into the mathematics behind 3D imagery.

Chapter 2

All That Math Jazz

No book on 3D programming would be complete without at least one chapter on the mathematics behind 3D transformations. If you care nothing about this, move on—there's nothing to see here. After all, doesn't OpenGL take care of this stuff automatically? Certainly. But it is helpful to be familiar with what's going on inside, if only to understand the lingo of 3D-speak.

Let's define some terminology first:

- *Translation:* Moving an object from its initial position (see Figure 2-1, left)

- *Rotation:* Rotating an object around a central point of origin (see Figure 2-1, right)

- *Scaling:* Changing the size of an object

- *Transformation:* All of the above

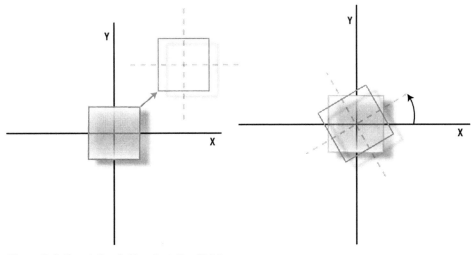

Figure 2-1. *Translation (left) and rotation (right)*

2D Transformations

Without knowing it, you probably have used 2D transformations already in the form of simple translations. If you create a `UIImageView` object and want to move it based on where the user is touching the screen, you might grab its `frame` and update the x and y values of the `origin`.

Translations

You have two ways to visualize this process. The first is having the object itself move relative to a common origin. This is called a *geometric transformation*. The second is having the world origin move while the object stays stationary. This is called a *coordinate transformation.* In OpenGL ES, both descriptions are commonly used together.

A translational operation can be expressed this way:

$$x' = x + T_x \qquad y' = y + T$$

The original coordinates are x and y, while the translations, T, will move the points to a new location. Simple enough. As you can tell, translations are naturally going to be very fast.

> **Note**   Lowercase letters, such as *xyz*, are the coordinates, while uppercase letters, such as *XYZ*, reference the axis.

Rotations

Now let's take a look at rotations. In this case, we'll rotate around the world origin at first to keep things simple. (See Figure 2-2.)

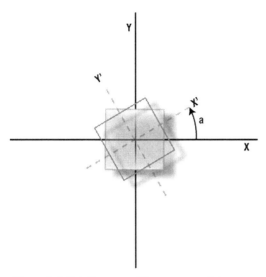

Figure 2-2. *Rotating around the common origin*

Naturally things get more complicated while we have to dust off the high school trig. The task at hand is to find out where the corners of the square would be after an arbitrary rotation, *a*. Eyes are glazing over across the land.

> **Note**   By convention counterclockwise rotations are considered positive, while clockwise are negative.

So, consider *x* and *y* as the coordinates of one of our square's vertices, and the square is normalized. Unrotated, any vertex would naturally map directly into our coordinate system of *x* and *y*. Fair enough. Now we want to rotate the square by an angle *a*. Although its corners are still at the "same" location in the square's own local coordinate system, they are different in ours, and if we're wanting to actually draw the object, we need to know the new coordinates of *x'* and *y'*.

Now we can jump directly to the trusty rotation equations, because ultimately that's what the code will express:

$$x' = x\cos(a) - y\sin(a) \qquad y' = x\sin(a) + y\cos(a)$$

Doing a really quick sanity check, you can see that if *a* is 0 degrees (no rotation), *x'* and *y'* reduce to the original *x* and *y* coordinates. If the rotation is 90 degrees, then *sin(a)=1*, *cos(a)=0*, so *x'=-y*, and *y'=x*. It's exactly as expected.

Mathematicians are always fond of expressing things in the most compact form possible. So 2D rotations can be "simplified" using matrix notation:

$$R_a = \begin{bmatrix} \cos(a) & -\sin(a) \\ \sin(a) & \cos(a) \end{bmatrix}$$

> **Note**   One of the most overused words in *Star Trek* is *matrix*. Pattern-matrix here, buffer-matrix there—"Number One, I have a headache-matrix and need to take a nap-matrix." (And don't get me started on the use of *protocol* in *24*.) Every self-respecting *Star Trek* drinking game (as if any drinking game would be self-respecting) should use *matrix* in its selection of words.

R_a is shorthand for our 2D rotation matrix. Although matrices might look busy, they are actually pretty straightforward and easy to code because they follow precise patterns. In this case, *x* and *y* can be represented as a teeny matrix:

$$\begin{bmatrix} x' \\ y' \end{bmatrix} = \begin{bmatrix} \cos(a) & -\sin(a) \\ \sin(a) & \cos(a) \end{bmatrix} \begin{bmatrix} x \\ y \end{bmatrix}$$

Translations can also be encoded in a matrix form. Because translations are merely moving the point around, the translated values of *x* and *y* come from adding the amount of movement to the point. What if you wanted to do a rotation and a translation on the same object? The translation matrix requires just a tiny bit of nonobvious thought. Which is the right one, the first or second shown here?

$$T = \begin{bmatrix} 1 & 1 \\ T_x & T_y \end{bmatrix} \quad \text{or} \quad T = \begin{bmatrix} 1 & 0 & 0 \\ 0 & 1 & 0 \\ T_x & T_y & 1 \end{bmatrix}$$

The answer is *obviously* the second one, or maybe it's not so obvious. The first one ends up as the following, which doesn't make much sense:

$$x' = x + yT_x \text{ and } y' = x + yT_y$$

So, to create a matrix for translation, we need a third component for our 2D point, commonly written as *(x,y, 1)*, as is the case in the second expression. Ignoring where the 1 comes from for a moment, notice that this can be easily reduced to the following:

$$x' = x + T_x \quad \text{and} \quad y' = y + T_y$$

The value of *1* is not to be confused with a third dimension of *z*, rather, it is a means used to express an equation of a line (in 2D space for this example) that is slightly different from the slope/intercept we learned in grade school. A set of coordinates in this form is called *homogeneous coordinates*, and in this case it helps to create a 3x3 matrix that can now be combined or concatenated to other 3x3 matrices.

Why would we want to do this? What if we wanted to do a rotation and translation together? Two separate matrices could be used for each point, and that would work just fine. But instead, we can precalculate a single matrix out of several using matrix multiplication (also known as *concatenation*) that in turn represents the cumulative effect of the individual transformations. Not only can this save some space, but it can substantially increase performance.

In Core Animation and Core Graphics, you will see a number of transformation methods with *affine* in their names. You can think of those as transformations (in this case, 2D) that can be decomposed into one or more of the following: rotation, translation, shear, and scale. All of the possible 2D affine transformations can be expressed as $x' = ax + cy + e$ and $y' = bx + dy + f$. That makes for a very nice matrix, a lovely one at that:

$$T = \begin{vmatrix} a & b & 0 \\ c & d & 0 \\ e & f & 1 \end{vmatrix} \text{ so } \begin{vmatrix} x' \\ y' \\ 1 \end{vmatrix} = \begin{vmatrix} a & b & 0 \\ c & d & 0 \\ e & f & 1 \end{vmatrix} \begin{vmatrix} x \\ y \\ 1 \end{vmatrix}$$

Now take a look at the structure `CGAffineTransform`:

```
struct CGAffineTransform {
    CGFloat a;
    CGFloat b;
    CGFloat c;
    CGFloat d;
    CGFloat tx;          //translation in x
    CGFloat ty;          //translation in y
};
```

Look familiar?

Scaling

Of the other two transforms, let's just take a look at the scaling, or simple resizing, of an object:

$$x' = xS_x \text{ and } y' = yS_y$$

In matrix form, this becomes as follows:

$$S = \begin{bmatrix} S_x & 0 & 0 \\ 0 & S_y & 0 \\ 0 & 0 & 1 \end{bmatrix}$$

With scaling, as with the other two transformations, the order is *very* important when applied to your geometry. Say, for example, you wanted to rotate and move your object. The results will clearly be different depending on whether you do the translation first or last. The more common sequence is to rotate the object first and then translate, as shown in Figure 2-3 (left). But if you invert the order, you'll get something like Figure 2-3 (right). In both these instances, the rotation is happening around the point of origin. If you wanted to rotate the object around its own origin, the first example is for you. If you meant for it to be rotated with everything else, the second works. (A typical situation might have you translate the object to the world origin, rotate it, and translate it back.)

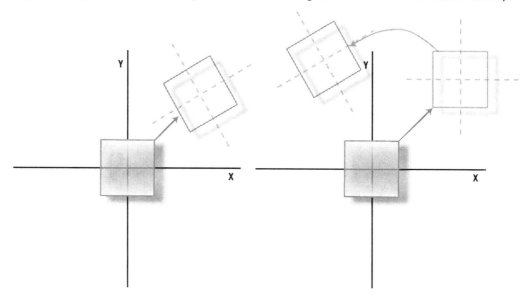

Figure 2-3. *Rotation around the point of origin followed by a translation (left) vs. translation followed by rotation (right)*

So, what does this have to do with the 3D stuff? Simple! Most if not all of the principles can be applied to 3D transformations and are more clearly illustrated with one less dimension.

3D Transformations

When moving everything you've learned to 3D space (also referred to as *3-space*), you'll see that, as in 2D, 3D transformations can be expressed as a matrix and as such can be concatenated with other matrices. The extra dimension of z is now the depth of the scene going in and out of the screen. OpenGL ES has $+z$ coming out and $-z$ going in. Other systems might have that reversed or even have Z being the vertical, with y now assuming depth. I'll stay with the OpenGL convention, as shown in Figure 2-4.

Note Moving back and forth from one frame of reference to another is the quickest road to insanity next to trying to figure out why Fox canceled *Firefly*. The classic 1973 book *Principles of Interactive Computer Graphics* has *z* going up and +*y* going into the screen. In his book, Bruce Artwick, the creator of Microsoft's Flight Simulator, shows *x* and *y* in the viewing plane but +*z* going *into* the screen. And yet another book has (get this!) *z* going up, *y* going *right*, and *x* coming toward the viewer. There oughtta be a law....

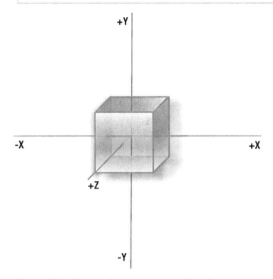

Figure 2-4. *The z-axis comes toward the viewer.*

First we'll look at 3D transformation. Just as the 2D variety was merely adding the desired deltas to the original location, the same thing goes for 3D. And the matrix that describes that would look like the following:

$$T = \begin{bmatrix} 1 & 0 & 0 & 0 \\ 0 & 1 & 0 & 0 \\ 0 & 0 & 1 & 0 \\ T_x & T_y & T_z & 1 \end{bmatrix} \text{ so } \begin{bmatrix} x' \\ y' \\ z' \\ 1 \end{bmatrix} = \begin{bmatrix} 1 & 0 & 0 & 0 \\ 0 & 1 & 0 & 0 \\ 0 & 0 & 1 & 0 \\ T_x & T_y & T_z & 1 \end{bmatrix} \begin{bmatrix} x \\ y \\ z \\ 1 \end{bmatrix}$$

And of course that would yield the following:

$$x' = x + T_x, \ y' = y + T_y \text{ and } z' = z + T_z$$

Notice the extra 1 that's been added; it's the same as for the 2D stuff, so our point location is now in *homogeneous* form.

So, let's take a look at rotation. One can safely assume that if we were to rotate around the *Z*-axis (Figure 2-5), the equations would map directly to the 2D versions. Using the matrix to express this, here is what we get (notice the new notation, where *R(z,a)* is used to make it clear which axis is being addressed). Notice that z remains a constant because it is multiplied by 1:

$$R(z,a) = \begin{bmatrix} \cos(a) & -\sin(a) & 0 & 0 \\ \sin(a) & \cos(a) & 0 & 0 \\ 0 & 0 & 1 & 0 \\ 0 & 0 & 0 & 1 \end{bmatrix}$$

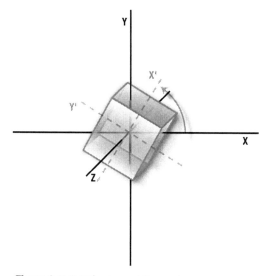

Figure 2-5. *Rotation around the z-axis*

This looks almost exactly like its 2D counterpart but with $z' = z$. But now we can also rotate around *x* or *y* as well. For *x* we get the following:

$$R(x,a) = \begin{bmatrix} 1 & 0 & 0 & 0 \\ 0 & \cos(a) & -\sin(a) & 0 \\ 0 & \sin(a) & \cos(a) & 0 \\ 0 & 0 & 0 & 1 \end{bmatrix}$$

And, of course, for *y* we get the following:

$$R(y,a) = \begin{bmatrix} \cos(a) & 0 & \sin(a) & 0 \\ 0 & 1 & 0 & 0 \\ -\sin(a) & 0 & \cos(a) & 0 \\ 0 & 0 & 0 & 1 \end{bmatrix}$$

But what about multiple transformations on top of each other? Now we're talking ugly. Fortunately, you won't have to worry too much about this because you can let OpenGL do the heavy lifting. That's what it's for.

Assume we want to rotate around the *y*-axis first, followed by *x* and then *z*. The resulting matrix might resemble the following (using *a* as the rotation around *x*, *b* for *y*, and *c* for *z*):

$$R = \begin{bmatrix} \cos(b)\cos(c) - \sin(b)\sin(a)\sin(c) & -\cos(b)\sin(c) + \sin(b)\sin(a)\cos(c) & \sin(b)\cos(a) & 0 \\ \sin(c)\cos(a) & \cos(c)\cos(a) & -\sin(a) & 0 \\ -\sin(b)\cos(c) + \cos(b)\sin(a)\sin(c) & \sin(c)\sin(b) + \cos(b)\sin(a)\cos(c) & \cos(a)\cos(b) & 0 \\ 0 & 0 & 0 & 1 \end{bmatrix}$$

Simple, eh? No wonder why the mantra for 3D engine authors is *optimize, optimize, optimize*. In fact, some of my inner loop in the original Amiga version of Distant Suns needed to be in 68K assembly. And note that this doesn't even include scaling or translation.

Now let's get to the reason for this book: all of this can be done by the following three lines:

```
glRotatef(b,0.0,1.0,0.0);
glRotatef(a,1.0,0.0,0.0);
glRotatef(c,0.0,0.0,1.0);
```

> **Note** There are many functions in OpenGL ES 1.1 that are not available in 2.0. The latter is oriented toward lower-level operations, sacrificing some of the ease-of-use utility routines for flexibility and control. The transformation functions have vanished, leaving it up to the developer to calculate their own matrices. Fortunately, there are a number of different libraries to mimic these operations. One such library was released by Apple's introduction of iOS 5. Called the ES Framework API (and described in Apple's official OpenGL ES 2.0 Programming Guide), it's designed to ease the transition to OpenGL ES 2.0.

When dealing with OpenGL, this particular matrix is called the *Modelview* because it is applied to anything that you draw, which are either models or lights. There are two other types that we'll deal with a little later: the *Projection* and *Texture* matrices.

It bears repeating that the actual order of the rotations is absolutely critical when trying to get this stuff to work. For example, a frequent task is to model an aircraft or spacecraft with a full six degrees of freedom: three translational components and three rotational components. The rotational parts are usually referred to as *roll, pitch,* and *yaw* (RPY). Roll would be rotations around the *z*-axis, pitch is around the *x* (in other words, aiming the nose up or down), and yaw is rotation around the *y*-axis, moving the nose left and right. Figure 2-6a, b, and c show this at work in the Apollo spacecraft from the moon landings in the 1960s. The proper sequence would be yaw, pitch, and roll, or rotation around *y, x,* and finally *z.* (This requires 12 multiplications and 6 additions, while premultiplying the three rotation matrices could reduce that down to 9 multiplications and 6 additions.) The transformations would be incremental, comprising the changes in the RPY angles since the last update, not the total ones from the beginning. In the good ol' days, round-off errors could compound distorting the matrix, leading to very cool but otherwise unanticipated results (but still cool nonetheless).

ENGINE LOCATION

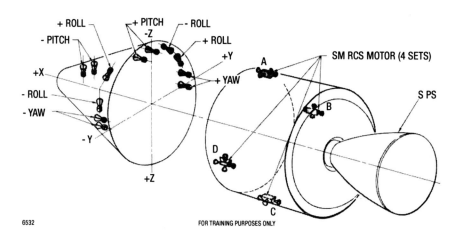

6532   FOR TRAINING PURPOSES ONLY

ROTATION CONTROL

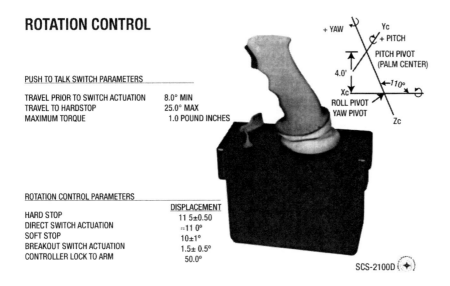

PUSH TO TALK SWITCH PARAMETERS

TRAVEL PRIOR TO SWITCH ACTUATION	8.0° MIN
TRAVEL TO HARDSTOP	25.0° MAX
MAXIMUM TORQUE	1.0 POUND INCHES

ROTATION CONTROL PARAMETERS

	DISPLACEMENT
HARD STOP	11 5±0.50
DIRECT SWITCH ACTUATION	≈11 0°
SOFT STOP	10±1°
BREAKOUT SWITCH ACTUATION	1.5± 0.5°
CONTROLLER LOCK TO ARM	50.0°

SCS-2100D

FLIGHT DIRECTOR ATTITUDE INDICATOR

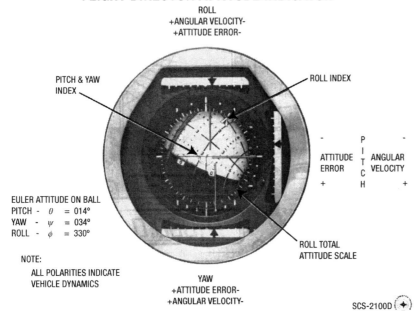

Figure 2-6. *Illustration of the Apollo's frame of reference, its joystick, and artificial horizon*

Picture This: Projecting the Object onto the Screen

Whew, even after all of that we're not quite done yet. Once you have performed all the rotations, scaling, and translations of your objects, you still need to get them *projected* onto your screen. Converting a 3D scene onto a 2D surface has troubled mankind since he sketched the first mammoth on a cave wall. But it is actually quite easy to grasp, as opposed to transformations.

There are two main kinds of projections at work here: *perspective* and *parallel*. Perspective projection is the way we see the 3D world on our 2D retina. Perspective views consist of vanishing points and foreshortening. Vanishing points are where all parallel lines converge in the distance, providing the perception of depth (think of railroad tracks heading toward the horizon). The result is that the closer something is, the bigger it appears, and vice versa, as shown in Figure 2-7. The parallel variety, also called *orthographic projection*, simply removes the effects of distance by effectively setting the z component of each vertex to 0 (the location of our viewing plane), as shown in Figure 2-8.

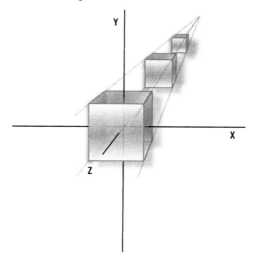

Figure 2-7. *Perspective projection*

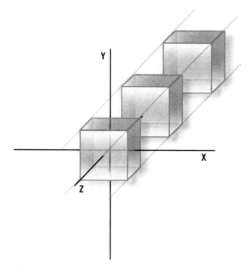

Figure 2-8. *Parallel projection*

In perspective projection, the distance component, *z*, is used to scale what will ultimately be the screen *x* and screen *y* values. So, the larger the *z*, or the distance away from the viewer, the smaller the pieces are visually. What one needs is the dimension of the *viewport* (OpenGL's version of your window or display screen) and its center point, which is typically the origin of the XY plane.

This final phase involves setting up the viewing *frustum*. The frustum establishes six clipping planes (top, bottom, left, right, near, and far) needed to precisely determine what should be visible to the user and how it is projected onto their *viewport*, which is OpenGL's version of your window or screen. This acts something like a lens into your OpenGL virtual world. By changing the values, you can zoom in or out and clip stuff really far away or not at all, as shown in Figures 2-9 and 2-10. The *perspective* matrix is defined by these values.

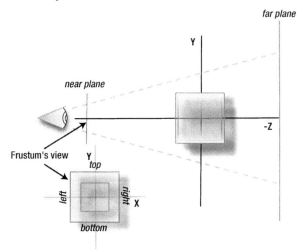

Figure 2-9. *Narrow bounds for the frustum give you a high-power lens.*

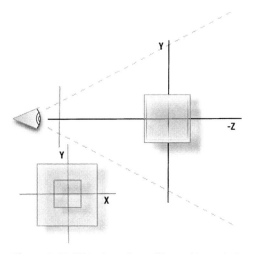

Figure 2-10. *Wider bounds are like a wide-angle lens.*

With these boundaries established, the one final transformation is that to the *viewport*, OpenGL's version of your screen. This is the point where OpenGL is fed the screen's dimensions, those of your display area, and the origin, which is likely the lower-left corner of the screen. On small devices such as the iPhone or iPad, you will likely fill up the entire screen and so will use the screen's width. But should you want to place the image into a subwindow of the main display, you could simply pass smaller values to the viewport. The law of similar triangles plays out here.

In Figure 2-11 we want to find what the projected *x'* is, given the *x* of an arbitrary vertex on the model. Consider two triangles, one formed by the corners CBA and the other smaller one by COA' (the *O* is for *origin*). The distance from C (where the eye is, to O is *d*). The distance from C to B is *d+z*. So, just taking the ratio of those, as follows:

$$\frac{x'}{d_{eye}} = \frac{x}{z + d_{eye}} \quad \text{and} \quad \frac{y'}{d_{eye}} = \frac{y}{z + d_{eye}}$$

yields the following:

$$x' = \frac{xd_{eye}}{z + d_{eye}} \quad \text{and} \quad y' = \frac{yd_{eye}}{z + d_{eye}} =$$

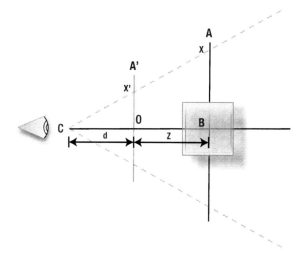

Figure 2-11. *Mapping a vertex to the viewport using the Law of Similar Triangles*

Figure 2-12 shows the final translations. Those can be added to *x'* and *y*:

$$x' = \frac{xd_{eye}}{z + d_{eye}} + T_x \quad \text{and} \quad y' = \frac{yd_{eye}}{z + d_{eye}} + T_y$$

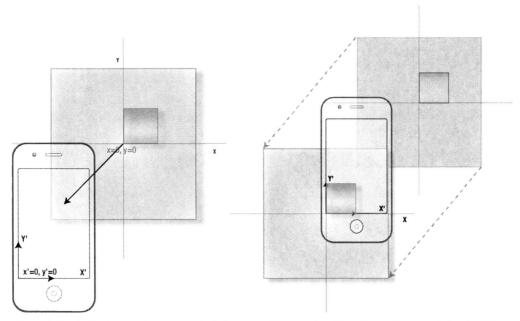

Figure 2-12. *Projecting x and y onto the device's screen. You can visuallize this as either translating the iPhone (or iPad) to the object's coordinates (left) or translating the object to the iPhone's coordinates (bright.*

And when the pixel dust settles, we have a nice matrixy form:

$$\begin{bmatrix} x' \\ y' \\ z' \\ 1 \end{bmatrix} = \begin{bmatrix} d & 0 & 0 & T_x \\ 0 & d & 0 & T_y \\ 0 & 0 & 0 & 0 \\ 0 & 0 & 1 & d \end{bmatrix} \begin{bmatrix} x \\ y \\ z \\ 1 \end{bmatrix}$$

Usually, some final scaling is required—for example, if the viewport is normalized. But that is left up to you.

Now Do it Backward and in High Heels

Such was a quote allegedly given by Ginger Rogers on how she felt about dancing with the great Fred Astaire. The response was that although he was very good, she had to do everything he did *and* do it backward and in high heels. (Rogers apparently never actually said that; its use has been traced back to a gag line from the comic strip Frank and Ernest.)

So, what does this have to do with transformations? Say you wanted to tell whether someone picked one of your objects by touching the screen. How do you know which of your objects has been selected? You must be able to do inverse transformations to "unmap" the screen coordinates back into something recognizable within your 3D space. But because the z-value gets dropped in the process, it will be necessary to search through your object list to find which was the most likely target. Untransforming something requires you to do everything backward. And this is done in the following way:

1. Multiply your Modelview matrix with your Projection matrix.

2. Invert the results.

3. Convert the screen coordinates of the touch point into the frame of reference for your viewport.

4. Take the results of that and multiply it by the inverted matrix from step 2.

Don't worry, this will be covered in more detail later in the book.

MATH IN ACTION

Let's prove that the previous math stuff really is what's going on in OpenGL ES.

Add the following code somewhere in your Chapter 1 exercise so that you know it will be called—after OpenGL has been initialized, of course. The best place is at the top of the drawFrame method:

```
GLfloat mvmatrix[16];

    glMatrixMode(GL_MODELVIEW);
    glLoadIdentity();                              //1
    glGetFloatv(GL_MODELVIEW_MATRIX,mvmatrix);
    glRotatef(30, 1.0, 0.0, 0.0);                  //2
    glGetFloatv(GL_MODELVIEW_MATRIX,mvmatrix);     //3
    glRotatef(60, 1.0, 0.0, 0.0);                  //4
    glGetFloatv(GL_MODELVIEW_MATRIX,mvmatrix);     //5
```

Put breakpoints after each call to glGetFloatv() and run.

Line 1 simply initializes the matrix to an unrotated state. Advance to line 2 after fetching the contents of the current matrix and then examine them in the debugger. You should see something like this:

$$\begin{bmatrix} 1 & 0 & 0 & 0 \\ 0 & 1 & 0 & 0 \\ 0 & 0 & 1 & 0 \\ 0 & 0 & 0 & 1 \end{bmatrix}$$

Line 2 rotates the matrix 30 degrees around the x-axis. (I'll cover glRotatef() in the next chapter.) Go to line 4 and do the same. What do you see?

What About Quaternions?

Quaternions are hyper-complex entities that can store the RPY information in a four-dimensional vector-type thingie. They are very efficient in both performance and space and are commonly used to model the instantaneous heading of an aircraft or spacecraft in flight simulation. They are a curious creature with great properties but are reserved for later.

GLKit and iOS5

Starting with iOS5, Apple introduced the GLKit, a collection of objects and helper functions that can make OpenGL a little easier to handle. Among those is an extensive math library with nearly 150 calls to handle vectors, matrices, and quaternions. OpenGL ES 1.*x* has wrappers around the transformations, hiding much of the inner workings, while OpenGL ES 2 does not. Up until the introduction of GLKit, hardy coders all across this fair land had to roll-their-own or find other places to get the needed math libraries. Apple added these both to make the lives of ES 2 coders a little better and to make it easier to manage ports from 1.1.

Summary

In this chapter, you learned the basics of 3D mathematics. First the chapter covered 2D transformations (rotation, translation, and scaling), and then 3D, with projection covered as well. Although you will not likely need to code any transformations yourself, being familiar with this chapter is key to understanding much of the OpenGL terminology later. My head hurts.

Building a 3D World

In the first two chapters, we covered the cool stuff and the math stuff (which could be either cool or boring). We went over Xcode's OpenGL ES 2 template just to give you a taste of the structure and design principles of a "simple" OpenGL app. Here in Chapter 3, we'll take a step back, examine a very simple 2D application at first, and then migrate it one step at a time to 3D. (4D hypercubes are beyond the scope of this work.) And during the process, more 3D theory about projections, rotations, and the like will be slipped in for good measure.

A Little More Theory

Remember that OpenGL ES objects are a collection of points in 3D space; that is, their location is defined by three values. These values are joined together to form faces, which are flat surfaces, that are triangles. The triangles are then joined together to form objects or pieces of objects.

To get a bunch of numbers that form vertices, other numbers that form colors, and still other numbers that combine the vertices and colors on the screen, it is necessary to tell the system about its graphic environment. Such things as the location of the viewpoint, the window (or viewport) that will receive the image, aspect ratios, and other bits of digital flotsam of sorts are needed to complete the 3D circuit. More specifically, I'll cover OpenGL's coordinates, how they relate to the frustum, how objects are clipped or culled from the scene, and drawing to your device's display.

OpenGL Coordinates

If you've done any sort of graphics at all on any system, you'll be acquainted with the run-of-the-mill X-Y coordinate system. X is always the horizontal axis, with right being positive, while Y is always the vertical axis, with down being positive, placing the origin in the upper-left corner. Known as *screen coordinates*, they are easily confused with *math coordinates,* which place the origin at the lower-left corner and where, for Y, up is positive. Fortunately, Apple's rendering framework, Quartz 2D, bucks tradition and uses math coordinates (although that can be adjusted as needed by using some of the Core Graphics transformation routines).

Now jumping to OpenGL 3D coordinates, we have a slightly different system using *Cartesian* coordinates, the standard of expressing locations in space. Going back to the math coordinates, OpenGL has the origin in the lower-left corner, with +Y going up. But now we add a third dimension expressed as Z. In this case, +Z is pointing out toward you, as shown in Figure 3-1.

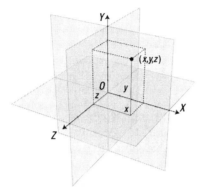

Figure 3-1. *OpenGL ES 3D Cartesian coordinate system (image by Jorge Stolfi)*

In fact, we have several kinds of coordinate systems, or *spaces*, in OpenGL, with each space being transformed to the next:

- Object space, which is relative to each of your objects.

- Camera (or *eye*) space, local to your viewpoint.

- Projection (or *clip*) space, which is the 2D screen or viewport that displays the final image.

- Normalized device coordinates (NDCs), which express the xyz values *normalized* from -1 to 1. That is, a value or set of values are normalized such that they fit inside a cube 2 units on a side.

- Windows (or *screen*) coordinates, which are the final locations of your scene when displayed in the actual screen.

These coordinate systems can be expressed in pipeline form, as shown in Figure 3-2.

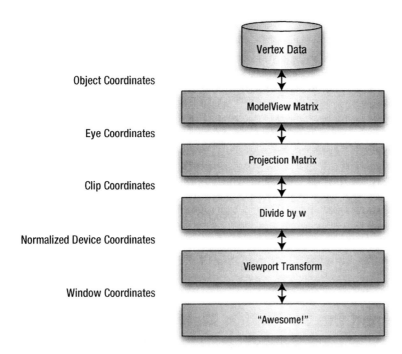

Figure 3-2. *Vertex transformation pipeline*

Object, eye, and clip space are the three you usually have to worry about. For example, object coordinates are generated with a local origin and then moved and rotated to *eye space*. If you have a bunch of airplanes for a combat game, for example, each will have its own local origin. You should be able to move the planes to any part of your world by moving, or *translating*, only the origin and letting the rest of the geometry just tag along for the ride. At this point, the visibility of objects is tested against the viewing frustum, which is the volume of space that defines what the virtual camera can actually see. If they lay outside the frustum, they are considered invisible and are clipped, or culled out, so that no further operations are done on them. As you may remember in Chapter 1, much of the work in graphics engine design focuses on the clipping part of the engine, to dump as many of the objects as early as possible yielding faster and more efficient systems.

And finally, after all that, the screen-oriented portions of OpenGL are ready to convert, or *project*, the remaining objects. And those objects are your planes, zeppelins, missiles, trucks on the road, ships at sea, squirrel trebuchets, and anything else you might want to stuff into your game.

> **Note**   OpenGL doesn't really define anything as "world space." However, the eye coordinates are the next best thing, in that you can define everything in relation to your location.

Eye Coordinates

There is no magical viewpoint object in OpenGL. So, instead of moving your viewpoint, you move all of the objects in relation to yourself. And yes, that is easy to get confused as you will find yourself constantly changing the signs of values. So, instead of moving away from an object, the object, in effect, is moving away from you. Imagine you are making a video of a car rushing by you. Under OpenGL, the car would be standing still; you and everything around you would be moving by it. This is done largely with the `glTranslate*()` and `glRotate*()` calls in OpenGL ES 1, or direct use of matrices in OpenGL ES 2, as you will see later. It is at this point where OpenGL's modelview matrix, referenced in previous chapters, comes into play. The modelview matrix handles the basic 3D transformations (as opposed to the projection matrix, which *projects* the 3D view onto the 2D space of your screen, or the texture matrix, which helps apply images to your object). You will refer to it frequently.

From here on out, assume that I am talking about OpenGL ES 1, unless otherwise specified.

Viewing Frustum and the Projection Matrix

In geometry, a *frustum* is that portion of (typically) a pyramid or cone that results after being cut by two parallel planes. In other words, think of the great Pyramid of Giza with the top third lopped off (not that I am condoning the destruction of Egyptian antiquities). In graphics, the viewing frustum defines the portion of the world that our virtual camera can actually see, as shown in Figure 3-3.

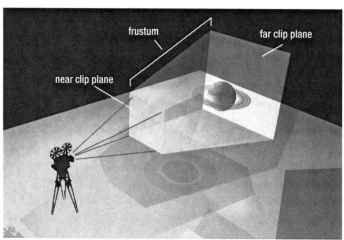

Figure 3-3. *Viewing frustum*

Unlike a number of things in OpenGL, the definition of the viewing frustum is very straightforward and follows the conceptual figures closely by simply defining a volume, sometimes called a "viewing pyramid," in space. Any objects that are whole or in part within the frustum may eventually find their way to the screen (if not obscured by a closer object).

The frustum also is used to specify your field of view (FOV), like your camera's wide-angle vs. telephoto lens. The larger the angle that the side planes form when compared to the center axis (that is, how they fan out), the larger the FOV. And a larger FOV will allow more of your world to be visible while a smaller one lets you concentrate on a smaller area.

Up to this point, the translations and rotations use the modelview matrix, easily set using the call glMatrixMode(GL_MODELVIEW);. But now at this stage of the rendering pipeline, you will define and work with the projection matrix (specified in Listing 1-2 in Chapter 1). This is done largely via the frustum definitions spelled out in the section "Picture This" in Chapter 2. And it is also a surprisingly compact means of doing a lot of operations.

The final steps to convert the transformed vertices to a 2D image are as follows:

1. A 3D point inside the frustum is mapped to a normalized cube to convert the XYZ values to NDC. NDC stands for normalized device coordinates, which is an intermediate system describing the coordinate space that lies inside the frustum. This is useful when it comes to mapping each vertex and each object to your device's screen, no matter what size or how many pixels it has, be it an iPhone, iPad, or something new with completely different screen dimesions. Once you have this form, the coordinates have "moved" but still retain their relative relationships with each other. And of course, in ndc, they now fall into values between -1 and 1. Note that internally the Z value is flipped. Now –Z is coming toward you, while +Z is going away, but thankfully that great unplesantness is all hidden.

2. These new NDCs are then mapped to the screen, taking into account the screen's aspect ratio and the "distance" the vertices are from the screen as specified by the near clipping plane. As a result, the further things are, the smaller they are. Most of the math is used for little more than determining the proportions of this or that within the frustum.

The preceding steps describe *perspective projection*, which is the way we normally view the world. That is, the further things are, the smaller they appear. When those inherent distortions are removed, we get *orthographic projection*. At that point, no matter how far an object is, it still displays the same size. Orthographic renderings are typically used in mechanical drawings when any perspective distortion would corrupt the intent of the original artwork.

> **Note**   You will often need to directly address which matrix you are dealing with. The call to glMatrixMode() is used to specify the current matrix, which all subsequent operations apply to. Forgetting which matrix is the current one is an easy error to make.

Back to the Fun Stuff: A Simpler Demo

When Xcode 4.2 was released (along with the iOS5 SDK), it changed the default project of the OpenGL wizard. Previously it produced an OpenGL ES 1 app showing a very simple 2D scene of a flat bouncing square, compared to the two 3D cubes rotating around a common center in the OpenGL ES 2 environment. The former was an ideal project to leverage early on because it was far less fussy than the later one, as described in Chapter 1. So we'll use the original demo and variants from here on out as a foundation project of sorts, starting from a known and easily understood codebase as a launchpad to bigger and better things.

The easiest way is to either fetch the source from the Apress site or take the example from Chapter 1 and copy the material from Listings 3-1 and 3-2 over the viewcontroller content in Chapter 1.

Listing 3-1. The header for the Listing 3-2.

```
#import <UIKit/UIKit.h>
#import <GLKit/GLKit.h>

@interface BouncySquareViewController : GLKViewController              //1

@end
```

Listing 3-2. The classic bouncing square demo with iOS5 modifications.

```
#import "BouncySquareViewController.h"

@interface BouncySquareViewController ()
{


}

@property (strong, nonatomic) EAGLContext *context;
@property (strong, nonatomic) GLKBaseEffect *effect;

@end


@implementation BouncySquareViewController

@synthesize context = _context;
@synthesize effect = _effect;

- (void)viewDidLoad
{
    [super viewDidLoad];

    self.context = [[EAGLContext alloc] initWithAPI:kEAGLRenderingAPIOpenGLES1];    //2
```

```
    if (!self.context)
    {
        NSLog(@"Failed to create ES context");
    }

    GLKView *view = (GLKView *)self.view;
    view.context = self.context;                                          //3
    view.drawableDepthFormat = GLKViewDrawableDepthFormat24;

[EAGLContext setCurrentContext:self.context];

}

#pragma mark - GLKView and GLKViewController delegate methods

- (void)glkView:(GLKView *)view drawInRect:(CGRect)rect                   //4
{
    static int counter=0;

    static const GLfloat squareVertices[] = {                            //5
        -0.5, -0.33,
         0.5, -0.33,
        -0.5,  0.33,
         0.5,  0.33,
    };

    static const GLubyte squareColors[] = {                              //6
        255, 255,   0, 255,
          0, 255, 255, 255,
          0,   0,   0,   0,
        255,   0, 255, 255,
    };

    static float transY = 0.0;

    glClearColor(0.5, 0.5, 0.5, 1.0);                                    //7
    glClear(GL_COLOR_BUFFER_BIT);

    glMatrixMode(GL_PROJECTION);                                         //8
    glLoadIdentity();                                                    //9
    glMatrixMode(GL_MODELVIEW);                                          //10
    glLoadIdentity();                                                    //11
    glTranslatef(0.0, (GLfloat)(sinf(transY)/2.0), 0.0);                //12

    transY += 0.075f;
```

```
    glVertexPointer(2, GL_FLOAT, 0, squareVertices);                      //13
    glEnableClientState(GL_VERTEX_ARRAY);
    glColorPointer(4, GL_UNSIGNED_BYTE, 0, squareColors);
    glEnableClientState(GL_COLOR_ARRAY);

    glDrawArrays(GL_TRIANGLE_STRIP, 0, 4);                                //14

    if(!(counter%100));                                                  //15
        NSLog(@"FPS: %d\n",self.framesPerSecond);

    counter++;
}
```

@end

You'll recognize a number of similar elements here from Chapter 1, but in a more compact form. All OpenGL ES 2 code has been removed for clarity.

- Line 1 defines our viewcontroller as a subclass of GLKViewController

- In line 2, the API is initialized, with OpenGL ES 1 as the chosen approach, by passing it the kEAGLRenderingAPIOpenGLES1 flag. The context is returned and fed to the GLKView.

- Lines 3ff bind the context that was fetched in line 2. Then the current context is set. Without that being set, OpenGL will fail on many calls coming up.

- The drawInRect() method in line 4 is a delegate call from GLKViewController. All of the geometry and attributes are specified here for clarity.

- Line 5 creates an array of vertices. Because this a 2D demo without lighting, only two values are needed for each vertex. Line 6 is our color array, using the standard RGBA format. One color for each of the four vertices.

- Lines 7f are identical to the first exercise, filling in the background with a medium gray.

- Line 8 sets the current matrix to be a projection matrix, and line 9 initializes it with an "identity matrix."

- Lines 10 and 11 do the same for the modelview.

- Instead of generating a matrix of our own and modifying it directly, as in Chapter 1, ES 1 handles those kind of housekeeping chores for us. So here in line 12, glTranslatef() moves the square along only the Z-axis (hence the middle value) using a sin function. Using a sin gives it a nice smooth motion that slows up at either end.

- Lines 13ff are similar to those in setupGL() in Listing 1-1, in that they tell OpenGL how much data we have of what type and where it can be found. glVertexPoint() hands off a pointer to the vertex array (see lines 5ff) and says that it has only two float values. Then the call glEnableClientState(GL_VERTEX_ARRAY) tells the system to make use of the vertex data. The next two lines do the same thing for the color array.

- Now draw things in line 14, and give us some metrics in line 15.

If it works, you should see something like Figure 3-4.

Figure 3-4. And the square goes bounce!

Going Beyond the Bouncy Square

Now let's change the preceding example to add a third dimension. Because we're getting seriously 3D here, several things will need to be added to handle the Z dimension, including a larger dataset for the cube's geometry and color, methods of handing off that data to OpenGL, the frustum definition, any face culling techniques if needed, and rotations instead of just the translations.

> **Note** *Translation* means to move an object around in your world up/down, left/right, and forward/backward, while *rotation* means to rotate the object and any arbitrary axis. Both are considered *transformations*.

Adding the Geometry

Now we need to double the number of vertices from the above example and extend them to support the extra z-value as shown in line 1 of Listing 3-3. You'll notice that all of the vertices are either .5 or -.5. Previously values for the Y-axis were -0.33 to 0.33. That compensated for the aspect ratio of the screen, stretching out the image so that the square really does look square. In this exercise, the viewing frustum will be added, which will enable us to specify the aspect ratio so that we don't have to compensate for non-square screens.

Following that, the color array is likewise doubled in size (lines 2ff). Then we need to specify how the vertices are all tied together so as to make 6 square faces out of 12 triangles. That is done via two additional arrays called tfan1 and tfan2. The numbers are indices into the vertex array, telling the system how to tie which points together in a form known as a "triangle fan." This will be covered shortly. So you will now be modifying the bouncy square app, either by using the original or just making a copy.

> **Note** You can rename an Xcode 4 project by going to the root of the project and renaming the project name at the very top of the tree. Unfortunately, it doesn't get everything like source files or references in the .xib files, so you'll still have to change those manually.

When ready, swap out the 2D data definitions in drawInRect()for the 3D-ified versions shown in Listing 3-3.

Listing 3-3. *Defining the 3D Cube*

```
static const GLfloat cubeVertices[] =                          //1
{
    -0.5, 0.5, 0.5,                    //vertex 0
     0.5, 0.5, 0.5,                    // v1
     0.5,-0.5, 0.5,                    // v2
    -0.5,-0.5, 0.5,                    // v3

    -0.5, 0.5,-0.5,                    // v4
     0.5, 0.5,-0.5,                    // v5
     0.5,-0.5,-0.5,                    // v6
    -0.5,-0.5,-0.5,                    // v7
};

static const GLubyte cubeColors[] = {                          //2
      255, 255,   0, 255,
      0,   255, 255, 255,
      0,     0,   0,   0,
      255,   0, 255, 255,

      255, 255,   0, 255,
      0,   255, 255, 255,
      0,     0,   0,   0,
      255,   0, 255, 255,
    };

static const GLubyte tfan1[6 * 3] =                            //3
{
    1,0,3,
    1,3,2,
    1,2,6,
    1,6,5,
    1,5,4,
    1,4,0
};

static const GLubyte tfan2[6 * 3] =                            //4
{
    7,4,5,
    7,5,6,
    7,6,2,
    7,2,3,
    7,3,0,
    7,0,4
};
```

Figure 3-5 shows the way the vertices are ordered. Under normal situations, you will never have to define geometry in this fashion. You'll likely load your objects from a file stored in one of the standard 3D data formats, such as those used by 3D Studio or Modeler 3D. And considering how complicated such files can be, it is not recommended that you write your own because importers for most of the major formats are available.

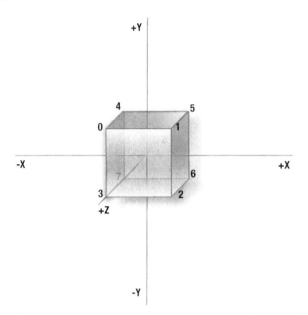

Figure 3-5. *Notice the various axes: X going right, Y is up, and Z is toward the viewer.*

Some new data is now needed to tell OpenGL in what order the vertices are to be used. With the square it was a no-brainer to order, or *sequence*, the data by hand so that the four vertices could represent the two triangles. The cube makes this considerably more complicated. We could have defined each of the six faces of the cube by separate vertex arrays, but that wouldn't scale well for more complex objects. And it would be less efficient than having to shove six sets of data through the graphics hardware. Thus, keeping all the data in a single array is the most efficient from both a memory and a performance standpoint. So, how do we tell OpenGL the layout of the data? In this case, we'll use the drawing mode called *triangle fans,* as shown in Figure 3-6. A triangle fan is a set of triangles that share a common vertex.

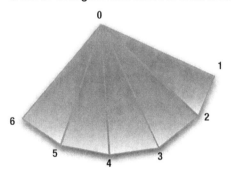

Figure 3-6. *A triangle fan has one common point with all triangles.*

Data can be stored and presented to OpenGL ES in many different ways. One format may be faster but uses more memory, while another may use less memory but at the cost of a little extra overhead. If you were to import data from one of the 3D files, chances are it is already optimized for one of the approaches, but if you really want to hand-tune the system, you may at some point have to repack the vertices into the format you prefer for your application.

Besides triangle fans, you will find other ways data can be stored or represented, called *modes*.

- ▓ Points and lines specify just that: points and lines. OpenGL ES can render your vertices as merely points of definable sizes or can render lines between the points to show the wireframe version (gl.h defines these by GL_POINTS and GL_LINES, respectively).

- ▓ Line strips, GL_LINE_STRIP, are a way for OpenGL to draw a series of lines in one shot, while line loops, GL_LINE_LOOP, are like line strips but will always connect the first and last vertices together.

- ▓ Triangles, triangle strips, and triangle fans round out the list of OpenGL ES primitives: GL_TRIANGLES, GL_TRIANGLE_STRIP, and GL_TRIANGLE_ FAN. Desktop OpenGL itself can handle additional modes such as quads (faces with four vertices/sides), quad strips, and polygons.

> **Note**   The term *primitive* denotes a fundamentally basic shape or form of data in graphics systems. Examples of primitives include cubes, spheres, and cones. The term can also be used for even simpler shapes such as points, lines, and, in the case of OpenGL ES, triangles and triangle fans.

When using elements, you will need to tell OpenGL what vertices are drawn when, using *index*, or *connectivity*, arrays. These will tell the pipeline the exact order the vertices need to be processed for each element, demonstrated in lines 3 and 4 in Listing 3-3. So, for example, the first three numbers in the array tfan1 are 1, 0, and 3. That means the first triangle is made up of vertices 1, 0, and 3, in that order. Therefore, back in the array cubeVertices, vertex 1 is located at x=0.5, y=0.5, and z=0.5. Vertex 0 is the point at x=-0.5, y=0.5, and z=0.5, while the third corner of our triangle is located at x=-0.5, y=-0.5, and z=0.5. The upside is that this makes it a lot easier to create the datasets because the actual order is now irrelevant, while the downside is that it uses up a little more memory to store the additional information.

The cube can be divided up into two different triangle fans, which is why there are two index arrays. The first incorporates the front, right, and top faces, while the second incorporates the back, bottom, and left faces, as shown in Figure 3-7.

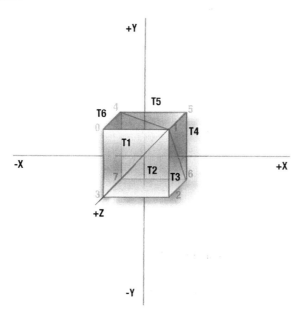

Figure 3-7. *The first triangle fan shares vertex 1 as the common vertex.*

Stitching It All Together

Now the rendering code must be modified to handle the new data. Listing 3-4 shows the rest of the drawInRect() method, right under the data definitions given in Listing 3-3. This will replicate much of the earlier example, complete with motion. The major difference is to be found in two calls to `glDrawArray()` because the cube is in two pieces, one each for of the three faces or six triangles that define the two triangle fans.

> **Note** You'll note that many of the OpenGL ES calls end in an *f*, such as `glScalef()`, `glRotatef()`, and so on. The *f* means that the parameters passed are floats, or GLfloat. The only other parameter types in OpenGL ES are fixed-point values, so `glScale` would now be `glScalex()`. Fixed point was useful for the older and slower devices, but with more current hardware, Apple recommends staying with floats.

The obsolete lines from the previous example have been commented out but left in place to more clearly show the differences.

Listing 3-4. *The rest of the drawInRect method for the Bouncy Cube*

```
static GLfloat transY = 0.0;
static GLfloat z=-2.0;                                                    //1

 glClearColor(0.5, 0.5, 0.5, 1.0);                                       //2
 glClear(GL_COLOR_BUFFER_BIT);
```

```
glEnable(GL_CULL_FACE);                                              //3
glCullFace(GL_BACK);

//    glMatrixMode(GL_PROJECTION);                                   //4
//    glLoadIdentity();

glMatrixMode(GL_MODELVIEW);                                          //5
glLoadIdentity();

//glTranslatef(0.0, (GLfloat)(sinf(transY)/2.0), 0.0);

glTranslatef(0.0, (GLfloat)(sinf(transY)/2.0), z);                  //6
transY += 0.075f;

//glVertexPointer(2, GL_FLOAT, 0, squareVertices);

glVertexPointer(3, GL_FLOAT, 0, cubeVertices);                       //7
glEnableClientState(GL_VERTEX_ARRAY);
glColorPointer(4, GL_UNSIGNED_BYTE, 0, cubeColors);                  //8
glEnableClientState(GL_COLOR_ARRAY);

// glDrawArrays(GL_TRIANGLE_STRIP, 0, 4);

glDrawElements( GL_TRIANGLE_FAN, 6 * 3, GL_UNSIGNED_BYTE, tfan1);    //9
glDrawElements( GL_TRIANGLE_FAN, 6 * 3, GL_UNSIGNED_BYTE, tfan2);

if(!(counter%100))
        NSLog(@"FPS: %d\n",self.framesPerSecond);

 counter++;
}
```

The following changes have been made:

- A z value has been added in at line 1. For the time being, this will be static because the animation remains only up and down. A negative value means that the object has moved away from us, as if it has moved deeper into the screen.

- Clear the background to the medium gray once again in line 2.

- Because we never want to process or draw anything that is not absolutely necessary, it is possible to just eliminate a bunch of the triangles that are "facing away" from the viewer, as on line 3. Face culling is used to remove the otherwise invisible faces. For our cube, the only triangles we need to see are the ones actually facing us, and that is determined by the *winding*, or the order, of the vertices for the face. If the winding is counterclockwise, it is facing us and should be visible; otherwise, it is culled. This may sound like a substitute for face normals, and, yes, it is when it comes to *backface elimination,* or culling. But normals are still needed to determine illumination striking a face.

> **Note**   "Windingness" is based on the direction the vertices describe. The first triangle formed by vertices 1, 0, and 3 is facing us because the vertices are ordered counterclockwise. All triangles in the first fan are counterclockwise.

- In line 4, the projection matrix initialization is turned off, leaving only the modelview matrix to be modified. Projection will be handled below.

- In line 5, only the `modelview` is set as the current matrix, in case someone else changed it elsewhere.

- In line 6, the final coordinate of the original `glTranslatef()` call, which had been fixed at 0 because it wasn't needed, is now changed to z (`-2.0`).

- The original `squareVertices` pointer is replaced by `cubeVertices` in line 7.

- Line 8 replaces the `squareColors` with `cubeColors`.

- The original `glDrawArrays()` is removed to be replaced by two calls to `glDrawElements()` on line 9, one for each of the triangle fans. Of note, the second argument is for the number of elements in the `tFan` connectivity arrays: six vertices times three elements on each vertex. OpenGL will take the connectivity arrays, `tfan1` and `tfan2`; look up each vertex in the vertex pointer array (line 7); and render the object.

You should be able to get a compile at this point, but you won't see anything because the viewing frustum has yet to be defined. The default far clip plane is -1.0, meaning that anything further than that will be culled, that is, not be visible. If you substitute -1.5 for z, in place of -2.0, the "cube" is moved closer and should be partially visible. Although it looks like the whole thing, it is actually just the closest face poking through. Change the z to -1.500001, and it vanishes. It's not going to look like much of a cube right now, because only a portion of it will be poking through. Also, because the frustum is not defined, the square viewport is stretched out when being adapted to fill the window. (The coordinate -1.5 is where the origin of the cube needs to be to ensure the closest face is at -1.0.) Now move it back to -2.0.

Defining the Frustum

The last step we need is to specify details on how the vertices are mapped to our screen using glFrustumf(), as in Listing 3-5. If you'll recall, the frustum is made of six planes that enclose the volume that specifies what we can see, something like a camera's lens.

Listing 3-5. Creating the viewing frustum, added to the View Controller file

```
-(void)setClipping
{
    float aspectRatio;
    const float zNear = .1;                                                //1
    const float zFar = 1000;                                               //2
    const float fieldOfView = 60.0;                                        //3
    GLfloat    size;

    CGRect frame = [[UIScreen mainScreen] bounds];                         //4

        //Height and width values clamp the fov to the height; flipping it would make it
relative to the width.
        //So if we want the field-of-view to be 60 degrees, similar to that of a wide
angle lens, it will be
        //based on the height of our window and not the width.  This is important to
know when rendering
// to a non-square screen.

    aspectRatio=(float)frame.size.width/(float)frame.size.height;          //5
    //Set the OpenGL projection matrix.

    glMatrixMode(GL_PROJECTION);                                           //6
    glLoadIdentity();

    size = zNear * tanf(GLKMathDegreesToRadians (fieldOfView) / 2.0);      //7

    glFrustumf(-size, size, -size /aspectRatio, size /aspectRatio, zNear, zFar);  //8
    glViewport(0, 0, frame.size.width, frame.size.height);                 //9

    //Make the OpenGL ModelView matrix the default.

    glMatrixMode(GL_MODELVIEW);                                            //10
}
```

Here is what is happening:

- Lines 1 and 2 specify the distances of the near and far clipping planes. These two values say that anything further than 1,000 or closer than .1 will be filtered out. ("A thousand what?" you might ask. Just a thousand; the units can be up to you. They could be light-years or cubits, it doesn't matter.)

- Line 3 sets the field of view to 60 degrees.

- Lines 4 and 5 calculate the aspect ratio of the final screen. Its height and width values clamp the FOV to the height; flipping it would make it relative to the width. So if we want the field-of-view to be 60 degrees, similar to that of a wide-angle lens, it will be based on the height of our window and not the width. This is important to know when rendering to a non-square screen.

- Because the frustum affects the projection matrix, we need to ensure that it is activated instead of the modelview matrix, in line 6.

- Line 7 has the duty of calculating a size value needed to specify the left/right and top/bottom limits of the viewing volume, as shown in Figure 3-3. This can be thought of as your virtual window into the 3D space. With the center of the screen being the origin, you need to go from −size to +size in both dimensions. That is why the field is divided by two—the window will go from -30 degrees to +30 degrees. Multiplying size by **zNear** merely adds a scaling hint of sorts. Finally, divide the bottom/top limits by the aspect ratio to ensure your square will really be a square.

- Now in line 8, we can plug those values into `glFrustumf()`; and in line 9, pass the actual pixel dimension of the viewport.

- Don't forget to reset the matrix mode back to modelview just to be a good neighbor, as in line 10.

`SetClipping()` needs to be called only once at the start unless you want to change the "power" of your lens. More complex situations might need to vary the **zNear/zFar** values to handle variances in depth or to use a different field of view to zoom in on a specific target. But you can add it into viewDidLoad() with the following two lines:

```
[EAGLContext setCurrentContext:self.context];

[self setClipping];
```

Any OpenGL call must have a current context to work, so it needs to be set ahead of everything else, hence the extra line ahead of setClipping(). If it works right, you should see something that looks exactly like the original bouncy cube! Wait, you're not impressed? OK, let's add some rotations to the thing.

Taking 'er Out for a Spin

Now it's time to add some more interesting animation to the scene. We're going to be spinning this slowly besides bouncing it up and down. To the top of `drawInRect()`, add the following:

```
static GLfloat spinX=0;
static GLfloat spinY=0;
```

Next add the following lines to the bottom of `drawInRect ()`:

```
spinY+=.25;
spinX+=.25;
```

And right *before* the `glTranslatef()` call, add the following:

```
glRotatef(spinY, 0.0, 1.0, 0.0);
glRotatef(spinX, 1.0, 0.0, 0.0);
```

Now run again. "Hey! Huh?" will be the mostly likely response. The cube doesn't seem to be spinning, but instead it's rotating around your viewpoint (while bouncing at the same time), as shown in Figure 3-8. This illustrates one of the most confusing elements in basic 3D animation: getting the order of the translations and rotations correct. (Remember the discussion in Chapter 2?)

Consider our cube. If you want to have a cube spinning in front of your face, which would be the proper order? Rotate and then translate? Or translate and then rotate? Reaching way back to fifth-grade math, you might remember learning something about addition and multiplication being *commutative*. That is, the order of operations was not critical: a+b=b+a, or a*b=b*a. Well, 3D transformations are *not* commutative (finally, a use for something I'd never thought I'd use!). That is, rotation*translation is not the same as translation*rotation. See Figure 3-9.

The right side is what you are seeing right now in the rotating cube example. The cube is being translated first and then rotated, but because the rotation takes place around the "world" origin (the viewpoint's location), you see it as if it's spinning around your head.

Now to the obvious does-not-compute moment: are the rotations not placed *before* the translations in the example code anyway?

Figure 3-8. *Translation first, rotation second*

Here is what should be causing the sudden outbreak of furrowed brows across the land:

```
glRotatef(spinY, 0.0, 1.0, 0.0);
glRotatef(spinX, 1.0, 0.0, 0.0);
glTranslatef(0.0, (GLfloat)(sinf(transY)/2.0), z);
```

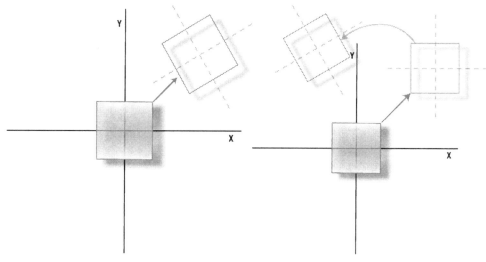

Figure 3-9. *Rotation first or translation first?*

However, in reality, the order of transformations is actually applied from *last to first*. Now put glTranslatef() *ahead* of the two rotations, and you should see something like Figure 3-10, which is exactly what we wanted in the first place. Here is the code needed to do that:

```
glTranslatef(0.0, (GLfloat)(sinf(transY)/2.0), z);

glRotatef(spinY, 0.0, 1.0, 0.0);
glRotatef(spinX, 1.0, 0.0, 0.0);
```

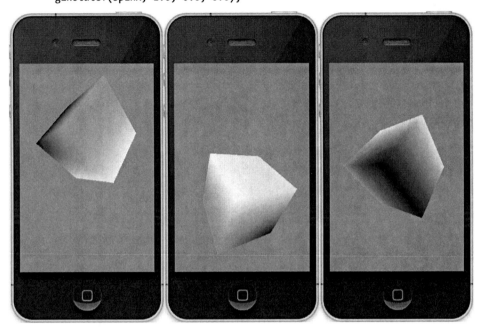

Figure 3-10. *Making the cube spin*

You can visualize transformation ordering in two different ways: the local coordinate or the world coordinate approach. Seeing things in the former, you move the objects to their final resting place and *then* perform the rotations. Because the coordinate system is local, the object will rotate around its own origin, making the previous sequence make sense when going from top to bottom. If you choose the world approach, which is in effect what OpenGL ES is doing, you must perform the rotations first around the object's local axis before performing the translation. In that way, the transformations actually happen from bottom to top. The net result is the same and so is the code, and both are confusing and easily can get out of sequence. That is why you'll see many a 3D guy or gal holding something at arm's length while moving themselves all around to help them figure out why their great-looking catapult model is flying below the ground. This is called the *3D shuffle*. And just to make things more confusing, this is only for *OpenGL ES 1*. The reason being is that the transformations are queued up until the rendering pass is done, and then processed from the first transformation call to the last. While in ES 2, you must perform all of the transforms yourself, in which case they are done immediately as called. Following is the same transformation sequence, but in OpenGL ES 2:

```
baseModelViewMatrix = GLKMatrix4Scale(baseModelViewMatrix,scale,scale,scale);
baseModelViewMatrix = GLKMatrix4Rotate(baseModelViewMatrix, _rotation, 1.0, 0.5, 0.0);
modelviewMatrix = GLKMatrix4MakeTranslation(0.0, offset, -6.0);
modelviewMatrix = GLKMatrix4Multiply(modelviewMatrix, baseModelViewMatrix);
```

One final transformation command to be aware of right now is glScalef(), used for resizing the model along all three axes. Let's say you need to double the height of the cube. You would use the line glScalef(1,2,1). Remember that the height is aligned with the Y-axis, while width and depth are X and Z, which we don't want to touch.

Now the question is, where would you put the line to ensure that the geometry of the cube is the only thing affected, as in Figure 3-11 (left), before or after the calls to glRotatef() in drawInRect()?

If you said after—as in the following example:

```
glTranslatef(0.0, (GLfloat)(sinf(transY)/2.0), z);

glRotatef(spinY, 0.0, 1.0, 0.0);
glRotatef(spinX, 1.0, 0.0, 0.0);
glScalef(1,2,1);
```

—you'd be right. The reason why this works is that because the last transformation in the list is actually the first to be executed, you must put scaling ahead of any other transformations if all you want is to resize the object's geometry. Put it anywhere else, and you could end up with something like Figure 3-11 (right). So, what's happening there? The following was generated with the code snippet:

```
glTranslatef(0.0, (GLfloat)(sinf(transY)/2.0), z);

glScalef(1,2,1);

glRotatef(spinY, 0.0, 1.0, 0.0);
glRotatef(spinX, 1.0, 0.0, 0.0);
```

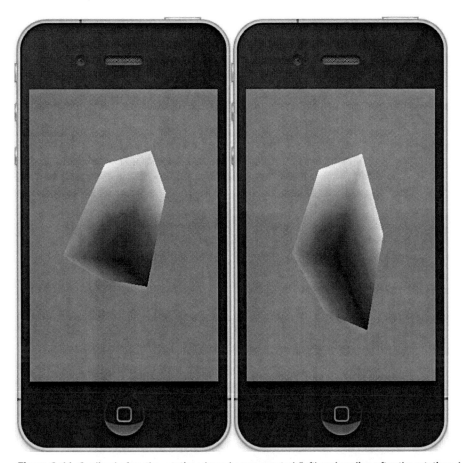

Figure 3-11. Scaling before the rotations have been executed (left) and scaling after the rotations (right)

The geometry is rotated first, and then the cube's local axis is rotated, which no longer aligns with the origin's axis. Following that with scale, it is stretched out along the world's y-axis, instead of its own. This would be as if you already started with a vertex list of a cube rotated partway and scaled it with nothing else. So if you make the scaling at the very end, your entire world is scaled.

Tweaking the Values

Now some more fun comes when we can start playing with various values. This section will demonstrate a number of the various principles that are not just relevant to OpenGL ES but found in nearly every 3D toolkit you're likely to stumble across.

Clipping Regions

With a working demo, we can have fun by tweaking some of values and observing the changes. First we'll change the far clipping plane in the frustum by changing the value of zFar from 1000 down to 1.5. Why? Remember that the cube's local origin is 2.0 and its size is 1.0. So when facing straight at us, the closest point would be 2.5 because each of the sides would straddle the origin with .5 on each side. So, by changing the value of zFar to 1.5, the cube would be hidden when it is exactly facing us. But portions will peek through, looking something like a piece of flotsam poking above the water. The reason is that when it rotates, the corners are naturally going to be a little closer to the viewing plane, as shown in Figure 3-12.

So, what happens when I move the near clipping plane farther away? Reset zFar back to 1000 (a number that is arbitrarily large enough to ensure we can see everything) and set zNear from .1 to 1.5. What do you think it will look like? It will be the opposite of the previous example. See Figure 3-13 for the results.

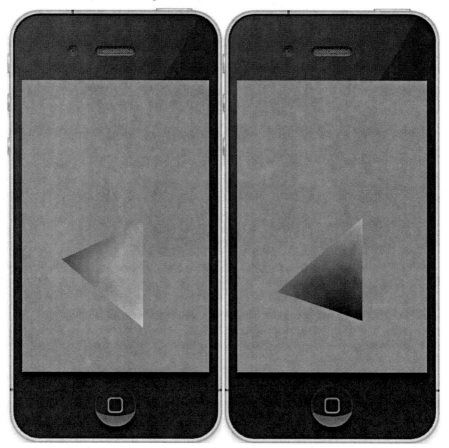

Figure 3-12. Peek-a-boo! The cube is clipped when any part of it is farther away than zFar.

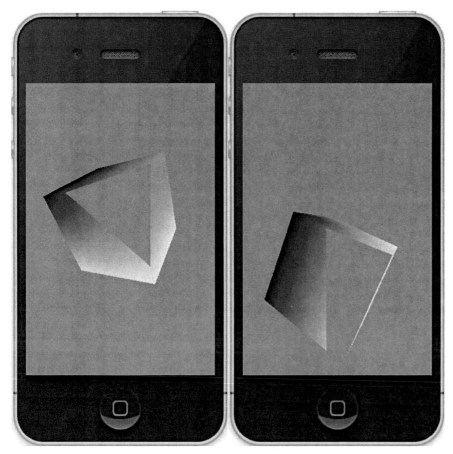

Figure 3-13. *The* zFar *plane is reset, while the* zNear *plane is moved back to clip any part of the cube that is too close.*

Using Z-axis clipping such as this is very helpful when dealing with large and complicated worlds. You'd likely not want all objects you might be "looking at" to be rendered, because many could be too far away to really see. Setting zFar and zNear to limit the visibility distance could speed up the system. However, this would not be the best substitute for preculling your objects before they get into the pipeline.

Field of View

Remember that the viewer's FOV can also be changed in the frustum settings. Go back to our bouncy friend again and make sure your zNear and zFar settings are back to the normal values of .1 and 1000. Now change the z value in drawInRect() to -20 and run again. Figure 3-14 (left) is what you should see.

Next we're going to zoom in. Go to setClipping() and change fieldOfView =5 degrees from 60 degrees. The results are depicted in Figure 3-14 (center). Notice how the cube has no apparent vanishing point or no perspective when compared to Figure 3-14 (right).

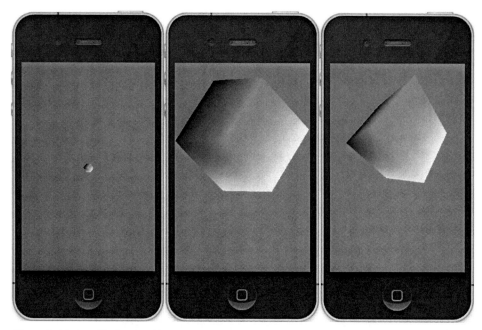

Figure 3-14a,b,c. *Moving the object away (left) and then zooming in on it (center). The rightmost image has the default FOV value set to 60 degrees with the cube at only 2 units away.*

Face Culling

Let's go back to the code you might remember from a few pages ago:

```
glEnable(GL_CULL_FACE);
glCullFace(GL_BACK);
```

As mentioned, the first line tells OpenGL to prepare to do face culling, while the second instructs which face is to be culled. In this case, the triangles facing away from us don't need to be rendered.

> **Note**   glEnable() is a frequent call and is used to change various states, from eliminating back faces, as shown earlier, to smoothing points (GL_POINT-SMOOTH), to performing depth tests (GL_DEPTH_TEST). It can also affect performance if you use it a lot. Best practice is to minimize use of glEnable() as much as possible.

Now replace GL_BACK with GL_FRONT, and run the program. See Figure 3-15.

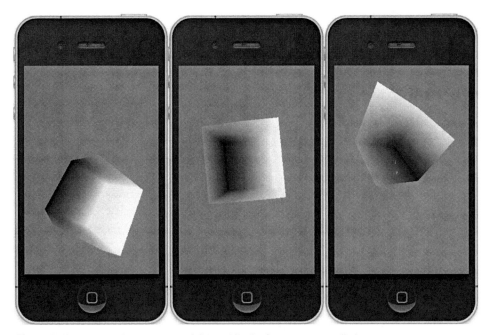

Figure 3-15. *The back faces are now visible, while the front ones are culled.*

Building a Solar System

With these basic tools in our 3D arsenal, we can actually start in the main project, building a small example solar system. What makes a solar system so ideal is that it has a very basic simple shape, several objects that must all move around each other in a hierarchical fashion, and a single light source. The reason why the cube example was used at first is that the shape is about as elementary as you can get for 3D, ensuring that the code was not full of extraneous geometry. When you get to something such as a sphere, most of the code will go to creating just the object, as you will see.

Although OpenGL is a great low-level platform, it still leaves a lot to be desired when it comes to anything remotely high level. As you saw in Chapter 1, when it comes to modeling tools, many available third-party frameworks could ultimately be used to do the job, but for now we're just going to be sticking with basic OpenGL ES.

> **Note**   Besides OpenGL itself, a popular helper toolkit called GL Utility Toolkit (GLUT) is available. GLUT provides a portable API support for basic windowing UI tasks and management functions. It can construct some basic primitives, including a sphere, so it can be very handy when doing small projects. Unfortunately, as of this writing, there is no official GLUT library for iOS, although a couple of efforts are currently in the works.

The first thing to do is create a new project derived from the bouncy square example. But instead of building up all the geometry in `drawInRect()`, you can create a new object called `Planet` and initialize the data, as in Listing 3-6a for the header and Listing 3-6b for the `init` method.

Listing 3-6a. *Building our 3D Planet*

```
#import <Foundation/Foundation.h>
#import <OpenGLES/ES1/gl.h>


@interface Planet : NSObject
{

        @private
            GLfloat     *m_VertexData;
            GLubyte      *m_ColorData;

            GLint         m_Stacks, m_Slices;
            GLfloat        m_Scale;
            GLfloat        m_Squash;
}
- (bool)execute;
- (id) init:(GLint)stacks slices:(GLint)slices radius:(GLfloat)radius squash:(GLfloat)
squash;

@end
```

Listing 3-6b. *3D Sphere generator*

```
- (id) init:(GLint)stacks slices:(GLint)slices radius:(GLfloat)radius squash:(GLfloat)
squash
{
    unsigned int colorIncrment=0;                                            //1
    unsigned int blue=0;
    unsigned int red=255;

    m_Scale=radius;
    m_Squash=squash;

    colorIncrment=255/stacks;                                                //2

    if ((self = [super init]))
    {
        m_Stacks = stacks;
        m_Slices = slices;
        m_VertexData = nil;
```

```
//Vertices

GLfloat *vPtr = m_VertexData =
(GLfloat*)malloc(sizeof(GLfloat) * 3 * ((m_Slices*2+2) * (m_Stacks)));        //3

        //Color data

GLubyte *cPtr = m_ColorData=
(GLubyte*)malloc(sizeof(GLubyte) * 4 * ((m_Slices *2+2) * (m_Stacks)));       //4

unsigned int    phiIdx, thetaIdx;

//latitude

for(phiIdx=0; phiIdx < m_Stacks; phiIdx++)                                    //5
{
    //Starts at -1.57 goes up to +1.57 radians.

    //The first circle.
                                                                             //6
    float phi0 = M_PI * ((float)(phiIdx+0) * (1.0/(float)( m_Stacks)) - 0.5);

    //The next, or second one.
                                                                             //7
    float phi1 = M_PI * ((float)(phiIdx+1) * (1.0/(float)( m_Stacks)) - 0.5);
    float cosPhi0 = cos(phi0);                                               //8
    float sinPhi0 = sin(phi0);
    float cosPhi1 = cos(phi1);
    float sinPhi1 = sin(phi1);

    float cosTheta, sinTheta;

                //longitude

    for(thetaIdx=0; thetaIdx < m_Slices; thetaIdx++)                         //9
    {
        //Increment along the longitude circle each "slice."

        float theta = 2.0*M_PI * ((float)thetaIdx) * (1.0/(float)( m_Slices -
1));

        cosTheta = cos(theta);
        sinTheta = sin(theta);

        //We're generating a vertical pair of points, such
        //as the first point of stack 0 and the first point of stack 1
        //above it. This is how TRIANGLE_STRIPS work,
        //taking a set of 4 vertices and essentially drawing two triangles
        //at a time. The first is v0-v1-v2 and the next is v2-v1-v3, and so on.
```

```
                        //Get x-y-z for the first vertex of stack.
    vPtr [0] = m_Scale*cosPhi0 * cosTheta;                           //10
    vPtr [1] = m_Scale*sinPhi0*m_Squash;
                vPtr [2] = m_Scale*cosPhi0 * sinTheta;


                        //The same but for the vertex immediately above the
                previous one.
    vPtr [3] = m_Scale*cosPhi1 * cosTheta;
    vPtr [4] = m_Scale*sinPhi1*m_Squash;
    vPtr [5] = m_Scale* cosPhi1 * sinTheta;

    cPtr [0] = red;                                                  //11
    cPtr [1] = 0;
    cPtr [2] = blue;
    cPtr [4] = red;
    cPtr [5] = 0;
    cPtr [6] = blue;
    cPtr [3] = cPtr[7] = 255;

    cPtr += 2*4;                                                     //12

    vPtr += 2*3;
    }

blue+=colorIncrment;                                                 //13
red-=colorIncrment;
    }
}

return self;
}
```

Okay, so it takes a lot of code to create something as basic as a sphere. Using the triangle lists is more involved than using the quads in standard OpenGL, but that's what we have to work with.

The basic algorithm divides the sphere into stacks and slices. Stacks are the lateral pieces while slices are vertical. The boundaries of the stacks are generated two at a time as partners. These form the boundaries of the triangle strip. So, stack A and B are calculated and subdivided into triangles based on the number of slices around the circle. The next time through, take stacks B and C and rinse and repeat. Two boundary conditions apply:

- The first and last stacks contain the two poles, in which case they are more of a triangle fan, as opposed to a strip, but we treat them as strips to simplify the code.

- Make sure that the end of each strip connects with the beginning to form a contiguous set of triangles.

So, let's break this down:

- The initialization routine uses the notion of stacks and slices to define the resolution of the sphere. Having more slices and stacks means a much smoother sphere but uses much more memory along with additional processing time. Think of a slice as similar to an apple wedge, representing a piece of the sphere from bottom to top. A stack is a slice that is lateral, defining sections of latitude. See Figure 3-16.

  The `radius` parameter is a form of scale. You could opt to normalize all your objects and use `glScalef()`, but that does add extra CPU overhead, so in this case `radius` is used as a form of prescaling. And `squash` is used to create a flattened sphere, necessary for Jupiter and Saturn. Both have very high rates of revolution. (Jupiter's day is only about 10 hours, while its diameter is more than 10 times the Earth's.) As a result, its polar diameter is about 93 percent of the equatorial diameter. And Saturn is even more flattened, with the polar diameter only 90 percent of the equatorial.

- Because we want something interesting to look at until we get to the cool texture stuff in Chapter 5, let's vary the colors from top to bottom. The top is blue, and the bottom is red. The `colorIncrement` is merely the color delta from stack to stack. Red starts at 255, and blue starts at 0, using unsigned chars.

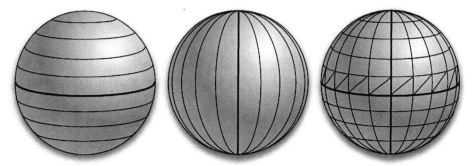

Figure 3-16. Stacks go up and down, slices go round and round, and faces are subdivided into triangle strips.

▨ Lines 3 and 4 allocate the memory for both the vertices and the colors.
Later other arrays will be needed to hold the texture coordinates and
face normals needed for lighting, but for now, let's keep things simple.
Notice that we're doing 32-bit colors, as with the cube. Three bytes
are for the RGB triplet, while the fourth is for *alpha* (translucency) but is
not needed in this example.

▨ Line 5 starts the outer loop, going from the bottom-most stack (or the
southern polar regions of our planet or altitude of -90 degrees) and up
to the northern pole, at +90 degrees.

Some Greek identifiers are used here for spherical coordinates. *Phi* is
commonly used for the latitude-like points, while *theta* is used for
longitude.

▨ Lines 6 and 7 generate the latitude for the boundaries of a specific
strip. For starters, when `phiIdx` is 0, we want `phi0` to be -90 degrees,
or -1.57. The -.5 shoves everything down by 90 degrees; otherwise,
our values would go from 0 to 180 degrees.

▨ In lines 8ff, some values are precalculated to minimize the CPU load.

▨ Line 9 is the inner loop, going from 0 to 360 degrees, and defines the
slices. The math is similar, so no need to go into extreme detail,
except that we are calculating the points on a circle, via line 10. Both
`m_Scale` and `m_Squash` come into play here. But for now, just assume
that they are both 1.0, so the sphere is normalized.

Notice that vertex 0 and vertex 2 are addressed here. Vertex 0 is x,
while vertex 2 is z—which are parallel to the ground, the X-Z plane.
Since vertex 1 is the same as y, it remains constant for each loop and
of course represents the latitude. Since we're doing the loops in pairs,
vertices 3, 4, and 5 cover up the
next loop.

In effect, we are generating pairs of points, namely, each point and its
mate immediately above it. And this is the format that GL expects for
the triangle strips, as shown in Figure 3-17.

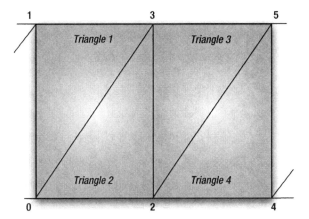

Figure 3-17. *A triangle strip of six vertices*

▨ In line 11, the color array is generated, and as with the vertices, they are generated in pairs. The green component is ignored for now.

▨ At lines 12f, the color array pointer and vertex array pointers are incremented.

▨ And finally in line 13, we increment the blue and decrement the red.

Now that the geometry is out of the way, we need to concentrate on the execute method. See Listing 3-7.

Listing 3-7. *Rendering the Planet*

```
- (bool)execute
{
    glMatrixMode(GL_MODELVIEW);                                      //1
    glEnable(GL_CULL_FACE);                                          //2
    glCullFace(GL_BACK);                                             //3

    glEnableClientState(GL_VERTEX_ARRAY);                           //4
    glEnableClientState(GL_COLOR_ARRAY);                            //5

    glVertexPointer(3, GL_FLOAT, 0, m_VertexData);                  //6

    glColorPointer(4, GL_UNSIGNED_BYTE, 0, m_ColorData);            //7
    glDrawArrays(GL_TRIANGLE_STRIP, 0, (m_Slices +1)*2*(m_Stacks-1)+2); //8

    return true;
}
```

You should now recognize many of the elements from the cube examples.

- First, in line 1, tell the system that we want to work with the GL_MODELVIEW matrix (the one that supports the transformation information).

- Lines 2 and 3 are identical to the ones used previously to cull out the back of the sphere that we cannot see.

- Lines 4 and 5 are again familiar and tell OpenGL to accept both vertex and color information.

- Next we supply the vertex data in line 6 and the color data in line 7.

- Line 8 does the heavy lifting in drawing the arrays, both color and vertices.

Now that the planet object is complete enough for this example, let's do the driver. First, create a new Objective-C object and call it something like OpenGLSolarSystemController. Now add the code from Listing 3-8a and 3-8b to initialize the object and universe.

Listing 3-8a. Initializing your universe: the header

```
#import <Foundation/Foundation.h>
#import <GLKit/GLKit.h>
#import "Planet.h"

@interface OpenGLSolarSystemController : NSObject
{
    Planet *m_Earth;
}

-(void)execute;
-(id)init;
-(void)initGeometry;

@end
```

Listing 3-8b. Initializing your universe: the rest of the stuff

```
-(id)init
{
    [self initGeometry];

    return self;
}

-(void)initGeometry
{
    m_Earth=[[Planet alloc] init:10 slices:10 radius:1.0 squash:1.0];
}
```

The earth model here is initialized at fairly low resolution: 10 stacks high, 10 slices around.

Listing 3-9 shows the master execute method. As with the cube, we translate the earth on the Z-axis and rotate it around the y-axis.

Listing 3-9. *Master execute method*

```
-(void)execute
{
    static GLfloat angle=0;

    glLoadIdentity();
    glTranslatef(0.0, -0.0, -3.0);

    glRotatef(angle,0.0,1.0,0.0);

    [m_Earth execute];

    angle+=.5;
}
```

For the final steps, go to the window's `viewcontroller` and change `viewDidLoad()` to Listing 3-10.

Listing 3-10. *The new* `viewDidLoad()` *method*

```
- (void)viewDidLoad
{
    [super viewDidLoad];

    self.context = [[EAGLContext alloc] initWithAPI:kEAGLRenderingAPIOpenGLES1];

    if (!self.context)
    {
        NSLog(@"Failed to create ES context");
    }

    GLKView *view = (GLKView *)self.view;
    view.context = self.context;
    view.drawableDepthFormat = GLKViewDrawableDepthFormat24;

    m_SolarSystem=[[ OpenGLSolarSystemController alloc] init];

    [EAGLContext setCurrentContext:self.context];

    [self setClipping];
}
```

Now change the `drawInRect()` method to the one in Listing 3-11.

Listing 3-11. *The new* drawInRect *for the Solar System*

```
- (void)glkView:(GLKView *)view drawInRect:(CGRect)rect
{

    glClearColor(0.0,0.0, 0.0, 1.0);
    glClear(GL_COLOR_BUFFER_BIT | GL_DEPTH_BUFFER_BIT);

    [m_SolarSystem execute];
}
```

Finally, add in setClipping() (used in the previous exercise), making sure you've reset the FOV to 50 or 60 degrees; modify the headers as needed; and compile. You should see something like Figure 3-18.

Figure 3-18. *The future planet Earth*

It is actually rotating but, because it has no features at all, you'll be hard-pressed to see the motion.

As with the previous examples, let's play around with some of the parameters and see what happens. First let's change the number of stacks and slices, from 10 to 20, in the initGeometry method. You should see something like Figure 3-19.

Figure 3-19. *The planet with double the stacks and slices*

If you want your curved objects to look smoother, there are generally three ways:

- Have as many triangles as possible.
- Use some special lighting and shading tools built into OpenGL.
- Use textures.

The next chapter will cover the second option. But for now, see how many slices and stacks it takes to make a really smooth sphere. (It works best with an equal number of both.) It really starts looking good at 100 each. For now, go back to 10 each when finished with this exercise.

If you want to look at the actual wireframe structure of the sphere, in Planet.m, change GL_TRIANGLE_STRIP in the execute method to GL_LINE_STRIP. And you may want to change the background color to a medium gray to make the lines stand out better (Figure 3-20, left). As an exercise, see what it takes to get Figure 3-20 (right). Now ask yourself why we're not seeing triangles there instead of that funky spiral pattern. It is simply the way OpenGL draws and connects line strips. We could have it render triangle outlines by specifying a connectivity array. But for our ultimate goal, that is not necessary.

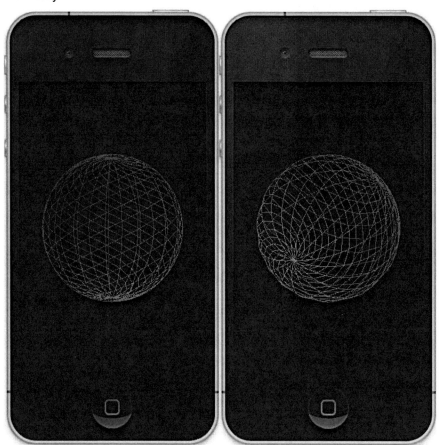

Figure 3-20. The planet In wireframe mode

On your own, change GL_LINE_STRIP to GL_POINTS. There you'll see each of the vertices rendered as a single dot.

Then try the frustum again. Set zNear from .1 to 2.15. (Why not 3? The distance of the object?) And you'll get Figure 3-21.

Figure 3-21. *Someone is setting the* zNear *clipping plane too close.*

And one final exercise: what would it take to get something that looks like Figure 3-22? (This is what you would need for Jupiter and Saturn; because they spin so fast, they are not spherical but rather oblate-spheroids.)

Figure 3-22. *What does it take to get this?*

And lastly, for extra credit, make it bounce like the cube.

Summary

In this chapter, we started by generating a 2D square, turned it into a 3D cube, and then learned how to rotate and translate it. We also learned about the viewing frustum and how it can be used to cull out objects and zoom in and out of our scene. Lastly, we constructed a much more complicated object that will be the root of the solar-system model. The next chapter will cover shading, lighting, and materials, and a second object will be added.

Chapter 4

Turning On the Lights

You must be strong now. You must never give up. And when people [or code] make you cry and you are afraid of the dark, don't forget the light is always there.

—Author Unknown

Light is the first of painters. There is no object so foul that intense light will not make it beautiful.

—Ralph Waldo Emerson

Everything's shiny, Cap'n. Not to fret.

—Kaylee Frye, Firefly

This chapter will cover perhaps the single biggest topic for OpenGL ES: the process of illuminating, shading, and coloring the virtual landscape. We touched on color in the previous chapter, but because it is so integral to both lighting and shading, we will cover it more in depth here. For those of you reading the quaint paper version of this book, yes, I know, it is odd to have a chapter on colors in a monochrome form. However, the ebook version is in color.

The Story of Light and Color

Without light, the world would be a dark place (duh). Without color, it would be hard to tell the difference between stoplights.

We all take for granted the wondrous nature of light—from the soft and gentle illumination off the morning mist to the ignition of a space shuttle's main engines to the shy pale radiance of a full moon on a snowy field in mid-winter. A lot has been written about the physics of light and its nature and perception. It might take an artist a lifetime to fully understand how to take colored pigments suspended in oil and to apply them on a canvas to create a believable rainbow at the base of a waterfall. Such is the task of OpenGL ES when it comes to turning on the lights in our scenes.

Sans poetry, light is merely a portion of the full electromagnetic spectrum that our eyes are sensitive to. The same spectrum also includes radio signals that our iPhones use, X-rays to aid a physician, gamma rays sent out from a dying star billions of years ago, and microwaves that can be used to reheat some pizza left over from Wii Bowling Night last Thursday.

Light is said to have four main properties: wavelength, intensity, polarization, and direction. The wavelength determines the color that we perceive, or whether we can actually see anything in the first place. The visible spectrum starts in the violet range, with wavelengths of around 380 nanometers, on up to red, with a wavelength of around 780 nanometers. Immediately below is ultraviolet, and right above the visible range you'll find infrared, which we can't directly see but can detect indirectly in the form of heat.

The way we perceive colors from objects has to do with what wavelengths the object or its material absorbs or otherwise *interferes* with the oncoming light. Besides absorption, it could be scattered (giving us the blue of the sky or the red of the sunset), reflected, and refracted.

If someone says that their favorite color is white, they must mean that all colors are their favorite because white is a summation of all colors of the visible spectrum. If it is black, they don't like any colors, because black is the absence of color. In fact, that is why you shouldn't wear black on a nice warm sunny day. Your clothing absorbs so much energy (in the form of light and infrared) that some of that ultimately turns into heat.

> **Note**   When the sun is straight overhead, it can deliver an irradiance of about 1 kilowatt for every square meter. Of that, a little more than half is infrared, sensed as a very warm day, while a little less than half is visible light, and a measly 32 watts are devoted to UV.

It is said that Aristotle developed the first known color theory. He considered four colors, each corresponding to one of the four elements of air, earth, water, and fire.

However, as we look at the visible spectrum, you will notice a nice contiguous spread from violet on one end to red on the other that has neither water nor fire in it. Nor will you see discrete values of red, green, or blue, typically used nowadays to define the individual shades. In the early 19th century, British polymath Thomas Young developed the tricolor model that uses three colors to simulate all visible hues. Young proposed that the retina was made up of bundles of nerve fibers, which would respond to varying intensities of red, green, or violet light. German scientist Hermann von Helmholtz later expanded this theory in the mid-19th century.

Note   Young was a particularly colorful fellow. (Someone had to say it.) Not only was he the founder of the field of *physiological optics*, in his spare time he developed the wave theory of light, including the invention of the classic double-slit experiment, which is a college physics staple. But wait! There's more! He also proposed the theory of capillary phenomena, was the first to use the term *energy* in the modern sense, partially deciphered some of the Egyptian portion of the Rosetta Stone, and devised an improved means of tuning musical instruments. The laddie must have been seriously sleep-deprived.

Today, colors are most frequently described via red-green-blue (RGB) triplets and their relative intensity. Each of the colors fades to black with zero intensity and shows varying hues as the intensity increases, ultimately perceived as white. Because the three colors need to be added together to produce the entire spectrum, this system is an *additive* model.

Besides the RGB model, printers use a subtractive mode known as CMYK, for cyan-magenta-yellow-black (the *key*). Because the three primaries cannot produce a really deep black, black is added as an accent for deep shadows or graphic details.

Another common model is HSV for hue-saturation-value, and you will frequently find it as an alternative to RGB in many graphics packages or color pickers. Developed in the 1970s specifically for computer graphics, HSV depicts color as a 3D cylinder (Figure 4-1). Saturation goes from the inside out, value goes from bottom to top, and hue goes around the edge. A variant on this is HSL, substituting value for lightness. Figure 4-2 shows the Mac OS X color picker in its many versions.

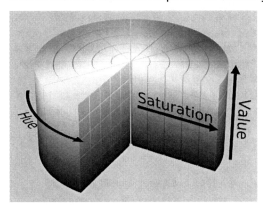

Figure 4-1. *HSV color wheel or cylinder (source: Wikipedia Commons)*

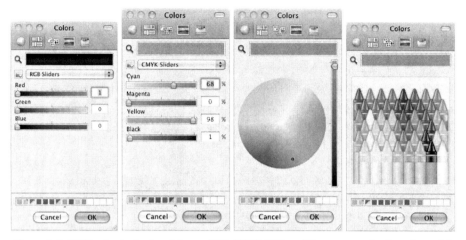

Figure 4-2. *OS X's standard color pickers—RGB, CMYK, HSV, and the ever-popular Crayola model*

Let There Be Light

In the real world, light comes at us from all sides and with all colors and, when combined, can create the details and rich scenes of everyday life. OpenGL doesn't attempt to duplicate anything like the real-world lighting models, because those are very complex and time-consuming and generally reserved for Disney's rendering farms. But it can approximate it in a way that is certainly good enough for real-time gaming action.

The lighting model used in OpenGL ES 1 permits us to place several lights of varying types around our scene. We can switch them on or off at will, specifying direction, intensity, colors, and so on. But that's not all, because we also need to describe various properties of our model and how it interacts with the incoming light. *Lighting* defines the way light sources interact with objects and the materials those objects are created with. *Shading* specifically determines the coloring of the pixel based on the lighting and material. Notice that a white piece of paper will reflect light completely differently than a pink, mirrored Christmas ornament. Taken together, these properties are bundled up into an object called a *material*. Blending the material's attributes and the light's attributes together generates the final scene.

> **Note**   OpenGL ES 2 has no lights whatsoever, leaving that up to the programmer via the use of shaders. The GLKit framework, new in iOS5, adds a few lights via the GLKBaseEffect object, but that is not meant to be a general-purpose substitute for version 1.

The colors of OpenGL lights can consist of up to three different components:

- Diffuse
- Ambient
- Specular

Diffuse light can be said to come from one direction such as the sun or a flashlight. It hits an object and then scatters off in all directions, producing a pleasant soft quality. When a diffuse light hits a surface, the reflected amount is largely determined by the angle of incidence. It will be at its brightest when directly facing the light but drops as it tilts further and further away.

Ambient light is that which comes from no particular direction, having been reflected off all the surfaces that make up the environment. Look around the room you are in, and the light that is bouncing off the ceiling, walls, and your furniture all combine to form the ambient light. If you are a photographer, you know how important ambient lighting is to make a scene much more realistic than a single point source can, particularly in portrait photography where you would have a soft "fill light" to offset the brighter main light.

Specular light is that which is reflected off a shiny surface. It comes from a specific direction but bounces off a surface in a much more directed fashion. It makes the hot spot that we'd see on a disco ball or a newly cleaned and waxed car. It is at its brightest when the viewpoint is directly in line with the source and falls off quickly as we move around the object.

When it comes to both diffuse and specular lighting, they are typically the same colors. But even though we're limited to the eight light objects, having different colors for each component actually means that a single OpenGL "light" can act like three different ones at the same time. Out of the three, you might consider having the ambient light be a different color, usually one that is opposing the main coloring so as to make the scene more visually interesting. In the solar-system model, a dim blue ambient light helps illuminate the dark side of a planet and lends a greater 3D quality to it.

> **Note**   You don't have to specify all three types for a given light. Diffuse usually works just fine in simple scenes.

Back to the Fun Stuff (for a While)

We're not done with the theory yet, but let's get back to coding for a while. After that, I'll cover more on light and shading theory.

You saw in the previous examples how colors defined with the standard RGB version on a per-vertex basis would let us see our world without any lighting at all. Now we will create lights of various types and position them around our so-called planet. OpenGL ES must support at least eight lights total, which is the case for iOS. But of course you can create more and add or remove them as needed. If you are really picky, you can check at runtime for just how many lights a particular implementation of OpenGL supports by using one of the many variants of glGet* to retrieve the values of this:

```
int numLights;
glGetIntegerv(GL_MAX_LIGHTS,&numLights);
```

> **Note** OpenGL ES has a number of utility functions, with glGet*() being one of the most commonly used. The glGet* calls let you inquire about the states of various parameters, such as the current modelview matrix to the current line width. The exact call depends on the type of data requested. Be careful about using these calls too frequently, particularly in production code, because they are very inefficient.

Let's go back to the example code from Chapter 3, where you had a squashed red and blue planet, and make the following changes:

1. Ensure that the squash value is 1.0, and the planet is made up of 10 stacks and 10 slices.

2. *In* Planet.m, *comment out the line* blue+=colorIncrment *at* the end of the init() method.

What should you see? C'mon, no peeking. Cover up Figure 4-3 and guess. Got it? Now you can compile and run. Figure 4-3 (left) is what you should see. Now go back to the initGeometry method and increase the number of slices and stacks to 100 each. That should yield Figure 4-3 (right). So, by simply changing a few numbers around, we have a crude lighting and shading scheme. But this is only a fixed lighting scheme that breaks down the moment you want to start moving things around. That's when we let OpenGL do the heavy lifting.

Unfortunately, the process of adding lights is a little more complicated than just calling something like glMakeAwesomeLightsDude(), as we will see.

Figure 4-3. *Simulated lighting from below (left) and a higher polygon count to simulate shading (right)*

1. Create a new header to hold some of the systemwide values, and call it OpenGLSolarSystem.h. For now, it should contain just the following two lines:

   ```
   #import <OpenGLES/ES1/gl.h>
   #define SS_SUNLIGHT    GL_LIGHT0    //GL uses  GL_LIGHTx
   ```

2. Add #import "OpenGLSolarSystem.h" to the top of the solar-system view controller.

3. Add the code in Listing 4-1, and call it from your viewDidLoad() method in the viewcontroller where all of the other initializers reside. And make sure to set the current *context*; otherwise, you'll not see a thing.

Listing 4-1. *Initializing the lights*

```
-(void)initLighting
{
    GLfloat diffuse[]={0.0,1.0,0.0,1.0};                          //1
    GLfloat pos[]={0.0,10.0,0.0,1.0};                            //2

    glLightfv(SS_SUNLIGHT,GL_POSITION,pos);                     //3
    glLightfv(SS_SUNLIGHT,GL_DIFFUSE,diffuse);                  //4

    glShadeModel(GL_FLAT);                                       //5

    glEnable(GL_LIGHTING);                                       //6
    glEnable(SS_SUNLIGHT);                                       //7
}
```

This is what's going on:

▨ The lighting components are in the standard RGBA normalized form. So in this case, there is no red, maximum green, and no blue. The final value of alpha should be kept at 1.0 for now, because it will be covered in more detail later.

▨ Line 2 specifies the position of the light. It is at a y of +10 so, it will be hovering above our sphere.

▨ In lines 3 and 4, we set the light's position and the diffuse component to the diffuse color. `glLightfv()` is a new call and is used to set various light-related parameters. You can retrieve any of this data at a later time using `glGetLightfv()`, which retrieves any of the parameters from a specific light.

▨ In line 5 we specify a shading model. Flat means that a face is a single solid color, while setting it to `GL_SMOOTH` will cause the colors to blend smoothly across the face and from face to face.

▨ And finally, line 6 tells the system we want to use lighting, while line 7 enables the one light we've created.

> **Note** The final parameter of `glLightfv()` takes an array of four `GLfloat` values; the *fv* suffix means "float-vector." There is also a `glLightf()` call to set single-value parameters.

Now compile and run. Eh? What's that, you say? You see only a black thing about the size of the super-massive black hole at the center of the galaxy M31? Oh yes, we forgot something, sorry. As previously mentioned, OpenGL in all of its varieties still remains a relatively low-level library, so it is up to the programmer to handle all sorts of housekeeping tasks that you'd expect a higher-level system to manage (and it gets much worse on OpenGL ES 2.0). And once the lights are turned on, the predefined vertex colors are ignored, so we get black. With that in mind, our sphere model needs an extra layer of data to tell the system just how to light its facets, and that is done through an array of *normals* for each vertex.

What is a vertex normal? *Face* normals are normalized vectors that are *orthogonal* (perpendicular) to a plane or face. But in OpenGL, vertex normals are used instead because they provide for better shading down the road. It sounds odd that a vertex can have a "normal" of its own. After all, what is the "direction" of a vertex? It is actually quite simple conceptually, because vertex normals are merely the normalized sum of the normals of the faces adjacent to the vertex. See Figure 4-4.

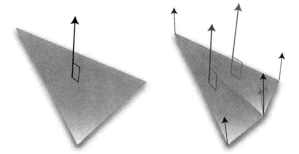

Figure 4-4. *A face normal is illustrated on the right, while vertex normals for a triangle fan are on the left.*

OpenGL needs all of this information to tell what "direction" the vertex is aiming at so it can calculate just how much illumination is falling on it, if at all. It will be its brightest when aiming directly at the light source and dims as it starts tilting away. This means we need to modify our planet generator to create a normal array along with the vertex and color arrays, as shown in Listing 4-2.

Listing 4-2. *Adding the normal generator to* planet.m

```
- (id) init:(GLint)stacks slices:(GLint)slices radius:(GLfloat)radius squash:(GLfloat)
squash
{
    unsigned int colorIncrment=0;
    unsigned int blue=0;
    unsigned int red=255;
    int numVertices=0;

    m_Scale=radius;
    m_Squash=squash;

    colorIncrment=255/stacks;

    if ((self = [super init]))
    {
        m_Stacks = stacks;
        m_Slices = slices;
        m_VertexData = nil;

        // Vertices

        GLfloat *vPtr = m_VertexData =
            (GLfloat*)malloc(sizeof(GLfloat) * 3 * ((m_Slices*2+2) * (m_Stacks)));
```

```
// Color data

GLubyte *cPtr = m_ColorData =
    (GLubyte*)malloc(sizeof(GLubyte) * 4 * ((m_Slices*2+2) * (m_Stacks)));

// Normal pointers for lighting.

GLfloat *nPtr = m_NormalData =                                          //1
            (GLfloat*)malloc(sizeof(GLfloat) * 3 * ((m_Slices*2+2) *
        (m_Stacks)));
unsigned int phiIdx, thetaIdx;

// Latitude

for(phiIdx=0; phiIdx < m_Stacks; phiIdx++)
{
    // Starts at -1.57 and goes up to +1.57 radians.

    // The first circle.

    float phi0 = M_PI * ((float)(phiIdx+0) * (1.0/(float)(m_Stacks)) - 0.5);

    // The next, or second one.

    float phi1 = M_PI * ((float)(phiIdx+1) * (1.0/(float)(m_Stacks)) - 0.5);
    float cosPhi0 = cos(phi0);
    float sinPhi0 = sin(phi0);
    float cosPhi1 = cos(phi1);
    float sinPhi1 = sin(phi1);

    float cosTheta, sinTheta;

    // Longitude

    for(thetaIdx=0; thetaIdx < m_Slices; thetaIdx++)
    {
        // Increment along the longitude circle each "slice."

        float theta = 2.0*M_PI * ((float)thetaIdx) * (1.0/(float)(m_Slices-1));
        cosTheta = cos(theta);
        sinTheta = sin(theta);

        // We're generating a vertical pair of points, such
        // as the first point of stack 0 and the first point of stack 1
        // above it. This is how TRIANGLE_STRIPS work,
        // taking a set of 4 vertices and essentially drawing two triangles
        // at a time. The first is v0-v1-v2 and the next is v2-v1-v3, etc.
```

```
            // Get x-y-z for the first vertex of stack.

            vPtr[0] = m_Scale*cosPhi0 * cosTheta;
            vPtr[1] = m_Scale*sinPhi0*m_Squash;
            vPtr[2] = m_Scale*cosPhi0 * sinTheta;

            // The same but for the vertex immediately above
            // the previous one

            vPtr[3] = m_Scale*cosPhi1 * cosTheta;
            vPtr[4] = m_Scale*sinPhi1*m_Squash;
            vPtr[5] = m_Scale* cosPhi1 * sinTheta;

            // Normal pointers for lighting.

            nPtr[0] = cosPhi0 * cosTheta;                          //2
            nPtr[1] = sinPhi0;
                        nPtr[2] = cosPhi0 * sinTheta;

            nPtr[3] = cosPhi1 * cosTheta;                          //3
                        nPtr[4] = sinPhi1;
                        nPtr[5] = cosPhi1 * sinTheta;

            cPtr[0] = red;
            cPtr[1] = 0;
            cPtr[2] = blue;
            cPtr[4] = red;
            cPtr[5] = 0;
            cPtr[6] = blue;
            cPtr[3] = cPtr[7] = 255;

            cPtr += 2*4;
            vPtr += 2*3;
            nPtr +=2*3;                                            //4

        }

        blue+=colorIncrment;
        red-=colorIncrment;
    }

    numVertices=(vPtr-m_VertexData)/6;
}

return self;
}
```

What's happening here:

▨   In line 1, the normal array is allocated with one three-component
     normal per vertex. (And while you're at it, don't forget to add the
     instance variable GLfloat *m_NormalData; to Planet.h.)

▨   Lines 2ff and 3ff generate the normal data. It doesn't look like any
     fancy-schmancy normal averaging scheme covered earlier, so what
     gives? Since we're dealing with a very simple symmetrical form of a
     sphere, the normals are identical to the vertices without any scaling
     values (to ensure they are unit vectors—that is, of length 1.0). Notice
     that the calculations for the vPtr values and the nPtrs are virtually the
     same as a result.

▨   And as with the other two pointers, nPtr is incremented.

> **Note**   You'll rarely need to actually generate your own normals. If you do any real work in
> OpenGL ES, you'll likely be importing models from third-party applications, such as 3D-Studio
> or Strata. They will generate the normal arrays along with the others for you. More will be
> covered on this later.

Add the following to the planet's interface in Planet.h:

GLfloat   *m_NormalData;

The final step is to modify the execute() method in Planet.m to look like Listing 4-3.

Listing 4-3. Supporting lighting in the Planet Execute routine

```
- (bool)execute
{
    glMatrixMode(GL_MODELVIEW);
    glEnable(GL_CULL_FACE);
    glCullFace(GL_BACK);

    glEnableClientState(GL_NORMAL_ARRAY);                          //1
    glEnableClientState(GL_VERTEX_ARRAY);
    glEnableClientState(GL_COLOR_ARRAY);

    glVertexPointer(3, GL_FLOAT, 0, m_VertexData);
    glNormalPointer(GL_FLOAT, 0, m_NormalData);                    //2

    glColorPointer(4, GL_UNSIGNED_BYTE, 0, m_ColorData);
    glDrawArrays(GL_TRIANGLE_STRIP, 0, (m_Slices+1)*2*(m_Stacks-1)+2);

    return true;
}
```

It's not much different than the original, except with the addition of lines 1 and 2 for
sending the normal data to the OpenGL pipeline alongside the color and vertex
information. If you have a very simple model in which many of the vertices all share the

same normal, you can dump the normal array and use `glNormal3f()` instead, saving a little memory and CPU overhead in the process.

Let's make one final tweak. For this example, ensure that the planet is allocated with the stack and slice values set back to 10 each This makes it easier to see how some of the lighting works. Now you can compile and run it for real, and if you get something similar to Figure 4-5, relax and take a pause for a cool refreshing beverage.

Figure 4-5. Flat lighting

Now that you're back, I am sure you've spotted something a little odd. Supposedly the geometry is based on strips of triangles, so why are the faces those weird four-sided triangle things?

When set for flat shading, OpenGL picks up its illumination cue from only a single vertex, the last one of the respective triangle. Now, instead of the strips being drawn from triangles in horizontal pairs, think of them loosely coupled in vertical pairs, as you see in Figure 4-6.

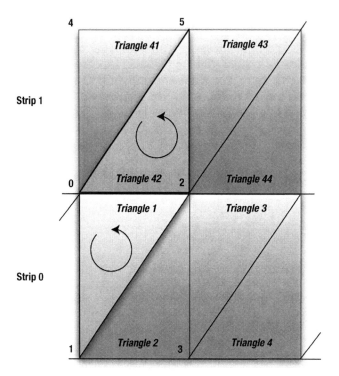

Figure 4-6. *"Stacked" triangle pairs*

In Strip 0, Triangle 1 will be drawn using vertices 0, 1, and 2, with vertex 2 used for the shading. Triangle 2 will use 2, 1, and 3. Lather, rinse, and repeat for the rest of the strip. Next for Strip 1, Triangle 41 will be drawn with vertices 4, 0, and 5. But Triangle 42 will use vertices 5, 0, and 2, with the same vertex as Triangle 1 for its shading. That is why the vertical pairs combine to form a "bent" quadrilateral.

There are few reasons nowadays to use flat shading, so in `initLighting()`, swap out `GL_FLAT` for `GL_SMOOTH`.

And now you probably know the drill: compile, run, and compare. Then for fun, decrease the sphere's resolution from 10 slices and segments down to 5. Go back to flat shading on this one, and then compare to smooth shading. See Figure 4-7a, b, and c. Figure 4-7c is particularly interesting because the shading model starts to break down, showing some artifacting along the face edges. Now reset the sphere's resolution back up to 20 or 30 to make it nice and smooth for the next section.

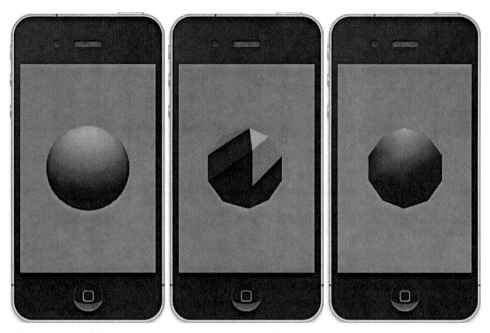

Figure 4-7. *From left to right, smooth shading a sphere with 20 stacks and 20 slices, flat shading on a sphere of only 5 stacks and slices, followed by smooth shading*

Fun with Light and Materials

Now, since we have a nice smooth sphere to play with, we can start tinkering with the other lighting models and materials. But first a thought experiment: say you have a green sphere as shown earlier but your diffuse light is red. What color will the sphere be? (Pause for the *Jeopardy* theme.) Ready? Well, in the real world what would it be? Reddish green? Greenish red? A mauvy shade of pinky russet? Let's try it and find out. Modify initLighting() again, as shown in Listing 4-4. Note that the light vectors have been renamed to their specific colors to make it a little more readable.

Listing 4-4. *Adding Some More Light Types and Materials*

```
-(void)initLighting
{
    GLfloat pos[]={0.0,3.0,0.0,1.0};

    GLfloat white[]={1.0,1.0,1.0,1.0};
    GLfloat red[]={1.0,0.0,0.0,1.0};
    GLfloat green[]={0.0,1.0,0.0,1.0};
    GLfloat blue[]={0.0,0.0,1.0,1.0};

    GLfloat cyan[]={0.0,1.0,1.0,1.0};
    GLfloat yellow[]={1.0,1.0,0.0,1.0};
    GLfloat magenta[]={1.0,0.0,1.0,1.0};
```

```
    GLfloat halfcyan[]={0.0,.5,.5,1.0};

    //Lights go here.

    glLightfv(SS_SUNLIGHT,GL_POSITION,pos);
    glLightfv(SS_SUNLIGHT,GL_DIFFUSE,green);

    //Materials go here.

    glMaterialfv(GL_FRONT_AND_BACK, GL_DIFFUSE, red);                          // 1

    glShadeModel(GL_SMOOTH);

    glEnable(GL_LIGHTING);
    glEnable(SS_SUNLIGHT);

    glLoadIdentity();
}
```

If you see our old friend, the supermassive black hole from M31, you've done well. So, why is it black? That's simple; remember the discussion at the start of this chapter on colors and reflectance? A red object looks red only when the lighting hitting it has a red component, precisely the way our green light doesn't. If you had a red balloon in a dark room and illuminated it with green light on it, it would look black, because no green would come back to you. And if someone asks you what you're doing with a red balloon in a dark room, just growl "Physics!" Then tell them that they just wouldn't understand in a dismissive tone.

So, with this understanding, replace the red diffuse material with green in line 1. What should you get? Right, the green sphere is illuminated again. But you may notice something really interesting. The green now looks a little bit brighter than before adding the material. Figure 4-8 (left) shows it without any material specified, and Figure 4-8 (right) shows it with the green diffuse material added.

Figure 4-8. *Without green material defined (left) and with it defined (right)*

Let's do one more experiment. Let's make the diffuse light be a more traditional white. What should now happen with the green? Red? How about blue? Since the white light has *all* those components, the colored materials should all show up equally well. But if you see the black ball again, you changed the material's color, not the lighting.

Specular Lighting

Well, how about the specular stuff? Add the following line to the lights section:

```
glLightfv(SS_SUNLIGHT,GL_SPECULAR,red);
```

To the material section, add this:

```
glMaterialfv(GL_FRONT_AND_BACK, GL_SPECULAR, red);
```

And change the light's position to the following:

```
GLfloat pos[]={10.0,3.0,0.0,1.0};
```

> **Note**   The first value to `glMaterial*` must always be `GL_FRONT_AND_BACK`. In normal OpenGL, you're permitted to have different materials on both sides of a face, but not so in OpenGL ES. However, you still must use the front and back values in OpenGL ES, or materials will not work properly.

Reset the diffuse material back to green. You should see something that looks like a big mess of something yellowish-reddish. Shorthand for what's happening is that there's yet another value we can use to play with the lighting. Called *shininess*, it specifies just how shiny the object's surface is and ranges from 0 to 128. The higher the value, the more focused the reflection will be, and hence the shinier it appears. But since it defaults to 0, it spreads the specular wealth across the entire planet. It overpowers the green so much that when mixed with the red, it shows up as yellow. So, in order to get control of this mess, add this line:

```
glMaterialf(GL_FRONT_AND_BACK,GL_SHININESS, 5);
```

I'll explain shortly the real math behind this, but for right now see what happens with the value of 5. Next try 25, and compare it with Figure 4-9. Shininess values from 5 to 10 correspond roughly to plastics; greater than that, and we get into serious metal territory.

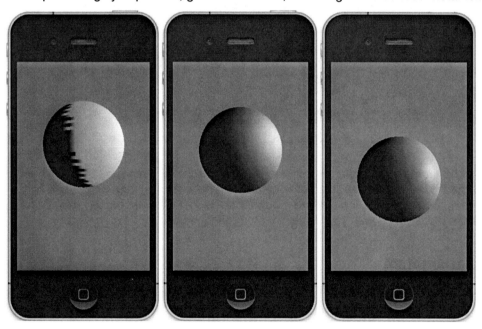

Figure 4-9. *Shininess set to 0, 5.0, and 25.0, respectively (left to right)*

Ambient Lighting

It's time for some fun with the ambient lighting. Add the following line to `initLighting()` then compile and run:

```
glLightfv(SS_SUNLIGHT,GL_AMBIENT,blue);
```

Does it look like Figure 4-10 (left)? And what should you do to get the image in Figure 4-10 (right)? You need to add the following line:

```
glMaterialfv(GL_FRONT_AND_BACK, GL_AMBIENT, blue);
```

Figure 4-10. *Blue ambient light only (left), both ambient light and ambient material (right)*

Besides the ambient attribute for each light, you can also set a world ambient value. The light-based values are variables, as are all of light parameters, so they vary as a function of the distance, attenuation, and so on. The world value is a constant across your entire OpenGL ES universe and can be set as follows:

```
GLfloat colorVector[4]={r,g,b,a};

glLightModelfv(GL_LIGHT_MODEL_AMBIENT,colorVector);
```

The default value is a dim gray formed by a color with red=.2, green=.2, and blue=.2. This helps ensure that your objects are always visible no matter what. And while we're at it, there is one other value for `glLightModelfv()`, and that is defined by the parameter of `GL_LIGHT_MODEL_TWO_SIDE`. The parameter is actually a Boolean float. If it is 0.0, only one side will be illuminated; otherwise, both will. The default is 0.0. And if for any reason you wanted to change which faces were front ones, you may use `glFrontFace()` and specify the triangles ordered clockwise or counterclockwise represent the front face. CCW is the default.

Taking a Step Back

So, what is actually happening here? Quite a lot, actually. There are three general shading models in use for real-time computer graphics. OpenGL ES 1 uses two of those, both of which we've seen. The first, the flat model, simply shades each triangle with one constant value. You've seen that that looks like in Figure 4-5. And in the good ol' days, this was a valid option, considering it was much faster than any others. However, when the iPhone in your pocket is roughly the equivalent of a handheld Cray-1 (minus about 3 tons and liquid cooling), those kinds of speed tricks are really a thing of the past. The smooth model uses *interpolative* shading, calculating the colors at each vertex and then interpolating them across the faces. The actual kind of shading OpenGL uses is a special form of this called *Gouraud shading*. This is why the vertex normals are generated based on normals of all the adjacent faces.

The third kind of shading is called *Phong* and is not used in OpenGL because of high CPU overhead. Instead of interpolating color values across the face, it interpolates normals, generating a normal for each fragment (that is, pixel). This helps remove some of the artifacting along edges defined by high curvatures, which produce very sharp angles. Phong can diminish that effect, but so can using more triangles to define your object.

There are numerous other models. Jim Blinn of the JPL-Voyager animations in the 1970s created a modified form of Phong shading, now called the Blinn-Phong model. If the light source and viewer can be treated as if they are at infinity, it can be less computationally intensive.

The Minnaert model tends to add a little more contrast to diffuse materials. Oren-Nayer adds a "roughness" component to the diffuse model in order to match reality just a little bit better.

Emissive Materials

Still another significant parameter we need to cover here that factors into the final color is `GL_EMISSION`. Unlike the diffuse, ambient, and specular bits, `GL_EMISSION` is for materials only and specifies that a material is *emissive* in quality. An emissive object has its own internal light source such as the sun, which will come in handy in the solar-system model. To see this in action, add the following line to the other material code in `initLighting()` and remove the ambient material:

```
glMaterialfv(GL_FRONT_AND_BACK, GL_EMISSION, yellow);
```

Because the yellow is at full intensity, what do you expect to see? Probably Figure 4-11a. Next cut the values down by half so you have this:

```
GLfloat yellow[]={.5,.5,0.0,1.0};
```

Now what do you see? I'll bet it looks something like Figure 4-11 (right).

Figure 4-11. *A body with emissive material set to full intensity for the yellow (left); the same scene but with just 50 percent intensity (right)*

Superficially, emissive materials may look just like the results of using ambient lighting. But unlike ambient lights, only a single object in your scene will be affected. And as a side benefit, they don't use up additional light objects. However, if your emissive objects do represent real lights of any sort such as the sun, putting a light object inside definitely adds another layer of authenticity to the scene.

One further note regarding materials: if your object has had the color vertices specified, as both our cube and sphere have, those values can be used instead of setting materials. You must call glEnable(GL_COLOR_MATERIAL). This will apply the vertex colors to the shading system, instead of those specified by the glMaterial calls.

Attenuation

In the real world, of course, light decreases the further an object is from the light source. OpenGL ES can model this factor as well using one or more of the following three attenuation factors:

- GL_CONSTANT_ATTENUATION

- GL_LINEAR_ATTENUATION

- GL_QUADRATIC_ATTENUATION

All three are combined to form one value that then figures into the total illumination of each vertex of your model. They are set using gLightf(GLenum light, GLenum pname, GLfloat param), where light is your light ID such as GL_LIGHT0, pname is one of the three attenuation parameters listed earlier, and the actual value is passed using param.

Linear attenuation can be used to model attenuation caused by factors such as fog. The quadratic attenuation models the natural falloff of light as the distance increases, which changes exponentially. As the distance of the light doubles, the illumination is cut to one quarter of the previous amount.

Let's just look at one, GL_LINEAR_ATTENUATION, for the time being. The math behind all three will be unveiled in a moment. Add the following line to initLighting():

```
glLightf(SS_SUNLIGHT,GL_LINEAR_ATTENUATION,.025);
```

And just to make things a little clearer visually, ensure that the emissive material is turned off. What do you see? Now increase the distance down the X-axis from 10 to 50 in the pos vector. Figure 4-12 illustrates the results.

Figure 4-12. *The light's x distance is 10 (left) and 50 (right), with a constant attenuation of 0.025.*

Spotlights

The standard lights default to an isotropic model; that is, they are like a desk light without a shade, shining equally (and blindingly) in all directions. OpenGL provides three additional lighting parameters that can turn the run-of-the-mill light into a directional light:

- GL_SPOT_DIRECTION
- GL_SPOT_EXPONENT
- GL_SPOT_CUTOFF

Since it is a directional light, it is up to you to aim it using the GL_SPOT_DIRCTION vector. It defaults to 0,0,-1, pointing down the $-Z$-axis, as shown in Figure 4-13. Otherwise, if you want to change it, you would use a call similar to the following that aims it down the +X-axis:

```
GLfloat direction[]={1.0,0.0,0.0};

glLightfv(GL_LIGHT0, GL_SPOT_DIRECTION, direction);
```

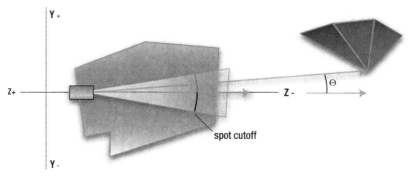

Figure 4-13. *A spotlight aimed at the default direction*

GL_SPOT_CUTOFF specifies the angle at which the spotlight's beam fades to 0 intensity from the center of the spotlight's cone and is naturally half the angular diameter of the full beam. The default value is 45 degrees, for a beam width of 90 degrees. And the lower the value, the narrower the beam.

The third and final spotlight parameter, GL_SPOT_EXPONENT, establishes the rate of drop-off of the beam's intensity, which is still another form of attenuation. OpenGL ES will take the cosine of the angle formed by the beam's center axis and that of an arbitrary vertex, Θ, and raise it to the power of GL_SPOT_EXPONENT. Because its default is 0, the light's intensity will be the same across all parts of the illuminated region until the cutoff value is reached, and then it drops to zero.

Light Parameters in Play

Table 4-1 summarizes the various light parameters covered in this section.

Table 4-1. *All of the Possible Lighting Parameters for* glLight*() *Calls in OpenGL ES 1.1*

Name	Purpose
GL_AMBIENT	Sets the ambient component of a light
GL_DIFFUSE	Sets the diffuse component of a light
GL_SPECULAR	Sets the specular component of a light
GL_POSITION	Sets the x,y,z coordinates of the light
GL_SPOT_DIRECTION	Aims a spotlight

Name	Purpose
GL_SPOT_EXPONENT	Specifies the rate of falloff from the center of a spotlight's beam
GL_SPOT_CUTOFF	Specifies the angle from the center of a spotlight's beam and drops to 0 intensity
GL_CONSTANT_ATTENUATION	Specifies the constant of the attenuation factor
GL_LINEAR_ATTENUATION	Specifies the linear component of the attenuation factor; simulates fog or other natural phenomena
GL_QUADRATIC_ATTENUATION	Specifies the quadratic portion of the attenuation factor, simulating the normal decrease in intensity as a function of distance

The Math Behind Shading

The diffuse shading model gives a very smooth look to objects, as you have seen. It uses something called the *Lambert lighting model*. Lambert lighting states simply that the more directly aimed a specific face is to the light source, the brighter it will be. The ground beneath your feet is going to be brighter the higher the sun is in the sky. Or in the more obscure but precise technical version, the reflective light increases from 0 to 1 as the angle, Θ, between the incident light, *l*, and the face's normal, *N*, decrease from 90 to 0 degrees based on cos (Θ). See Figure 4-14. Here's a quickie thought experiment: when Θ is 90 degrees, it is coming from the side; cos(90) is 0, so the reflected light along N is naturally going to be 0. When it is coming straight down, parallel to N, cos(0) will be 1, so the maximum amount will be reflected back. And this can be more formally expressed as follows:

$$I_d = k_d I_i \cos(\Theta)$$

I_d is the intensity of the diffuse reflection, I_i is the intensity of the incoming ray of light, and k_d represents the *diffuse reflectance* that is loosely coupled to the roughness of the object's material. *Loosely* means that in a lot of real-world materials, the actual surface may be somewhat polished but yet translucent, while the layers immediately underneath perform the scattering. Materials such as this may have both strong diffuse and specular components. Also, each color band may have its own *k* value in real life, so there would be one for red, green, and blue.

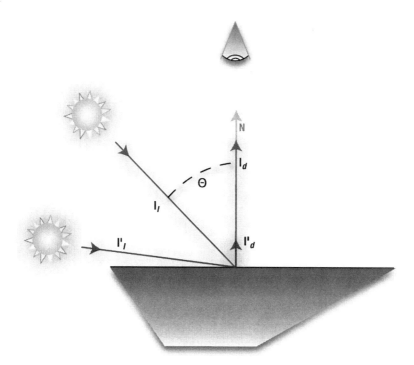

Figure 4-14. *For a perfectly diffuse surface, the reflected intensity of an incoming beam will be the vertical component of that beam, or cosine of the angle between the incoming beam and the surface normal.*

Specular Reflections

As referenced earlier, specular reflections serve to give your model a shiny appearance besides the more general diffuse surface. Few things are perfectly flat or perfectly shiny, and most lay somewhere in between. In fact, the earth's oceans are good specular reflectors, and on images of the earth from long distances, the sun's reflection can clearly be seen in the oceans.

Unlike a diffuse "reflection," which is equal in all directions, a specular reflection is highly dependent on the viewer's angle. We've been taught that the *angle of incidence=angle of reflectance*. This is true enough for the perfect reflector. But with the exception of mirrors, the nose of a '51 Studebaker, or the nicely polished forehead of that Cylon centurion right before he blasts you 150,000 years into the past, few things are perfect reflectors. And as such, there will be a slight scattering of the incoming ray; see Figure 4-15.

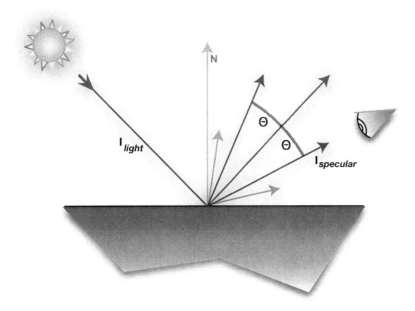

Figure 4-15. *For a specular reflection, the incoming ray is scattered but only around the center of its reflected counterpart.*

The equation of the specular component can be expressed as follows:

$$I_{specular} = W(q)I_{light}\cos^n \Theta$$

where:

I_{light} is the intensity of the incoming ray.

$W(q)$ is how reflective the surfaces is based on the angle of I_{light}.

n is the *shininess factor* (sound familiar?).

Θ is the angle between the reflected ray and the ray hitting the eye.

This is actually based on what's called the Fresnel Law of Reflection, which is where the W(q) value comes from. Although W(q) is not directly used by OpenGL ES 1 because it varies with the angle of incidence and is therefore a little more complicated than the specular lighting model, it could be used in a shader for version OpenGL ES 2. In that case, it would be particularly useful in doing reflections off the water, for example. In its place is a constant that is based on the specular values from the material setting.

The shininess factor, also called the *specular exponent*, is what we played with earlier. However, in real life *n* can go far higher than the max of 128.

Attenuation

Now back to the three kinds of attenuation listed earlier: constant, linear, and quadratic. The total attenuation is calculated as follows, where k_c is the constant, k_l is the linear value, k_q is the quadratic component, and d stands for the distance from the light and an arbitrary vertex:

$$k_l = \frac{1}{\left(k_c + k_l d + k_q d^2\right)}$$

Summing It All Up

So, now you can see that there are many factors in play to merely generate the color and intensity of that color for any of the vertices of any models in our scene. These include the following:

- Attenuation because of distance
- Diffuse lights and materials
- Specular lights and materials
- Spotlight parameters
- Ambient lights and materials
- Shininess
- Emissivity of the material

You can think of all of these as acting on the entire color vector or on each of the individual R, G, and B components of the colors.

So, to spell it all out, the final vertex color will be as follows:

$$color = ambient_{world\ model} + ambient_{material} + emissive_{material} + intensity_{light}$$

where:

$$intensity_{light} = \sum_{i=0}^{n-1} (attenuation\ \ factor)_i (spotlight\ \ factor)_i$$

$$\left[ambient_{light} ambient_{material} + \cos(\Theta)^{shininess} specular_{light} specular_{material} \right]$$

In other words, the color is equal to the some of the things not controlled by the lights added to the intensity of all the lights once we take into account the attenuation, diffuse, specular, and spotlight elements.

When calculated, these values act individually on each of the R, G, and B components of the colors in question.

What's This All For?

One reason why it is handy to understand what's going on beneath the hood is that it helps make OpenGL and related tools less mysterious. Just like when you learn a foreign language, say Klingon (and if you, dear reader, are Klingon, *majQa' nuqDaq 'oH puchpa' 'e!*), it ceases to be the mystery that it once was; where growls were growls and snarls were snarls, now you might recognize it as a lovely poem about fine tea.

And another reason is, as mentioned early on, all of these nice "high-level" tools are absent in OpenGL ES 2.0. Most any of the earlier shading algorithms will have to be implemented by you in little bits o' code that are called *shaders*. Fortunately, information on the most common shaders is available on the Internet and, replicating the previous information, relatively straightforward.

More Fun Stuff

Now, armed with all of this photonic goodness, it's time to get back to coding and introduce more than one light. Secondary lights can make a surprisingly large difference in the authenticity of the scene for little effort.

Go back to `initLighting()` and make it look like Listing 4-5. Here we add two more lights, named `SS_FILLLIGHT1` and `SS_FILLLIGHT2`, respectively. Add their definitions to the header file:

```
#define SS_FILLLIGHT1    GL_LIGHT1
#define SS_FILLLIGHT2    GL_LIGHT2
```

Now compile and run. Do you see Figure 4-16 (left)? Here is where the Gouraud shading model breaks down, as mentioned earlier, exposing the edges of the triangles. And what is the solution? At this point, simply increase the number of slices and stacks from 20 to 50 each, and you'll get the much more pleasing image, shown in Figure 4-16 (right).

Listing 4-5. Adding Two Fill Lights

```
-(void)initLighting
{
    GLfloat posMain[]={5.0,4.0,6.0,1.0};
    GLfloat posFill1[]={-15.0,15.0,0.0,1.0};
    GLfloat posFill2[]={-10.0,-4.0,1.0,1.0};

    GLfloat white[]={1.0,1.0,1.0,1.0};
    GLfloat red[]={1.0,0.0,0.0,1.0};
    GLfloat dimred[]={.5,0.0,0.0,1.0};
```

```
GLfloat green[]={0.0,1.0,0.0,0.0};
GLfloat dimgreen[]={0.0,.5,0.0,0.0};
GLfloat blue[]={0.0,0.0,1.0,1.0};
GLfloat dimblue[]={0.0,0.0,.2,1.0};

GLfloat cyan[]={0.0,1.0,1.0,1.0};
GLfloat yellow[]={1.0,1.0,0.0,1.0};
GLfloat magenta[]={1.0,0.0,1.0,1.0};
GLfloat dimmagenta[]={.75,0.0,.25,1.0};

GLfloat dimcyan[]={0.0,.5,.5,1.0};

//Lights go here.

glLightfv(SS_SUNLIGHT,GL_POSITION,posMain);
glLightfv(SS_SUNLIGHT,GL_DIFFUSE,white);
glLightfv(SS_SUNLIGHT,GL_SPECULAR,yellow);

glLightfv(SS_FILLLIGHT1,GL_POSITION,posFill1);
glLightfv(SS_FILLLIGHT1,GL_DIFFUSE,dimblue);
glLightfv(SS_FILLLIGHT1,GL_SPECULAR,dimcyan);

glLightfv(SS_FILLLIGHT2,GL_POSITION,posFill2);
glLightfv(SS_FILLLIGHT2,GL_SPECULAR,dimmagenta);
glLightfv(SS_FILLLIGHT2,GL_DIFFUSE,dimblue);

glLightf(SS_SUNLIGHT,GL_QUADRATIC_ATTENUATION,.005);

//Materials go here.

glMaterialfv(GL_FRONT_AND_BACK, GL_DIFFUSE, cyan);
glMaterialfv(GL_FRONT_AND_BACK, GL_SPECULAR, white);

glMaterialf(GL_FRONT_AND_BACK,GL_SHININESS,25);

glShadeModel(GL_SMOOTH);
glLightModelf(GL_LIGHT_MODEL_TWO_SIDE,0.0);

glEnable(GL_LIGHTING);
glEnable(SS_SUNLIGHT);
glEnable(SS_FILLLIGHT1);
glEnable(SS_FILLLIGHT2);

glLoadIdentity();
}
```

Figure 4-16. *Three lights, one main and two fill. The left-hand image has a low-resolution sphere, whereas the one on the right is high-resolution.*

In the previous examples, a number of new API calls were covered, which are summarized in Table 4-2. Get to know them—they are your friends, and you'll be using them a lot.

Table 4-2. *New API Calls Covered*

Name	Purpose
glGetLight	Retrieves any of the parameters from a specific light
glLight*	Sets the parameters for the lights
glLightModel	Specifies the light model, either GL_LIGHT_MODEL_AMBIENT or GL_LIGHT_MODEL_TWO_SIDE
glMaterialfv	Defines the attributes for the current material

Continued

Name	Purpose
glNormal	Assigns a single normal to an array of faces
glNormalPointer	Specifies the current normal array for an object in the execute method
glShadeModel	Either GL_FLAT or GL_SMOOTH
glPopMatrix	Pops a matrix off the current stack
glPushMatrix	Pushes a matrix on the current stack

Back to the Solar System

Now we have enough tools to get back to the solar-system project. Hold on, there is a lot of material to cover here. In particular are some other aspects of OpenGL that have nothing to do with lighting or materials but need to be addressed before the solar-system model gets much more complex.

First we need to add some new method declarations and instance variables to OpenGLSolarSystemController.h. See Listing 4-6.

Listing 4-6. Header additions to support the Solar System

```
#import <Foundation/Foundation.h>
#import <GLKit/GLKit.h>
#import "OpenGLSolarSystem.h"
#import "Planet.h"

#define X_VALUE                              0
#define Y_VALUE                              1
#define Z_VALUE                              2


@interface OpenGLSolarSystemController : NSObject
{
    Planet *m_Earth;
    Planet *m_Sun;
    GLfloat   m_Eyeposition[3];
}

-(void)execute;
-(void)executePlanet:(Planet *)planet;
-(id)init;
-(void)initGeometry;

@end
```

Next, a second object, in this case, our sun, needs to be generated, sized, and placed. And while we're at it, change the size of the earth to make it smaller than the sun. So, replace the initGeometry() method in OpenGLSolarSystemController with Listing 4-7.

Listing 4-7. *Add a second object and initialize the viewer's position*

```
-(void)initGeometry
{
    m_Eyeposition[X_VALUE]=0.0;                                              //1
    m_Eyeposition[Y_VALUE]=0.0;
    m_Eyeposition[Z_VALUE]=5.0;

    m_Earth=[[Planet alloc] init:50 slices:50 radius:.3 squash:1.0];        //2
    [m_Earth setPositionX:0.0 Y:0.0 Z:-2.0];                                //3

    m_Sun=[[Planet alloc] init:50 slices:50 radius:1.0 squash:1.0];         //4
    [m_Sun setPositionX:0.0 Y:0.0 Z:0.0];
}
```

Here's what's going on:

- Our eyepoint now has a well-defined location of +5 on the Z-axis as defined in line 1ff.

- In line 2, the earth's diameter is reduced to .3.

- And in line 3 we initialize the earth's location to be behind the sun from our standpoint, at z=-2.

- Now we can create the sun and place it at the exact center of our relatively fake solar system.

InitLighting() needs to look like Listing 4-8, cleaned up from all of the mucking around in the previous examples.

Listing 4-8. *Expanded lighting for the Solar-System model*

```
-(void)initLighting
{
    GLfloat sunPos[]={0.0,0.0,0.0,1.0};
    GLfloat posFill1[]={-15.0,15.0,0.0,1.0};
    GLfloat posFill2[]={-10.0,-4.0,1.0,1.0};

    GLfloat white[]={1.0,1.0,1.0,1.0};
    GLfloat dimblue[]={0.0,0.0,.2,1.0};

    GLfloat cyan[]={0.0,1.0,1.0,1.0};
    GLfloat yellow[]={1.0,1.0,0.0,1.0};
    GLfloat magenta[]={1.0,0.0,1.0,1.0};
    GLfloat dimmagenta[]={.75,0.0,.25,1.0};
```

```
    GLfloat dimcyan[]={0.0,.5,.5,1.0};

    //Lights go here.

    glLightfv(SS_SUNLIGHT,GL_POSITION,sunPos);
    glLightfv(SS_SUNLIGHT,GL_DIFFUSE,white);
    glLightfv(SS_SUNLIGHT,GL_SPECULAR,yellow);

    glLightfv(SS_FILLLIGHT1,GL_POSITION,posFill1);
    glLightfv(SS_FILLLIGHT1,GL_DIFFUSE,dimblue);
    glLightfv(SS_FILLLIGHT1,GL_SPECULAR,dimcyan);

    glLightfv(SS_FILLLIGHT2,GL_POSITION,posFill2);
    glLightfv(SS_FILLLIGHT2,GL_SPECULAR,dimmagenta);
    glLightfv(SS_FILLLIGHT2,GL_DIFFUSE,dimblue);

    //Materials go here.

    glMaterialfv(GL_FRONT_AND_BACK, GL_DIFFUSE, cyan);
    glMaterialfv(GL_FRONT_AND_BACK, GL_SPECULAR, white);

    glLightf(SS_SUNLIGHT,GL_QUADRATIC_ATTENUATION,.001);

    glMaterialf(GL_FRONT_AND_BACK,GL_SHININESS,25);

    glShadeModel(GL_SMOOTH);
    glLightModelf(GL_LIGHT_MODEL_TWO_SIDE,0.0);

    glEnable(GL_LIGHTING);
    glEnable(SS_SUNLIGHT);
    glEnable(SS_FILLLIGHT1);
    glEnable(SS_FILLLIGHT2);
}
```

Naturally, the top-level execute method solar-system controller has to be completely overhauled, along with the addition of a small utility function, as shown in Listing 4-9.

Listing 4-9. Solar-System execute methods

```
-(void)execute
{
    GLfloat paleYellow[]={1.0,1.0,0.3,1.0};                    //1
    GLfloat white[]={1.0,1.0,1.0,1.0};
    GLfloat cyan[]={0.0,1.0,1.0,1.0};
    GLfloat black[]={0.0,0.0,0.0,0.0};                         //2
    static GLfloat angle=0.0;
    GLfloat orbitalIncrement=1.25;                             //3
    GLfloat sunPos[3]={0.0,0.0,0.0,1.0};
```

```
    glPushMatrix();                                                          //4

    glTranslatef(-m_Eyeposition[X_VALUE],-m_Eyeposition[Y_VALUE],            //5
            -m_Eyeposition[Z_VALUE]);

    glLightfv(SS_SUNLIGHT,GL_POSITION,sunPos);                               //6
    glMaterialfv(GL_FRONT_AND_BACK, GL_DIFFUSE, cyan);
    glMaterialfv(GL_FRONT_AND_BACK, GL_SPECULAR, white);

    glPushMatrix();                                                          //7

    angle+=orbitalIncrement;                                                 //8

    glRotatef(angle,0.0,1.0,0.0);                                            //9

    [self executePlanet:m_Earth];                                            //10

    glPopMatrix();                                                           //11

    glMaterialfv(GL_FRONT_AND_BACK, GL_EMISSION, paleYellow);                //12
    glMaterialfv(GL_FRONT_AND_BACK, GL_SPECULAR, black);                     //13

    [self executePlanet:m_Sun];                                             //14

    glMaterialfv(GL_FRONT_AND_BACK, GL_EMISSION, black);                     //15

    glPopMatrix();                                                           //16
}

-(void)executePlanet:(Planet *)planet
{
    GLfloat posX, posY, posZ;

    GLfloat angle=0;

    glPushMatrix();

    [planet getPositionX:&posX Y:&posY Z:&posZ];                             //17

    glTranslatef(posX,posY,posZ);                                           //18

    [planet execute];                                                       //19

    glPopMatrix();
}
```

Here's what's going on:

- Line 1 creates a lighter shade of yellow. This just colors the sun a slightly more accurate hue.

- We need a black color to "turn off" some of the material characteristics if needed, as in line 2.

- In line 3, the orbital increment is needed to get the earth to orbit the sun.

- glPushMatrix() in line 4 is a new API call. When combined with glPopMatrix(), it helps isolate the transformations for one part of the world from another part. In this case, the first glPushMatrix() actually prevents the following call to glTranslate() from adding new translations upon itself. You could dump the glPush/PopMatrix pair and put the glTranslate() out of execute(), into the initialization code, just as long as it is called only once.

- The translation in line 5 ensures that the objects are "moved away" from our eyepoint. Remember that everything in an OpenGL ES world effectively revolves around the eyepoint. I prefer to have a common origin that doesn't rely on viewer's location, and in this case, it is the position of the sun as expressed in offsets from the eyepoint.

- Line 6 merely enforces the sun's location as being at the origin.

- Ooh! Another glPushMatrix() in line 7. This ensures that any transformations on the earth don't affect the sun.

- Lines 8 and 9 get the earth to orbit the sun. How? In line 10 a little utility function is called. That performs any transitions and moves an object away from the origin if need be. As you recall, the transformations can be thought of being last called/first used. So, the translation in executePlanets() is actually performed first, followed by the glRotation(). Note that this method will have the earth orbiting in a perfect circle, whereas in reality, no planets will have a perfectly circular orbit, so glTranlsation() will be used.

- glPopMatrix() in line 11 dumps any of the transformations unique to the earth.

- Line 12 sets the sun's material to be emissive. Note that the calls to glMaterialfv() are not bound to any specific object. They set the current material used by all following objects only until the next calls are made. Line 13 turns off any specular settings used for the earth.

- Line 14 calls our utility again, this time with the sun.

- The emissive material attribute is switched off, here in line 15, followed by another glPopMatrix(). Note that every time you do use a push matrix, it must be paired with a pop. OpenGL ES can handle stacks up to 16 deep. Also, since there are three kinds of matrices in use in OpenGL (the modelview, projection, and texture), make sure that you are pushing/popping the proper stack. You can ensure this by remembering to use glMatrixMode().

- Now in executePlanet(), line 17 gets the planet's current position so line 18 can translate the planet to the proper position. In this case, it never actually changes, because we're letting glRotatef() handle the orbital duties. Otherwise, the xyz would constantly change as a factor of time.

- Finally, call the planet's own execute routine in line 19.

We're almost done. Planet.h (Listing 4-10) and Planet.m (Listing 4-11) need to be modified to hold some state information. Note that I am very old-school and prefer to write my own setter/getters.

Listing 4-10. *Modifications to Planet.h to support the Solar-System model*

```objc
#import <Foundation/Foundation.h>
#import <OpenGLES/ES1/gl.h>


@interface Planet : NSObject
{

@private
    GLfloat         *m_VertexData;
    GLubyte         *m_ColorData;
    GLfloat         *m_NormalData;
    GLint           m_Stacks, m_Slices;
    GLfloat         m_Scale;
    GLfloat         m_Squash;
    GLfloat         m_Angle;
    GLfloat         m_Pos[3];
    GLfloat         m_RotationalIncrement;
}

-(bool)execute;
-(id) init:(GLint)stacks slices:(GLint)slices radius:(GLfloat)radius squash:(GLfloat)
squash;
-(void)getPositionX:(GLfloat *)x Y:(GLfloat *)y Z:(GLfloat *)z;
-(void)setPositionX:(GLfloat)x Y:(GLfloat)y Z:(GLfloat)z;
-(GLfloat)getRotation;
-(void)setRotation:(GLfloat)angle;
-(GLfloat)getRotationalIncrement;
-(void)setRotationalIncrement:(GLfloat)inc;
-(void)incrementRotation;

@end
```

To `Planet.m` add the following initialization code at the very end of the `init()` method:

```
m_Angle=0.0;
m_RotationalIncrement=0.0;

m_Pos[0]=0.0;
m_Pos[1]=0.0;
m_Pos[2]=0.0;
```

And after the execute method, add the code in Listing 4-11, defining the new methods.

Listing 4-11. Modifications to Planet.m

```
-(void)getPositionX:(GLfloat *)x Y:(GLfloat *)y Z:(GLfloat *)z
{
    *x=m_Pos[0];
    *y=m_Pos[1];
    *z=m_Pos[2];
}

-(void)setPositionX:(GLfloat)x Y:(GLfloat)y Z:(GLfloat)z
{
    m_Pos[0]=x;
    m_Pos[1]=y;
    m_Pos[2]=z;
}

-(GLfloat)getRotation
{
    return m_Angle;
}

-(void)setRotation:(GLfloat)angle
{
    m_Angle=angle;
}

-(void)incrementRotation
{
    m_Angle+=m_RotationalIncrement;
}

-(GLfloat)getRotationalIncrement
{
    return m_RotationalIncrement;
}

-(void)setRotationalIncrement:(GLfloat)inc
{
    m_RotationalIncrement=inc;
}
```

And while you're at it, let's turn down the gray in the background. It's supposed to be space, and space isn't gray. Go to `OpenGLSolarSystemViewController` and the main `drawInRect()` routine and change the call to `glClearColor` to read as follows:

```
glClearColor(0.0,0.0, 0.0, 1.0);
```

Now compile and run. You should see something like Figure 4-17.

Figure 4-17. *What's happening in the middle?*

There's something odd here. When running, you should see the earth come out from behind the sun on the left side, orbit toward us to cross in front of the sun, and then move away to repeat the orbit again. But what is happening when it should be in front of the sun in Figure 4-17 (center)?

In all graphics, computer or otherwise, the order of drawing plays a big role. If you're painting a portrait, you draw the background first. If you are generating a little solar system, the sun should be drawn first (er, maybe not…or not always).

Rendering order, or *depth sorting,* and how to determine what objects occlude other objects has always been a big part of computer graphics. Before the sun was added, render order was irrelevant, because there was only a single object. But as the world gets a lot more complicated, you'll find that there are two general ways this problem is solved.

The first is called the *painter's algorithm*. This means simply to draw the furthest objects first. This is very easy in something as simple as one sphere orbiting another. But what happens when you have very complicated 3D immersive worlds like World of Warcraft or Second Life? These would actually use a variant of painter's algorithm, but with some precomputed information ahead of time that determines all possible orders of occlusion. That information is then used to form a *binary space partitioning* (BSP) tree. Any place in the 3D world can be mapped to an element in the tree, which can then be traversed to fetch the optimum order for viewer's location. This is very fast in execution but complicated to set up. Fortunately, it is way overkill for our simple universe. The second means of depth sorting isn't sorting at all but actually uses the z component of each individual pixel. A pixel on the screen has an x and y value, but it can also have a z value as well, even though the Viewsonic in front of me is a flat 2D surface. As one pixel is ready to draw on top of another, the z values are compared, and the closer of the two wins out. Called *z-buffering*, it is very simple and straightforward but can chew up extra CPU time and graphics memory for very complicated scenes. I prefer the latter, and OpenGL makes z-buffering very easy to implement, but GLKit makes it easier. As this book was being written, iOS5 was announced, and with great delight, I was able to gleefully delete about 1½ pages of code and comments to replace them with a single line to add somewhere to your view controller's initialization code:

```
glEnable(GL_DEPTH_TEST);
```

The GLKViewController manages all of setup code now, and Apple's wizard produced code defaults to a depth buffer using:

```
view.drawableDepthFormat = GLKViewDrawableDepthFormat24;
```

You can select to have no buffer, one that's 16 bits or 24 bits of resolution. The extra 8 bits is reserved for use by stencils, which will be covered later.

If it works right, you should now see the earth eclipsing the sun when in front or being hidden while in back. See Figure 4-18.

***Figure 4-18**. Using the z-buffer*

Summary

This chapter covered the various approaches to lighting and shading the scene, along with the mathematical algorithms used to determine the color at each vertex. You also studied diffuse, specular, emissive, and ambient lighting along with various parameters having to do with turning the lights into spotlights. The solar-system model was updated to support multiple objects and to use z-buffering to handle object occlusion properly.

Chapter 5

Textures

The true worth of a man is not to be found in man himself but in the colours and textures that come alive in others.

—Albert Schweitzer

People would be a rather dull bunch without texture in their lives. Removing those interesting little foibles and eccentricities would remove a little of the sheen in our daily wanderings, be they odd but beguiling little habits or unexpected talents. Imagine the high-school janitor who happens to be an excellent ballroom dancer, the famous comedian who must wear only new white socks every day, the highly successful game engineer who's afraid to write letters by hand—all can make us smile and add just a little bit of wonder through the day. And so it is when creating artificial worlds. The visual perfection that computers can generate might be pretty, but it just doesn't feel right if you want to create a sense of authenticity to your scenes. That's where texturing comes in.

Texture makes that which is perfect become that which is real. The American Heritage Dictionary describes it this way: "The distinctive physical composition or structure of something, especially with respect to the size, shape, and arrangement of its parts." Nearly poetic, huh?

In the world of 3D graphics, texturing is as vital as lighting in creating compelling images and can be incorporated with surprisingly little effort nowadays. Much of the work in the graphics chip industry is rooted in rendering increasingly detailed textures at higher rates than each previous generation of hardware.

Because texturing in OpenGL ES is such a vast topic, this chapter will be confined to the basics, with more advanced topics and techniques reserved for the next chapter. With that in mind, let's get started.

The Language of Texturing

Say you wanted to create an airstrip in a game you're working on. How would you do that? Simple, take a couple of black triangles and stretch them really long. Bang! You've got your landing strip! Not so fast there, sport. What about the lines painted down the center of the strip? How about a bunch of small white faces? That could work. But don't forget those yellow chevrons at the very end. Well, add a bunch of additional faces and color them yellow. And don't forget about the numbers. How about the curved lines leading to the tarmac? Pretty soon you might be up to hundreds of triangles, but that still wouldn't help with the oil spots, repairs, skid marks, and roadkill. Now it starts getting complicated. Getting all of the fine detail could require thousands if not tens of thousands of faces. Meanwhile, your buddy, Arthur, is also creating a strip. You are comparing notes, telling him about polygon counts, and you haven't even gotten to the roadkill yet. Arthur says all he needed was a couple of triangles and one image. You see, he used texture maps, and using texture maps can create a highly detailed surface such as an airstrip, brick walls, armor, clouds, creaky weathered wooden doors, a cratered terrain on a distant planet, or the rusting exterior of a '56 Buick.

In the early days of computer graphics, texturing (or texture mapping) used up two of the most precious resources: CPU cycles and memory. Texture mapping was used sparingly, and all sorts of little tricks were done to save on both resources. With memory now virtually free (compared to 20 years ago) and with modern chips having seemingly limitless speed, using textures is no longer a decision one should ever have to stay up all night and struggle with.

All About Textures (Mostly)

Textures come in two broad types: *procedural* and *image*. Procedural textures are generated on the fly based on some algorithm. There are "equations" for wood, marble, asphalt, stone, and so on. Nearly any kind of material can be reduced to an algorithm and hence drawn onto an object, as shown in Figure 5-1.

Figure 5-1. *A golden chalice (left). By using procedural texture mapping (right), the chalice can be made up of gold ore instead, while the cone uses a marble map.*

Procedural textures are very powerful because they can produce an infinite variety of scalable patterns that can be enlarged to reveal increasingly more detail, as shown in Figure 5-2. Otherwise, this would require a massive static image.

Figure 5-2. *Close-up on the goblet from Figure 5-1 (right). Notice the fine detailing that would need a very large image to accomplish.*

The 3D rendering application Strata Design 3D-SE, which was used for the images in Figure 5-2, supports both procedural and image-based textures. Figure 5-3 shows the dialog used to specify the parameters of the gold ore texture depicted in Figure 5-2.

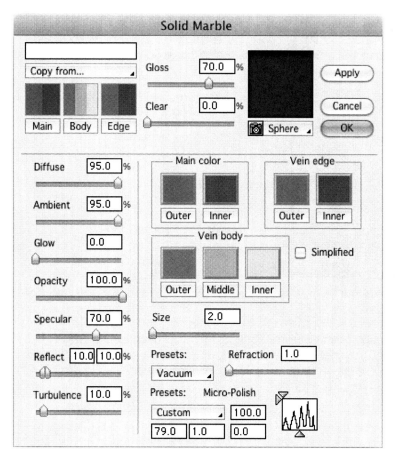

Figure 5-3. *All of the possible settings used to produce the gold ore texture in Figure 5-2.*

Procedural textures, and to a lesser degree image textures, can be classified in a spectrum of complexity from random to structured. Random, or *stochastic* textures, can be thought of as "looking like noise," like a fine-grained material such as sand, dust, gravel, the grain in paper, and so on. Near stochastic could be flames, grass, or the surface of a lake. On the other hand, structured textures have broad recognizable features and patterns. A brick wall, wicker basket, plaid, or herd of geckos would be structured.

Image Textures

As referenced earlier, image textures are just that. They can serve as a surface or material texture such as mahogany wood, steel plating, or leaves scattered across the ground. If done right, these can be seamlessly tiled to cover a much larger surface than the original image would suggest. And because they come from real life, they don't need the sophisticated software used for the procedural variety. Figure 5-4 shows the chalice scene, but this time with wood textures, mahogany for the chalice, and alder for the cone, while the cube remains gold.

Figure 5-4. *Using real-world image textures*

Besides using image textures as materials, they can be used as pictures themselves in your 3D world. A rendered image of an iPad can have a texture dropped into where the screen is. A 3D city could use real photographs for windows on the buildings, for billboards, or for family photos in a living room.

OpenGL ES and Textures

When OpenGL ES renders an object, such as the mini solar system in Chapter 4, it draws each triangle and then lights and colorizes them based on the three vertices that make up each face. Afterward it merrily goes to the next one, singing a jaunty little tune no doubt. A texture is nothing more than an image. As you learned earlier in the chapter, it can be generated on the fly to handle context-sensitive details (such as cloud patterns), or it can be a JPEG, PNG, or anything else. It is made up of pixels, of course, but when operating as a texture, they are called *texels*. You can think of an OpenGL ES texture as a bunch of little colored "faces" (the texels), each of the same size and stitched together in one sheet of, say, 256 such faces on a side. Each face is the same size as each other one and can be stretched or squeezed so as to work on surfaces of any size or shape. They don't have corner geometry to waste memory storing xyz values, can come in a multitude of lovely colors, and give a lot of bang for the buck. And of course they are extraordinarily versatile.

Like your geometry, textures have their own coordinate space. Where geometry denotes locations of its many pieces using the trusty Cartesian coordinates known as x, y, and z, textures use s and t. The process that applies a texture to some geometric object is called *UV mapping*. (s and t are used only for OpenGL world, whereas others use u and v. Go figure.)

So, how is this applied? Say you have a square tablecloth that you must make fit a rectangular table. You need to attach it firmly along one side and then tug and stretch it along the other until it just barely covers the table. You can attach just the four corners, but if you really want it to "fit," you can attach other parts along the edge or even in the middle. That's a little how a texture is fitted to a surface.

Texture coordinate space is *normalized*; that is, both *s* and *t* range from 0 to 1. They are unitless entities, abstracted so as not to rely on either the dimensions of the source or the destination. So, the face to be textured will carry around with its vertices *s* and *t* values that lay between 0.0 to 1.0, as shown in Figure 5-5.

Figure 5-5. *Texture coordinates go from 0 to 1.0, no matter what the texture is.*

In the most elementary example, we can apply a rectangular texture to a rectangular face and be done with it, as illustrated in Figure 5-5. But what if you wanted only part of the texture? You could supply a PNG that had only the bit you wanted, which is not very convenient if you wanted to have many variants of the thing. However, there's another way. Merely change the *s* and *t* coordinates of the destination face. Let's say all you wanted was the upper-left quarter of the Easter Island statue I call Hedly. All you need to do is change the coordinates of the destination, and those coordinates are based on the proportion of the image section you want, as shown in Figure 5-6. That is, because you want the image to be cropped halfway down the *s*-axis, the *s* coordinate will no longer go from 0 to 1 but instead from 0 to .5. And the *t* coordinate would then go from .5 to 1.0. If you wanted the lower-left corner, you'd use the same 0 to .5 ranges as the *s* coordinate.

Also note that the texture coordinate system is resolution independent. That is, the center of an image that is 512 on a side would be (.5,.5), just as it would be for an image 128 on a side.

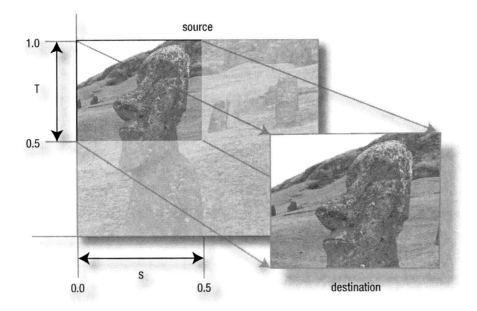

Figure 5-6. *Clipping out a portion of the texture by changing the texture coordinates*

Textures are not limited to rectilinear objects. With careful selections of the *st* coordinates on your destination face, you can do some of the more colorful shapes depicted in Figure 5-7.

Figure 5-7. *Mapping an image to unusual shapes*

If you keep the image coordinates the same across the vertices of your destination, the image's corners will follow those of the destination, as shown in Figure 5-8.

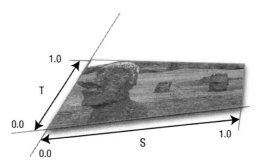

Figure 5-8. *Distorting images can give a 3D effect on 2D surfaces.*

Textures can also be *tiled* so as to replicate patterns that depict wallpaper, brick walls, sandy beaches, and so on, as shown in Figure 5-9. Notice how the coordinates actually go beyond the upper limit of 1.0. All that does is to start the texture repeating so that, for example, an *s* of .6 equals an *s* of 1.6, 2.6, and so on.

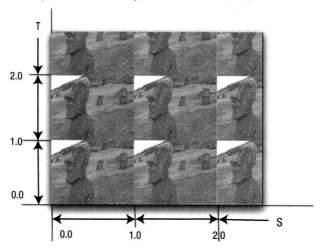

Figure 5-9. *Tiled images are useful for repeated patterns such as those used for wallpaper or brick walls.*

Besides the tiling model shown in Figure 5-9, texture tiles can also be "mirrored," or clamped, which is a mechanism for dealing with *s* and *t* when outside of the 0 to 1.0 range.

Mirrored tiling repeats textures as above, but also flips columns/rows of alternating images, as shown in Figure 5-10 (left). Clamping an image means that the last row or column of texels repeats, as shown in Figure 5-10 (right). Clamping looks like a total mess with my sample image but is useful when the image has a neutral border. In that case, you can prevent any image repetition on either or both axes if *s* or *v* exceeds its normal bounds.

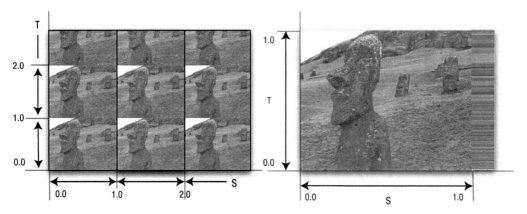

Figure 5-10. A mirrored-repeat for just the s-axis (left), the texture clamped (right)

Note   The problem with the right edge in Figure 5-10 suggests that textures designed to be clamped should have a 1-pixel-wide border to match the colors of the object to which they are bound. Unless you think it's really cool, then of course that trumps nearly everything.

OpenGL ES, as you know by now, doesn't do quadrilaterals—that is, faces with four sides (as opposed to its big desktop brother). So, we have to fabricate them using two triangles, giving us structures such as the triangle strips and fans that we experimented with in Chapter 3. Applying textures to this "fake" quadrilateral is a simple affair. One triangle has texture coordinates of (0,0), (1,0), and (0,1), while the other has coordinates of (1,0), (1,1), and (0,1). It should make more sense if you study Figure 5-11.

Figure 5-11. Placing a texture across two faces

And finally, let's take a look at how a single texture can be stretched across a whole bunch of faces, as shown in Figure 5-12, and then we can get back to the fun stuff.

Figure 5-12. *Stretching a texture across many faces*

Image Formats

OpenGL ES supports many different image formats, and I'm not talking about PNG vs. JPEG, but I mean the form and layout in memory. The standard is 32 bits, which assigns 8 bits of memory each for red, green, blue, and alpha. Referred to as RGBA, it is the standard used for most of the exercises. It is also the "prettiest" because it provides more than 16 million colors and translucency. However, you can often get away with 16-bit or even 8-bit images. In doing that, you can save a lot of memory and crank up the speed quite a bit, with careful selection of images. See Table 5-1 for some of the more popular formats.

Table 5-1. *Some of the More Popular Image Formats*

Format	Details
RGBA	8 bits per channel, including alpha.
RGB	8 bits per channel, no alpha.
ALPHA	A single 8-bit channel used for stencils.
LUMINANCE	A single 8-bit channel for grayscale images.
RGB565	16 bits total: 5 for red, 6 for green, and 5 for blue. The green is given a little more color fidelity because the eye is more sensitive to that than to either red or blue.
RGBA4444	16 bits, 4 for each channel.
RGBA5551	5 bits per color channel, and 1 for alpha.

Also a format requirement of sorts is that, generally, OpenGL can use only texture images that are power-of-two on a side. Some systems can get around that, such as iOS with certain limitations, but for the time being, just stick with the standard.

So, with all of this stuff out of the way, it's time to start coding.

Back to the Bouncy Square One

Let's take a step back and fetch the generic bouncy square again example again, which we first worked on in Chapter 3. We'll apply a texture to it and then manipulate it to show off some of the tricks detailed in this chapter, such as repeating, animating, and distortion.

Previous to iOS 5, programmers needed to create their own texture conversion code or use code supplied by Apple, which took nearly 40 lines of Core Graphics to convert a .png to OpenGL compatible format. Now we have two nice shiney new toys to play with called GLKTexture, and GLKTextureInfo.

In your view controller add Listing 5-1.

Listing 5-1. *Loading and converting a texture to OpenGL format.*

```
-(GLKTextureInfo *)loadTexture:(NSString *)filename
{
    NSError *error;
    GLKTextureInfo *info;

    NSString *path=[[NSBundle mainBundle]pathForResource:filename ofType:NULL];

    info=[GLKTextureLoader textureWithContentsOfFile:path options:NULL error:&error];

    glTexParameteri(GL_TEXTURE_2D,GL_TEXTURE_WRAP_S,GL_REPEAT);
    glTexParameteri(GL_TEXTURE_2D,GL_TEXTURE_WRAP_T,GL_REPEAT);

    return info;
}
```

Table 5-2. *All the* `GL_TEXTURE` *Parameters for* `glTexParameter*` *Calls in OpenGL ES 1.1*

Name	Purpose
GL_TEXTURE_MIN_FILTER	Sets the minification type (see Table 5-3)
GL_TEXTURE_MAG_FILTER	Sets the magnification type (see Table 5-4)
GL_TEXTURE_WRAP_S	Specifies how textures are to be *wrapped* in the S direction, GL_CLAMP or GL_REPEAT
GL_TEXTURE_WRAP_T	Specifies how textures are to be *wrapped* in the T direction, GL_CLAMP or GL_REPEAT

This can now be initialized from viewDidLoad() using the following:

```
[EAGLContext setCurrentContext:self.context];
m_Texture=[self loadTexture:@"hedly.png"];
```

The two texture parameters specify how to handle repeating textures, covered below. My image, **hedly.png**, is the photo of one of the mysterious huge stone heads on Easter Island in the Pacific. For ease of testing, use a power-of-two (POT) image, 32 bits, RGBA.

> **Note** By default, OpenGL requires each row of texels in the image data to be aligned on a 4-byte boundary. Our RGBA textures adhere to that; for other formats, consider using the call `glPixelStorei(GL_PACK_ALIGNMENT,x)`, where x can be 1, 2, 4, or 8 bytes for alignment. Use 1 to cover all cases.

Note that there is usually a size limitation for textures, which depends on the actual graphics hardware used. On both the first- and second-generation iPhones (the original and 3G) and iPod/Touch devices, textures were limited to no larger than 1024×1024 because of using the Power VR MBX platform. On all others, the newer PowerVR SGX is used, which doubles the max size of textures to 2048×2048. You can find out how big a texture a particular platform can use by calling the following, where maxSize is an integer, and then compensate at runtime:

```
glGetIntegerv(GL_MAX_TEXTURE_SIZE,&maxSize);
```

Now change the **drawInRect**() routine, as shown in Listing 5-2. Most of this you have seen before, with the new stuff detailed below. And while you're at it, go ahead and add GLKTextureInfo *m_Texture to the header.

Listing 5-2. Render the geometry with the texture

```
- (void)glkView:(GLKView *)view drawInRect:(CGRect)rect
{

    static const GLfloat squareVertices[] =
    {
        -0.5f, -0.33f,
        0.5f, -0.33f,
        -0.5f,  0.33f,
        0.5f,  0.33f,
    };

    static const GLubyte squareColors[] = {
        255, 255,   0, 255,
        0,   255, 255, 255,
        0,     0,   0,   0,
        255,   0, 255, 255,
    };
```

```
static const GLfloat textureCoords[] =                                  //1
{
    0.0, 0.0,
    1.0, 0.0,
    0.0, 1.0,
    1.0, 1.0
};

static float transY = 0.0f;

glClearColor(0.5f, 0.5f, 0.5f, 1.0f);
glClear(GL_COLOR_BUFFER_BIT);


glMatrixMode(GL_MODELVIEW);
glLoadIdentity();
glTranslatef(0.0f, (GLfloat)(sinf(transY)/2.0f), 0.0f);

transY += 0.075f;

glVertexPointer(2, GL_FLOAT, 0, squareVertices);
glEnableClientState(GL_VERTEX_ARRAY);
glColorPointer(4, GL_UNSIGNED_BYTE, 0, squareColors);
glEnableClientState(GL_COLOR_ARRAY);


glEnable(GL_TEXTURE_2D);                                                 //2
glEnable(GL_BLEND);                                                      //3
glBlendFunc(GL_ONE, GL_SRC_COLOR);                                       //4
glBindTexture(GL_TEXTURE_2D,m_Texture.name);                            //5
glTexCoordPointer(2, GL_FLOAT,0,textureCoords);                         //6
glEnableClientState(GL_TEXTURE_COORD_ARRAY);                            //7

glDrawArrays(GL_TRIANGLE_STRIP, 0, 4);                                   //8

glDisableClientState(GL_COLOR_ARRAY);
glDisableClientState(GL_VERTEX_ARRAY);

glDisableClientState(GL_TEXTURE_COORD_ARRAY);                           //9
}
```

So, what's going on here?

▨ The texture coordinates are defined here in lines 1ff. Notice that as referenced earlier they are all between 0 and 1. We'll play with these values a little later.

▨ In line 2, the GL_TEXTURE_2D target is enabled. Desktop OpenGL supports 1D and 3D textures but not ES.

▨ Here is where blending can be enabled. Blending is where the source color of the image and the destination color of the background are blended (mixed) according to some equation that is switched on in line 4.

The blend function determines how the source and destination pixels/fragments are mixed together. The most common form is where the source overwrites the destination, but others can create some interesting effects. Because this is such a large topic, it deserves its own chapter, which as it turns out is Chapter 6.

▨ Line 5 ensures that the texture we want is the current one. Like the other OpenGL objects, textures are assigned a "name," (a unique integer ID number), which will be referenced until it's deleted.

▨ Line 6 is where the texture coordinates are handed off to the hardware.

▨ And just as you had to tell the client to handle the colors and vertices, you need to do the same for the texture coordinates here in line 7.

▨ Line 8 you'll recognize, but this time besides drawing the colors and the geometry, it now takes the information from the current texture, matches up the four texture coordinates to the four corners specified by the squareVertices[] array (each vertex of the textured object needs to have a texture coordinate assigned to it), and blends it using the values specified in line 4.

▨ Finally, disable the client state for texture, line 9, the same way it was disabled for color and vertices.

If everything works right, you should see something like Figure 5-13a. You don't you say? It's upside down? Depending on the format used, your texture could very well be inverted, with its internal origin in the upper-left corner instead of the lower left. The fix is easy for this. Change loadTexture to look like:

```
-(GLKTextureInfo *)loadTexture:(NSString *)filename
{
    NSError *error;
    GLKTextureInfo *info;
    NSDictionary *options=[NSDictionary dictionaryWithObjectsAndKeys:
                            [NSNumber numberWithBool:YES],
                            GLKTextureLoaderOriginBottomLeft,nil];

    NSString *path=[[NSBundle mainBundle]pathForResource:filename ofType:NULL];

    info=[GLKTextureLoader textureWithContentsOfFile:path options:options error:&error];

    glBindTexture(GL_TEXTURE_2D, info.name);

    glTexParameteri(GL_TEXTURE_2D,GL_TEXTURE_WRAP_S,GL_REPEAT);
    glTexParameteri(GL_TEXTURE_2D,GL_TEXTURE_WRAP_T,GL_REPEAT);

    return info;
}
```

What you're telling the loader to do is to flip the origin of the texture to anchor it at the bottom left of the screen. Now does it look like 5-13 (left)?

Notice how the texture is also picking up the colors from the vertices? Comment out the line `glEnableClientState(GL_COLOR_ARRAY) in drawInRect()`, and you should now see Figure 5-13 (right). If you don't see any image, double-check your file and ensure that it really is a power-of-two in size, such as 128×128 or 256×256.

Figure 5-13. *Applying texture to the bouncy square. Using vertex colors (left) and not (right).*

So, now we can replicate some of the examples in the first part of this chapter. The first is to pick out only a portion of the texture to display. Change `textureCoords` in `drawInRect` to the following:

```
static  GLfloat textureCoords[] =
{
        0.0, 0.5,
        0.5, 0.5,
        0.0, 1.0,
        0.5, 1.0
};
```

Did you get Figure 5-14?

Figure 5-14. *Cropping the image using s and t coordinates*

The mapping of the texture coordinates to the real geometric coordinates looks like Figure 5-15. Spend a few minutes to understand what is happening here if you're not quite clear yet. Simply put, there's a one-to-one mapping of the texture coordinates in their array with the geometric coordinates in theirs.

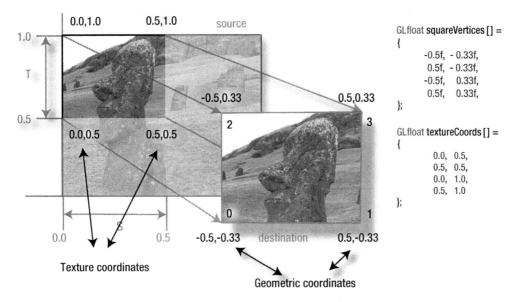

Figure 5-15. *The texture coordinates have a one-to-one mapping with the geometric ones.*

Now change the texture coordinates to the following. Can you guess what will happen (Figure 5-16)?

```
static  GLfloat textureCoords[] =
{
        0.0, 0.0,
        2.0, 0.0,
        0.0, 2.0,
        2.0, 2.0
};
```

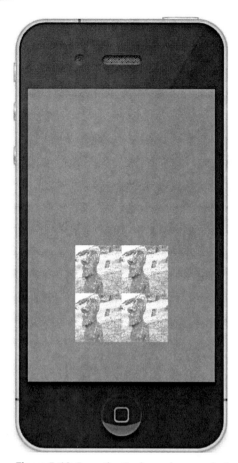

Figure 5-16. *Repeating the image is convenient when you need to do repetitive patterns such as wallpaper.*

Now let's distort the texture by changing the vertex geometry, and to make things visually clearer, restore the original texture coordinates to turn off the repeating:

```
static const GLfloat squareVertices[] =
 {
      -0.5f, -0.33f,
       0.5f, -0.15f,
      -0.5f,  0.33f,
       0.5f,  0.15f,
 };
```

This should pinch the right side of the square and take the texture with it, as shown in Figure 5-17.

Figure 5-17. *Pinching down the right side of the polygon*

Armed with all of this knowledge, what would happen if you changed the texture coordinates *dynamically?* Add the following code to **drawInRect**—anywhere should work:

```
static float texIncrease=0.01;
textureCoords[0]+=texIncrease;
textureCoords[2]+=texIncrease;
textureCoords[4]+=texIncrease;
textureCoords[6]+=texIncrease;
textureCoords[1]+=texIncrease;
textureCoords[3]+=texIncrease;
textureCoords[5]+=texIncrease;
textureCoords[7]+=texIncrease;
```

This will increase the texture coordinates just a little from frame to frame. Run, and stand in awe. This is a really simple trick to get animated textures. A marquee in a 3D world might use this. You could create a texture that was like a strip of movie film with a cartoon character doing something and change the *s* and *t* values to jump from frame to frame like a little flip book. Another is to create a texture-based font. Because OpenGL has no native font support, it's up to us, the long-suffering engineers of the world, to add it ourselves. Sigh. This could be done by placing the characters of the desired font onto a single mosaic texture, called a "font atlas," and then selecting them by carefully using texture coordinates.

Mipmaps

Mipmaps are a means of specifying multiple levels of detail for a given texture. That can help in two ways: it can smooth out the appearance of a textured object as its distance to the viewpoint varies, and it can save resource usage when textured objects are far away.

For example, in Distant Suns, I may use a texture for Jupiter that is 1024×512. But that would be a waste of both memory and CPU if Jupiter was so far away that it was only a few pixels across. Here is where mipmapping can come into play. So, what is a mipmap?

From the Latin phrase "multum in parvo" (literally: "much in little"), a *mipmap* is a family of textures of varying levels of detail. Your root image might be 128 on a side, but when a part of a mipmap, it would have textures that were also 64, 32, 16, 8, 4, 2, and 1 pixel on a side, as shown in Figure 5-18.

Figure 5-18. *Hedly the head, the mipmapped edition*

In iOS5, switching on mipmapping is done by adding only one additional parameter to the `GLKTextureLoader:textureWithContentsOfFile()` call. So swap in the options dictionary in place of the previous one, as follows:

```
NSDictionary *options=[NSDictionary dictionaryWithObjectsAndKeys:
                        [NSNumber
numberWithBool:YES],GLKTextureLoaderOriginBottomLeft,
                        [NSNumber
numberWithBool:TRUE],GLKTextureLoaderGenerateMipmaps,nil];
```

Naturally, `drawInRect()` also needs some changes. Swap out your old `drawInRect()` for the new and improved version in Listing 5-5. This will cause the z value to oscillate back and forth.

Listing 5-5. *Subsitute this for your drawInRect.*

```
- (void)glkView:(GLKView *)view drawInRect:(CGRect)rect
{
    static int counter=1;
    static float direction=-1.0;
    static float transZ=-1.0;
    static GLfloat rotation=0;
    static bool initialized=NO;

    static const GLfloat squareVertices[] =
    {
        -0.5f, -0.5f,-0.5f,
         0.5f, -0.5f,-0.5f,
        -0.5f,  0.5f,-0.5f,
         0.5f,  0.5f,-0.5f
    };

    static  GLfloat textureCoords[] =
    {
        0.0, 0.0,
        1.0, 0.0,
        0.0, 1.0,
        1.0, 1.0
    };

    glClearColor(0.5f, 0.5f, 0.5f, 1.0f);
    glClear(GL_COLOR_BUFFER_BIT);


    glMatrixMode(GL_MODELVIEW);
    glLoadIdentity();
    glTranslatef(0.0f,0.0f,transZ);
    glRotatef(rotation,0.0,0.0,1.0);

    glVertexPointer(3, GL_FLOAT, 0, squareVertices);
    glEnableClientState(GL_VERTEX_ARRAY);

    glEnable(GL_TEXTURE_2D);
    glEnable(GL_BLEND);

    glTexCoordPointer(2, GL_FLOAT,0,textureCoords);
    glEnableClientState(GL_TEXTURE_COORD_ARRAY);

    glTexParameteri(GL_TEXTURE_2D,GL_TEXTURE_MIN_FILTER,GL_NEAREST);
    glTexParameteri(GL_TEXTURE_2D,GL_TEXTURE_MAG_FILTER,GL_LINEAR);
```

```
        glTranslatef(0.0f,0.5f,0.0f);

        glDrawArrays(GL_TRIANGLE_STRIP, 0, 4);

        glTranslatef(0.0f,-1.0f,0.0f);

        glTexParameteri(GL_TEXTURE_2D,GL_TEXTURE_MIN_FILTER,GL_LINEAR_MIPMAP_NEAREST);
        glTexParameteri(GL_TEXTURE_2D,GL_TEXTURE_MAG_FILTER,GL_LINEAR_MIPMAP_NEAREST);

        glDrawArrays(GL_TRIANGLE_STRIP, 0, 4);

        glDisableClientState(GL_VERTEX_ARRAY);

        glDisableClientState(GL_TEXTURE_COORD_ARRAY);

        if(!(counter%100))
        {
            if(direction==1.0)
                direction=-1.0;
            else
                direction=1.0;
        }

        transZ+=(.10*direction);

        rotation += 1.0;
        counter++;
}
```

Grab a copy of setClipping() and move it over here, then call it from your initialzation code in viewDidLoad().

If that compiles and runs OK, you should see something like Figure 5-19.

Figure 5-19. *Two images, both mipmapped, but one's better looking. What gives?*

You've probably noticed that the two images look a little different. The top image is shimmery, and the bottom image is noticably smoother, making it easier to look at. That brings me to the topic of filtering.

Filtering

An image, when used as a texture, may exhibit various artifacting depending on its content and final size when projected onto the screen. Very detailed images might be seen with an annoying shimmering effect. However, it is possible to dynamically modify an image to minimize these effects through a process called *filtering*. Filtering is typically used in conjunction with mipmapping because the former can make use of the latter's multiple images.

Let's say you have a texture that is 128×128 but the texture face is 500 pixels on a side. What should you see? Obviously the image's original pixels, now called *texels*, are going to be much larger than any of the screen pixels. This is a process referred to as *magnification*. Conversely, you could have a case where the texels are much smaller than a pixel, and that is called *minification*. Filtering is the process used to determine how to correlate a pixel's color with the underlying texel, or texels. Tables 5-3 and 5-4, respectively, show the possible variants of this.

Table 5-3. *Texture Filter Types in OpenGL ES for Minification*

Name	Purpose
GL_LINEAR	Smooths texturing using the four nearest texels closest to the center of the pixel being textured
GL_LINEAR_MIPMAP_LINEAR	Similar to GL_LINEAR but uses the two nearest mipmaps closest to the rendered pixel
GL_LINEAR_MIPMAP_NEAREST	Similar to GL_LINEAR but uses the one nearest mipmap closest to the rendered pixel
GL_NEAREST	Returns the nearest texel value to the pixel being rendered
GL_NEAREST_MIPMAP_NEAREST	Similar to GL_NEAREST but uses the texel from the nearest mipmap

Table 5-4. *Texture Filter Types in OpenGL ES for Magnification*

Name	Purpose
GL_LINEAR	Smooths texturing using the four nearest texels closest to the center of the pixel being textured
GL_NEAREST	Returns the nearest texel value to the pixel being rendered

There are three main approaches to filtering:

- *Point sampling (called* nearest *in OpenGL lingo)*: A pixel's color is based on the texel that is nearest to the pixel's center. This is the simplest, is the fastest, and naturally yields the least satisfactory image.

- *Bilinear sampling, otherwise called just linear*: A pixel's coloring is based on a weighted average of a 2×2 array of texels nearest to the pixel's center. This can smooth out an image considerably.

- *Trilinear sampling*: Requires mipmaps and takes the two closest mipmap levels to the final rendering on the screen, performs a bilinear selection on each, and then takes a weighted average of the two individual values.

It's the trilinear sampling that you saw in action in the previous exercise, and it results in a pretty dramatic increase in perceived image quality.

Figure 5-20a shows a close-up of Hedly with the filtering off, while Figure 5-20b has it switched on. If you go back and look at the mipmap code, you'll see that both images are actually using filtering. The shimmery one on top is using the GL_LINEAR and the GL_NEAREST filtering. The bottom is doing the same but using the additional information that the mipmaps provide. Just for kicks, you might want to do comparisons of some of the other settings. For example, which is better: GL_NEAREST or GL_LINEAR?

Filtering might eventually go the way of 8-bit coloring as the retina-level displays become more common.

One more thing: if you look really closely at the bottom image, you might actually see it swap to another texture size. It's subtle, but it's there.

Figure 5-20. *All filtering turned off (left), bilinear filtering turned on (right)*

OpenGL Extensions and PVRTC Compression

Even though OpenGL is a standard, it was designed with extensibility in mind, letting various hardware manufacturers add their own special sauce to the 3D soup using *extension strings*. In OpenGL, developers can poll for possible extensions and then use them if they exist. To get a look at this, use the following line of code:

```
char *extentionList=glGetString(GL_EXTENSIONS);
```

This will return a space-separated list of the various extra options in iOS for OpenGL ES, looking something like this (from iOS 4.3):

```
GL_OES_blend_equation_separate GL_OES_blend_func_separate GL_OES_blend_subtract
GL_OES_compressed_paletted_texture GL_OES_depth24 GL_OES_draw_texture
GL_OES_fbo_render_mipmap GL_OES_framebuffer_object GL_OES_mapbuffer
GL_OES_matrix_palette GL_OES_packed_depth_stencil GL_OES_point_size_array
GL_OES_point_sprite GL_OES_read_format GL_OES_rgb8_rgba8 GL_OES_stencil_wrap
GL_OES_stencil8 GL_OES_texture_mirrored_repeat GL_OES_vertex_array_object
GL_EXT_blend_minmax GL_EXT_discard_framebuffer GL_EXT_read_format_bgra
GL_EXT_texture_filter_anisotropic GL_EXT_texture_lod_bias
GL_APPLE_framebuffer_multisample GL_APPLE_texture_2D_limited_npot
GL_APPLE_texture_format_BGRA8888 GL_APPLE_texture_max_level GL_IMG_read_format
GL_IMG_texture_compression_pvrtc
```

The last line, in bold, points out that iOS can handle a special compressed texture format called PVRTC used by the brand of graphics processing units (GPUs) in iOS devices. The first two generations of iPhones and iPod/Touches used a PowerVR MBX chip, while the later ones use the more powerful PowerVR SGX GPU. The advantage of the later ones is that it can accept highly compressed textures in their own format and display them on the fly. This can save substantial memory while increasing framerate, by compressing textures down as small as 1/16th uncompressed size.

Of course, this comes with one main caveat: images must have a square power-of-two (POT) form. The compression works best on photographic type of images as opposed to contrasty graphics.

> **Note**   Another interesting extra feature is found in the string `GL_APPLE_texture_2D_limited_npot` GL. NPOT means "nonpower-of-two." Remember that more recent versions of iOS can use NPOT images? So if you have reason to use an NPOT image, check the extensions beforehand and handle the results accordingly.

Here we're going to generate and import a PVRTC. First you will have to compress your existing files down to the PVR format using the a nice little tool that Imagination Technologies, the manufacturer of the PowerVR graphics chips, used in all iOS devices.

You can fetch it at `www.imgtec.com`. Look for *PowerVR Insider Utilities* under the developer's section. It is called PVRTexTool.

> **Note**   Apple also supplies a texture convertor called texturetool. While it is only a command-line based tool, it is very powerful in its own right and could be used to handle large batch jobs if you had a lot of files to compress at once.

Do not be alarmed when you launch it! It might look like Windows NT, but there is nothing wrong with your picture. It actually uses the X11 windowing platform that makes it usable across many different operation systems.

To convert a texture to PVRTC, simply load it into the editor, and select the *Encode Current Texture* button. That will open up a new dialog that will let you select which 3D platform you want to encode to; in this case, select the OpenGL ES 1.x tab. Select either the PVRTC 2BPP or PVRTC 4BPP button in the Compressed Formats section, and then the encode button on the bottom.

That's it!

Table 5-5 shows the formats generated by the tool. Even though you have a selection of only two, four are possible depending on whether the source bitmap has alpha or not. The 2BPP format means two bits-per-pixel while 4BPP means, well you guessed it, four-bits-per-pixel.

Many other image formats supported as well, and those are covered in Chapter 9 in the discussion on performance issues.

Table 5-5. The Four PVR Formats Generated by PVRTexTool

Format	Compression	Details
GL_COMPRESSED_RGBA_PVRTC_4BPPV1_IMG	8:1	4 bits/pixel with alpha
GL_COMPRESSED_RGB_PVRTC_4BPPV1_IMG	6:1	4 bits/pixel no alpha
GL_COMPRESSED_RGBA_PVRTC_2BPPV1_IMG	16:1	2 bits/pixel with alpha
GL_COMPRESSED_RGB_PVRTC_2BPPV1_IMG	12:1	2 bits/pixel no alpha

Say you have a 512×512 PNG texture that will consume 1 MB of memory. The least compression using PVRTexTool will take less than 200 KB. The greatest compression format, 2 bits/pixel with alpha, would be a mere 64 KB.

PVRTC textures are also readable by GLKTextureLoader() but will fail to load if you specify GLKTextureLoaderGenerateMipmaps in the option dictionary. However, you can use PVRTexTool to embed a mipmap chain in the host file for you. Because the compression is a lossy one, you can see the various resolution files pop in and out when using the preceding code, more readily than the sharper images.

> **Note**   Because PVRTC is hardware specific, Apple has issued a precautionary note to not necessarily rely on PVRTC support in future devices. This simply means that Apple may at some point use a different GPU manufacturer that is not likely to support another company's format.

More Solar System Goodness

Now we can go back to our solar-system model from the previous chapter and add a texture to the Earth so that it can really look like the Earth. Examine Planet.m, and swap out init() for Listing 5-6.

Listing 5-6. Modified sphere generator with texture support added

```
-(id) init:(GLint)stacks slices:(GLint)slices radius:(GLfloat)radius     //1
    squash:(GLfloat) squash textureFile:(NSString *)textureFile
{
    unsigned int colorIncrment=0;
    unsigned int blue=0;
    unsigned int red=255;
    int numVertices=0;

    if(textureFile!=nil)
        m_TextureInfo=[self loadTexture:textureFile];                    //2
```

```
m_Scale=radius;
m_Squash=squash;

colorIncrment=255/stacks;

if ((self = [super init]))
{
        m_Stacks = stacks;
        m_Slices = slices;
        m_VertexData = nil;

        m_TexCoordsData = nil;

        //Vertices

        GLfloat *vPtr = m_VertexData =
                (GLfloat*)malloc(sizeof(GLfloat) * 3 * ((m_Slices*2+2) *↵
                (m_Stacks)));

        //Color data

        GLubyte *cPtr = m_ColorData =
                (GLubyte*)malloc(sizeof(GLubyte) * 4 * ((m_Slices*2+2) *↵
                (m_Stacks)));

        //Normal pointers for lighting

        GLfloat *nPtr = m_NormalData = (GLfloat*)
                malloc(sizeof(GLfloat) * 3 * ((m_Slices*2+2) * (m_Stacks)));

        GLfloat *tPtr=nil;                                              //3

        if(textureFile!=nil)
        {
                tPtr=m_TexCoordsData =
                (GLfloat *)malloc(sizeof(GLfloat) * 2 * ((m_Slices*2+2) *↵
                (m_Stacks)));
        }

        unsigned int phiIdx, thetaIdx;

        //Latitude

        for(phiIdx=0; phiIdx < m_Stacks; phiIdx++)
        {
                //Starts at -1.57 goes up to +1.57 radians.

                //The first circle

                float phi0 = M_PI * ((float)(phiIdx+0) * (1.0/(float)↵
                (m_Stacks)) - 0.5);
```

```
                    //The second one

                    float phi1 = M_PI * ((float)(phiIdx+1) * (1.0/(float)↵
(m_Stacks)) - 0.5);

                    float cosPhi0 = cos(phi0);
                    float sinPhi0 = sin(phi0);
                    float cosPhi1 = cos(phi1);
                    float sinPhi1 = sin(phi1);

                    float cosTheta, sinTheta;

                    //Longitude

                    for(thetaIdx=0; thetaIdx < m_Slices; thetaIdx++)
                    {
                            //Increment along the longitude circle each "slice."

                            float theta = -2.0*M_PI * ((float)thetaIdx) *↵
 (1.0/(float)(m_Slices-1));

                            cosTheta = cos(theta);
                            sinTheta = sin(theta);

                            //We're generating a vertical pair of points, such
                            //as the first point of stack 0 and the first point↵
                            // of stack 1above it. This is how TRIANGLE_STRIPS work,
                            //taking a set of 4 vertices and essentially drawing↵
                            // two triangles at a time. The first is v0-v1-v2 and↵
the next is
                            // v2-v1-v3 etc. Get x-y-z for the first vertex of↵
stack.

                            vPtr[0] = m_Scale*cosPhi0 * cosTheta;
                            vPtr[1] = m_Scale*sinPhi0*m_Squash;
                            vPtr[2] = m_Scale*(cosPhi0 * sinTheta);

                            //The same but for the vertex immediately above the↵
previous one.

                            vPtr[3] = m_Scale*cosPhi1 * cosTheta;
                            vPtr[4] = m_Scale*sinPhi1*m_Squash;
                            vPtr[5] = m_Scale*(cosPhi1 * sinTheta);

                            //Normal pointers for lighting.

                            nPtr[0] = cosPhi0 * cosTheta;
                            nPtr[2] = cosPhi0 * sinTheta;
                            nPtr[1] = sinPhi0;

                            nPtr[3] = cosPhi1 * cosTheta;
                            nPtr[5] = cosPhi1 * sinTheta;
                            nPtr[4] = sinPhi1;

                            if(tPtr!=nil)                                    //4
                            {
                                    GLfloat texX = (float)thetaIdx *↵
```

```
                (1.0f/(float)(m_Slices-1));
                                            tPtr[0] = texX;
                                            tPtr[1] = (float)(phiIdx+0) *↵

                (1.0f/(float)(m_Stacks));
                                            tPtr[2] = texX;
                                            tPtr[3] = (float)(phiIdx+1) *↵

                (1.0f/(float)(m_Stacks));
                                        }

                                    cPtr[0] = red;
                                    cPtr[1] = 0;
                                    cPtr[2] = blue;
                                    cPtr[4] = red;
                                    cPtr[5] = 0;
                                    cPtr[6] = blue;
                                    cPtr[3] = cPtr[7] = 255;

                                    cPtr += 2*4;
                                    vPtr += 2*3;
                                    nPtr += 2*3;


                                    if(tPtr!=nil)                               //5
                                            tPtr += 2*2;
                                }

                            blue+=colorIncrment;
                            red-=colorIncrment;

                            // Degenerate triangle to connect stacks and maintain winding
        order.

                            vPtr[0] = vPtr[3] = vPtr[-3];
                            vPtr[1] = vPtr[4] = vPtr[-2];
                            vPtr[2] = vPtr[5] = vPtr[-1];

                            nPtr[0] = nPtr[3] = nPtr[-3];
                            nPtr[1] = nPtr[4] = nPtr[-2];
                            nPtr[2] = nPtr[5] = nPtr[-1];

                            if(tPtr!=nil)
                                    {
                                    tPtr[0] = tPtr[2] = tPtr[-2];               //6
                                    tPtr[1] = tPtr[3] = tPtr[-1];
                                    }
                        }
                    }

                numVertices=(vPtr-m_VertexData)/6;
            }

        m_Angle=0.0;
        m_RotationalIncrement=0.0;
```

```
m_Pos[0]=0.0;
m_Pos[1]=0.0;
m_Pos[2]=0.0;

return self;
}
```

So, here is what's happening:

- A file name for the image is added to the end of the parameter list in line 1. Remember to add it also to `init`'s declaration in `Planet.h`.

- In line 2, the texture is created and GLKTextureInfo is returned.

- In lines 3ff, the coordinates for the texture are allocated.

- Starting at line 4, calculate the texture coordinates. Because the sphere has x slices and y stacks and the coordinate space goes only from 0 to 1, we need to advance each value by increments of `1/m_slices` for *s* and `1/m_stacks` for *t.* Notice that this covers two pairs of coordinates, one above the other, matching the layout of the triangle strips that also produces stacked pairs of coordinates.

- In line 5, advance the pointer to the coordinate array to hold the next set of values.

- And finally, line 6 ties up some loose threads in preparation for going to the next stack in the loop.

Next, update `Planet.h` by adding the following to the interface:

```
#import <GLKit/GLKit.h>
```

Also add the following:

```
GLKTextureInfo *m_TextureInfo;
GLfloat *m_TexCoordsData;
```

Copy over the `loadTexture()` method from the first example to the planet object, and modify the header as needed. Feel free to remove the mipmap support if you like, but there's no harm in leaving it in; it's just not essential for this exercise.

For an earth texture, note that this will wrap around the *entire* sphere model, so not just any image will do; as such, it should resemble Figure 5-21. You can get the one I use for this exercise, which is available from the Apress website. Or you might want to check NASA first at `http://maps.jpl.nasa.gov/`.

Figure 5-21. *Textures typically fill out the entire frame, edge to edge. Planets use a Mercator projection (a cylindrical map).*

When you've found a suitable image, add it to your project and hand it off to the planet object when allocated back in your solar system's controller. Because you don't need a texture for the sun, you can just pass a nil pointer. And of course we'll need to update the execute() method, as shown in Listing 5-7.

Listing 5-7. *Ready to handle the new texture*

```
-(bool)execute
{
        glMatrixMode(GL_MODELVIEW);
        glEnable(GL_CULL_FACE);
        glCullFace(GL_BACK);
        glFrontFace(GL_CW);

        glEnableClientState(GL_NORMAL_ARRAY);
        glEnableClientState(GL_VERTEX_ARRAY);
        glEnableClientState(GL_COLOR_ARRAY);

    if(m_TexCoordsData!=nil)
    {
        glEnable(GL_TEXTURE_2D);
        glEnableClientState(GL_TEXTURE_COORD_ARRAY);

        if(m_TextureInfo!=0)
            glBindTexture(GL_TEXTURE_2D, m_TextureInfo.name);

        glTexCoordPointer(2, GL_FLOAT, 0, m_TexCoordsData);
    }

    glMatrixMode(GL_MODELVIEW);

    glVertexPointer(3, GL_FLOAT, 0, m_VertexData);
    glNormalPointer(GL_FLOAT, 0, m_NormalData);

    glColorPointer(4, GL_UNSIGNED_BYTE, 0, m_ColorData);
```

```
    glDrawArrays(GL_TRIANGLE_STRIP, 0, (m_Slices+1)*2*(m_Stacks-1)+2);

    glDisable(GL_BLEND);
    glDisable(GL_TEXTURE_2D);
    glDisableClientState(GL_TEXTURE_COORD_ARRAY);

    return true;
}
```

The main difference here is the addition of code to enable texturing, to set the current texture, and to hand off the pointer to OpenGL.

Compile and run, and ideally you'll see something like Figure 5-22.

Figure 5-22. *Sun and Earth*

If you examine the actual artwork used for this exercise, you'll notice that it is fairly bright but low in contrast. The main reason is that the real oceans are actually quite dark and it just did not look right under the lighting condition.

Summary

This chapter served as an introduction to textures and their uses. It covered basic texture theory, how texture coordinates are expressed, how mipmaps can be used for greater fidelity, and how textures can be filtered to smooth them out. The solar-system model was updated so that earth now really looks like the earth using a texture map. In the next chapter, we'll continue with textures, putting to use the iPhone's multiple texture units, along with blending techniques.

Chapter 6

Will It Blend?

Yes! It blends!

—Tom Dickson, owner of the Blendtec blender company

In 2006, Tom Dickson posted a goofy video to YouTube illustrating how tough his company's blenders were by blending some marbles into powder. Since then, his frequent videos have been viewed more than 100 million times and have featured blendings of everything from a tiki torch and a laser pointer to a Justin Bieber doll and a new camcorder. Tom's kind of blending has nothing to do with our kind of blending, though, unless the sadistic and unmerciful pulverization of a couple of iPads and an iPhone 4 count. After all, they are OpenGL ES devices—devices that have their own form of blending, albeit not nearly as destructive. (Yes, it's a stretch.)

Blending plays an important role in OpenGL ES applications. It is the process used to create translucent objects that can be used for something as simple as a window to something as complicated as a pond. Other uses include the addition of atmospherics such as fog or smoke, the smoothing out of aliased lines, and the simulation of various sophisticated lighting effects. OpenGL ES 2 has a complex mechanism that uses small modules called *shaders* to do specialized blending effects among other things. But before shaders there were blending functions, which were not nearly as versatile but considerably easier to use.

In this chapter, you'll learn the basics of blending functions and how to apply them for both color and alpha blending. After that, you'll use a different kind of blending involving multiple textures, used for far more sophisticated effects such as shadowing. Finally, I'll show how we can apply these effects in the solar-system project.

Alpha Blending

You have no doubt noticed the color quadruplet of RGBA. As mentioned earlier, the *A* part is the *alpha channel*, and it is traditionally used for specifying translucency in an image. In a bitmap used for texturing, the alpha layer forms an image of sorts, which can be translucent in one section, transparent in another, and completely opaque in a third.

If an object isn't using texturing but instead has its color specified via its vertices, lighting, or overall global coloring, alpha will let the entire object or scene have translucent properties. A value of 1.0 means the object or pixel is completely opaque, while 0 means it is completely invisible.

For alpha to work, as with any blending model, you work with both a source image and a destination image. Because this topic is best understood through examples, we're going to start with the first one now.

First let's go back to the original bouncy square exercise from Chapter 3. Then use Listing 6-1 in place of the original drawInRect() method, making sure you call setClipping in your initializer as before. Solid squares of colors are used here first, instead of textured ones, because it makes for a simpler example.

Listing 6-1. *The new* drawInRect() *method*

```
(void)glkView:(GLKView *)view drawInRect:(CGRect)rect
{
        static const GLfloat squareVertices[] =                           //1
        {
                -0.5, -0.5, 0.0,
                 0.5, -0.5, 0.0,
                -0.5,  0.5, 0.0,
                 0.5,  0.5, 0.0
        };

        static float transY = 0.0;

        glClearColor(0.0, 0.0, 0.0, 1.0);                                 //2

        glClear(GL_COLOR_BUFFER_BIT);

        glMatrixMode(GL_MODELVIEW);
        glLoadIdentity();

    //Do square one bouncing up and down.

        glTranslatef(0.0, (GLfloat)(sinf(transY)/2.0), -4.0);             //3

        glVertexPointer(3, GL_FLOAT, 0, squareVertices);
        glEnableClientState(GL_VERTEX_ARRAY);

    //SQUARE 1

        glColor4f(0.0, 0.0,1.0,1.0);                                      //4

        glDrawArrays(GL_TRIANGLE_STRIP, 0, 4);

    //SQUARE 2

        glColor4f(1.0, 0.0,0.0, .5);                                      //5
```

```
    glLoadIdentity();
    glTranslatef( (GLfloat)(sinf(transY)/2.0),0.0, -3.0);          //6

    glDrawArrays(GL_TRIANGLE_STRIP, 0, 4);                         //7

    transY += 0.075;                                              //8
}

(void)setClipping
{
    float aspectRatio;
    const float zNear = .01;
    const float zFar = 100;
    const float fieldOfView =30.0;
    GLfloat    size;

    CGRect frame = [[UIScreen mainScreen] bounds];

    //h/w clamps the fov to the height; flipping it would make it relative to the width.

    aspectRatio=(float)frame.size.height/(float)frame.size.width;

    //Set the OpenGL projection matrix.

    glMatrixMode(GL_PROJECTION);

    size = zNear * tanf((fieldOfView/57.3)/ 2.0);

    glFrustumf(-size, size, -size *aspectRatio,
            size *aspectRatio, zNear, zFar);

    glViewport(0, 0, frame.size.width, frame.size.height);

    //Make the OpenGL modelview matrix the default.

    glMatrixMode(GL_MODELVIEW);
}
```

And as before, let's take a close look at the code:

■   You should now recognize the bouncy square's coordinates. And in this case, the z component is added to make a 3D bouncy square.

■   Of course, in line 2, the buffer is cleared. But make the background black instead of the default gray.

■   In line 3 the square is moved back by 4 units.

■   Because there is no coloring per vertex, this call to glColor4f() in line 4 will set the entire square to blue. However, notice the last component of 1.0. That is the *alpha*, and it will be addressed shortly. Immediately following gColor4f() is the call to actually draw the square.

■ But we want two squares to show how they can blend. So in line 5, the color is changed to red and is given an alpha of .5, half that of the blue one.

■ Following that is a translation of only 3 units in line 6, and as a result, the red square will be larger because it is closer. Also, notice that the x value is now being translated. Instead of the up and down movement of the blue square, the closer red one will move left and right.

■ And in line 7, the red square is rendered. Because there is no depth buffer being used right now, the only reason why the red square covers the blue one is that it is drawn after the blue square.

■ In line 8 the value of the translation is cut down so as to decrease the motion, making it a little easier to catch the blending effects when turned on.

If all works, you should have something that looks like Figure 6-1.

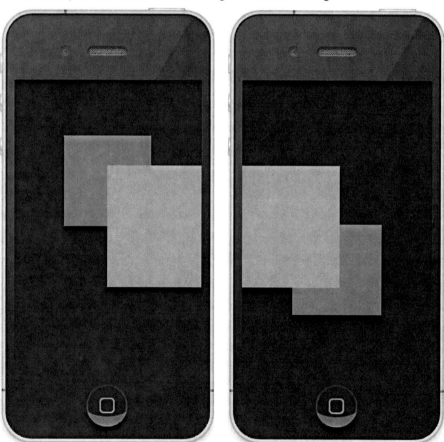

Figure 6-1. The blue square goes up and down; the red one goes left and right.

It's not much to look at, but this will be the framework for the next several experiments. The first will switch on the default blending function.

As with so many other OpenGL features, you turn blending on with the call `glEnable(GL_BLEND)`. Add that anywhere before the first call to `glDrawArray()`. Recompile, and what do you see? Nothing, or at least nothing has changed. It still looks like Figure 6-1. That's because there's more to blending than saying shaking your fist at the monitor shouting "Blend!" We must specify a blending *function* as well, which describes how the source colors (as expressed via its fragments or pixels) mix with those at the destination. The default, of course, is when the source fragments always replace those at the destination, when depth cueing is off. As a matter of fact, blending can take place only when z-buffering is switched off.

Blending Functions

To change the default blending, we must resort to using `glBlendFunc()`, which comes with two parameters. The first tells just what to do with the source, and the second specifies what to do with the destination. To picture what goes on, note that all that's ultimately happening is that each of the RGBA source components is added, subtracted, or whatever, with each of the destination components. That is, the source's red channel is mixed with the destination's red channel, the source's green is mixed with the destination's green, and so on. This is usually expressed the following way: call the source RGBA values *Rs*, *Gs*, *Bs*, and *As*, and call the destination values *Rd*, *Gd*, *Bd*, and *Ad*. But we also need both source and destination *blending factors*, expressed as *Sr*, *Sg*, *Sb*, and *Sa* and *Dr*, *Dg*, *Db*, and *Da*. (It's not as complicated as it seems, really.) And here's the formula for the final composite color:

$$(R, G, B) = ((Rs * Sr) + (Rd * Dr), (Gs * Sg) + (Gd * Dg), (Bs * Sb) + (Bd * Db))$$

In other words, multiply the source color by its blending factor and add it to the destination color multiplied by its blending factor.

One of the most common forms of blending is to overlay a translucent face on top of stuff that has already been drawn—that is, the destination. As before, that can be a simulated window pane, a heads-up display for a flight simulator, or other graphics that might just look nicer when mixed with the existing imagery. (The latter is used a lot in Distant Suns for a number of the elements such as the constellation names, the outlines, and so on.) Depending on the purpose, you may want the overlay to be nearly opaque, using an alpha approaching 1.0, or very tenuous, with an alpha approaching 0.0.

In this basic blending task, the source's colors are first multiplied by the alpha value, its blending factor. So if the source red is maxed out at 1.0 and the alpha is 0.75, the result is derived by simply multiplying 1.0 by 0.75. The same would be used for both green and blue. On the other hand, the destination colors are multiplied by *1.0 minus the source's alpha*. Why? That effectively yields a composite color that can never exceed the maximum value of 1.0; otherwise, all sorts of color distortion could happen. Or imagine it this way: the source's alpha value is the proportion of the color "width" of 1.0 that the source is permitted to fill. The leftover space then becomes 1.0 minus the source's alpha. The larger the alpha, the greater the proportion of the source color that can be used, with an increasingly smaller proportion reserved for the destination color. So as the alpha approaches 1.0, the greater the amount of the source color that is copied to the frame buffer, replacing the destination color.

> **Note**   In these examples, normalized color values are used because they make it much easier to follow the process instead of using unsigned bytes, which would express the colors from 0 to 255.

Now we can examine that in the next example. To set up the blending functions described earlier, you would use the following call:

```
glBlendFunc(GL_SRC_ALPHA, GL_ONE_MINUS_SRC_ALPHA);
```

GL_SRC_ALPHA and GL_ONE_MINUS_SRC_ALPHA are the blending factors described earlier. And remember that the first parameter is the source's blending, the object being written currently. Place that line immediately after where you enable blending. And to the red colors, compile and run. Do you see Figure 6-2?

Figure 6-2. *The red square has an alpha of .5, and the blue has an alpha of 1.0.*

So, what's happening? The blue has an alpha of 1.0, so each blue fragment completely replaces anything in the background. Then the red with an alpha of .5 means that 50 percent of the red is written to the destination. The black area will be a dim red but only 50 percent of the specified value of 1.0 given in `glColor4f()`. So far, so good. Now on top of the blue, 50 percent of the red value is mixing with a 50 percent blue value:

Blended color=Color Source*Alpha of source + (1.0-Alpha of Source)*Color of the destination

Or looking at each component based on the values in the earlier red square example, here are the calculations:

Red=1.0*0.5+(1.0-0.5)*0.0

Green=0.0*0.5+(1.0-0.5)*0.0

Blue=0.0*0.5+(1.0-0.5)*1.0

So, the final color of the fragment's pixels should be 0.5,0.0,0.5, or magenta. Now, the red and resulting magenta are a little on the dim side. What would you do if you wanted to make this much brighter? It would be nice if there were a means of blending the full intensities of the colors. Would you use alpha values of 1.0? Nope. Why? Well, with blue as the destination and a source alpha of 1.0, the preceding blue channel equation would be 0.0*1.0+(1.0-1.0)*1.0. And that equals 0, while the red would be 1.0, or solid. What you would want is to have the brightest red when writing to the black background, and the same for the blue. For that you would use a blending function that writes both colors at full intensity, such as GL_ONE. That means the following:

`glBlendFunc(GL_ONE, GL_ONE);`

Going back to the equations using the source triplet of red=1, green=0, blue=0 and the destination of red=0, green=0, blue=1 (with alpha defaulting to 1.0), the calculations would be as follows:

Red=1*1+0*1

Green=0* (1+(0-0)*1

Blue=0*1+(1-0)*1

And that yields a color in which red=1, green=0, blue=1. And that my friends, is magenta, as shown in Figure 6-3.

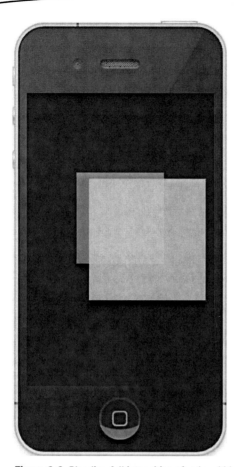

Figure 6-3. *Blending full intensities of red and blue*

Now it's time for another experiment of sorts. Take the code from the previous example, set both alphas to 0.5, and reset the blend function back to the traditional values for transparency:

```
glBlendFunc(GL_SRC_ALPHA, GL_ONE_MINUS_SRC_ALPHA);
```

After you run this modified code, take note of the combined color, and notice that the further square is blue at -4.0 away and is also the first to be rendered, with the red one as the second. Now reverse the order of the colors that are drawn, and run. What's wrong? You should get something like Figure 6-4.

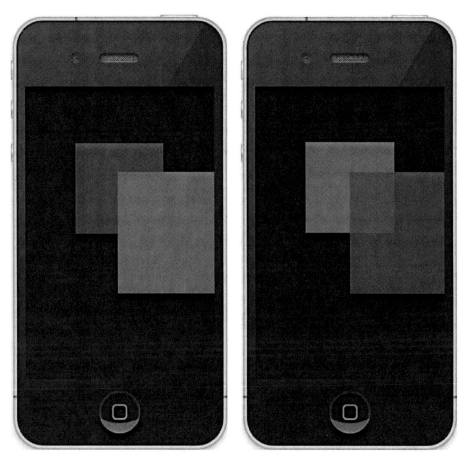

Figure 6-4. *The left is drawn with blue first (left), while the one on the right is drawn with red first (right).*

The intersections are slightly different colors. This shows one of the mystifying gotchas in OpenGL: like with most 3D frameworks, the blending will be slightly different depending on the order of the faces and colors when rendered. In this case, it is actually quite simple to figure out what's going on. In Figure 6-4 (left), the blue square is drawn first with an alpha of .5. So, even though the blue color triplet is defined as 0,0,1, the alpha value will knock that down to 0,0,.5 while it is written to the frame buffer. Now add the red square with similar properties. Naturally, the red will write to the black part of the frame buffer in the same manner as the blue, so the final value will be .5,0,0. But note what happens when red writes on top of the blue. Since the blue is already at half of its intensity, the blending function will cut that down even further, to .25, as a result of the destination part of the blending function, *(1.0-Source alpha)*blue+destination*, or (1.0-.5).5+0, or .25. The final color is then .5,0,.25. With the lower intensity of the blue, it contributes less to the composite color, leaving red to dominate. Now in Figure 6-4 (right), the order is reversed, so the blue dominates with a final color of .25,0,.5.

Table 6-1 has all of the allowable OpenGL ES blending factors, although not all are supported by both source and destination. As you can see, there is ample room for tinkering, with no set rules of what creates the best-looking effect. This will be highly reliant on your individual tastes and needs. It is a lot of fun to try different values, though. Make sure to fill the background with a dim gray, because some of the combinations will just yield black when written to a black background.

Table 6-1. *The Source and Destination Blending Values; Note That Not All Are Available to Both Channels*

Blend Factor	Description
GL_ZERO	Multiplies the operand by 0.
GL_ONE	Multiplies the operand by 1.
GL_SRC_COLOR	Multiplies the operand by the four components of the source color (destination only).
GL_ONE_MINUS_SRC_COLOR	Multiplies the operand by (1.0 – source colors) (destination only).
GL_DST_COLOR	Multiplies the operand by the four components of the destination color (source only).
GL_ONE_MINUS_DST_COLOR	Multiplies the operand by the 1.0 – destination colors (source only).
GL_SRC_ALPHA	Multiplies the operand by the source alpha.
GL_ONE_MINUS_SRC_ALPHA	Multiplies the operand by (1.0 – source alpha).
GL_DST_ALPHA	Multiplies the operand by the destination alpha.
GL_ONE_MINUS_DST_ALPHA	Multiplies the operand by (1.0 – destination alpha).
GL_SRC_ALPHA_SATURATE	Special mode for older graphics implementations to help anti-aliasing. You'll likely never use it. (Source only.)

In Chapter 5, we took a look at the GL extensions that OpenGL ES on iOS devices supported. Several of those are for more sophisticated blending solutions such as GL_OES_blend_equation_separate, GL_OES_blend_func_separate, GL_OES_blend_subtract, and GL_EXT_blend_minmax. These values are used with the methods glBlendEquation() and glBlendEquationSeparate().

Look back at the default blending equation, where the final color is determined by a *source value+a dest value*. But what if you wanted the source to subtract the destination instead of add? Calling glBlendEquation(GL_FUNC_SUBTRACT) will do the job. Add that line right below glBlendFunc(), ensure both squares have an alpha of .5, and reset the colors back to the original with red in front, compile and run. The results may be slightly nonobvious, as in Figure 6-5 (left). What is happening is that the operation really is "subtracting" blue from the red source, but there is no blue component in the red square's color. The math yields a final color with red=.5, green=0, and blue=-.25. But because negative colors do not occur in this plane of existence (or at least in San Jose,

California), the system clamps the blue component to 0. The result is a solid red where the intersection is. So, in order to see something here, the front square needs to be drawn with some blue already. So, change red's color to be 1,0,1, or magenta. Now when run, Figure 6-5 (right) is the result, because the blue destination can subtract from the blue in the source, leaving a positive value that the system understands. And in this case the value of the intersection is .5,0,.25, which is why we don't have a pure red but more of a magenta-ish red. Try importing it into a paint program, and verify the actual colors using the eyedropper function.

Figure 6-5a,b. *On the left, no blending takes place using the subtract operation, while it succeeds on the right.*

There are still two other function calls in the extended set, and they are `glBlendEquationSeparateOES()` and `glBlendFuncSeparateOES()`. These functions allow you to modify the RGB channels separately from alpha. The `OES` suffix specifies that these are extensions to OpenGL ES (but only for 1.1 of OpenGL—they are standard in 2.0, so you don't need the OES at the end), and are defined in glext.h. One way in which this is useful is to counteract the effects rendering order that Figure 6-4 illustrates.

And one final method here that might be really handy in some blending operations is that of `glColorMask()`. This function lets you block one or more color channels from being written to the destination. To see this in action, modify the red square's colors to be 1,1,0,1; set the two blend functions back to `GL_ONE`; and comment out the line `glBlendEquation(GL_FUNC_SUBTRACT);`. You should see something like Figure 6-6 (left) when run. The red square is now yellow and, when blended with blue, yields white at the intersection. Now add the following line:

```
glColorMask(GL_TRUE, GL_FALSE, GL_TRUE, GL_TRUE);
```

The preceding line masks, or turns off, the green channel when being drawn to the frame buffer. When run, you should see Figure 6-6 (right), which looks remarkably like Figure 6-3. And as a matter of fact, logically they are identical.

Figure 6-6. *The left one doesn't use* `glColorMask`, *so all colors are in play, while the right one masks off the green channel.*

Multicolor Blending

Now we can spend a few minutes looking at the effect of blending functions when the squares are defined with individual colors for each vertex. Add Listing 6-2 to the venerable `drawInRect()`. The first color set defines yellow, magenta, and cyan (the three complementary colors to the standard red-green-blue specified in the second set).

Listing 6-2. Vertex Colors for the Two Squares

```
static const GLfloat squareColorsYMCA[] =
{
        1.0, 1.0,   0, 1.0,
          0, 1.0, 1.0, 1.0,
          0,   0,   0, 1.0,
        1.0,   0, 1.0, 1.0,
};

 static const GLfloat squareColorsRGBA[] =
{
        1.0,   0,   0, 1.0,
          0, 1.0,   0, 1.0,
          0,   0, 1.0, 1.0,
        1.0, 1.0, 1.0, 1.0,
 };
```

Assign the first color array to the first square (which has been the blue one up until now), and assign the second to the former red square. And don't forget to enable the use of the color array. You should be familiar enough now to know what to do. Also, notice that the arrays are now normalized as a bunch of `GLfloat`s as opposed to the previously used unsigned bytes, so you'll have to tweak the calls to `glColorPointer()`. The solution is left up to the reader (I've always wanted to say that). With the blending disabled, you should see Figure 6-7 (left), and when enabled using the traditional function for transparency, Figure 6-7 (center) should be the result. What? It isn't? You say it still looks like the first figure? Why would that be?

Look back at the color arrays. Notice how the last value in each row, alpha, is at its maximum of 1.0. Remember that with this blending mode, any of the destination values are multiplied by: (1.0 – source alpha), or rather, 0.0, so that the source color reigns supreme as you saw in a previous example. One solution to seeing some real transparency would be to use the following:

`glBlendFunc(GL_ONE, GL_ONE);`

This works because it ditches the alpha channel altogether. If you want alpha with the "standard" function, merely change the 1.0 values to something else, such as .5. And the result is Figure 6-7 (right).

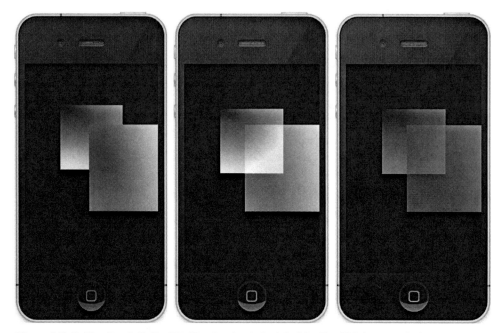

Figure 6-7*. No blending (left),* GL_ONE *blending (center), alpha blending (right), respectively*

Texture Blending

Now, with fear and trembling, we can approach the blending of textures. Initially this seems much like the earlier alpha blending, but all sorts of interesting things can be done by using *multitexturing*.

First let's rework the earlier code to support two textures at once and do vertex blending. Listing 6-3 merges some of the code from Chapter 5 with the framework from this chapter's examples.

Listing 6-3*. The* drawInRect() *Method Rejiggered to Support Two Textured Squares*

```
- (void)glkView:(GLKView *)view drawInRect:(CGRect)rect
{
        static const GLfloat squareVertices[] =
        {
                -0.5, -0.5, 0.0,
                 0.5, -0.5, 0.0,
                -0.5,  0.5, 0.0,
                 0.5,  0.5, 0.0
        };
```

```
static const GLfloat squareColorsYMCA[] =
{
        1.0, 1.0,   0, 1.0,
          0, 1.0, 1.0, 1.0,
          0,   0,   0, 1.0,
        1.0,   0, 1.0, 1.0,
};

static const GLfloat squareColorsRGBA[] =
{
        1.0,   0,   0, 1.0,
          0, 1.0,   0, 1.0,
          0,   0, 1.0, 1.0,
        1.0, 1.0, 1.0, 1.0,
};

static  GLfloat textureCoords[] =
{
        0.0, 0.0,
        1.0, 0.0,
        0.0, 1.0,
        1.0, 1.0
};

static float transY = 0.0;

glMatrixMode(GL_PROJECTION);
    glLoadIdentity();

    [self setClipping];

    glClearColor(0.0, 0.0,0.0, 1.0);

    glClear(GL_COLOR_BUFFER_BIT);

    glMatrixMode(GL_MODELVIEW);
    glLoadIdentity();

//Set up for using textures.
glEnable(GL_TEXTURE_2D);
glBindTexture(GL_TEXTURE_2D,m_Texture0.name);
glTexCoordPointer(2, GL_FLOAT,0,textureCoords);
glEnableClientState(GL_TEXTURE_COORD_ARRAY);

//Do square one bouncing up and down.

glTranslatef(0.0, (GLfloat)(sinf(transY)/2.0), -4.0);

glVertexPointer(3, GL_FLOAT, 0, squareVertices);
glEnableClientState(GL_VERTEX_ARRAY);
```

```
        //glEnable(GL_BLEND);

        glBlendFunc(GL_SRC_ALPHA, GL_ONE_MINUS_SRC_ALPHA);


    //SQUARE 1

        //glEnableClientState(GL_COLOR_ARRAY);

        glColorPointer(4, GL_FLOAT, 0, squareColorsYMCA);

        glDrawArrays(GL_TRIANGLE_STRIP, 0, 4);

    //SQUARE 2

    glLoadIdentity();
    glTranslatef( (GLfloat)(sinf(transY)/2.0),0.0, -3.0);

    glColorPointer(4, GL_FLOAT, 0, squareColorsRGBA);
    glBindTexture(GL_TEXTURE_2D,m_Texture1.name);

    glDrawArrays(GL_TRIANGLE_STRIP, 0, 4);

    transY += 0.075f;
}
```

In addition to this, make sure to add loadTexture() from the Chapter 5 examples, and initialize it in the usual place. Because we need two different textures, initialize the first as m_Texture0 and the second as m_Texture1. You will likely notice that while I have both blending and color stuff, I commented out some lines just for this first run-through to ensure that the basic stuff is working. If it's working, you should see something like Figure 6-8 (left). And if that works, unleash the vertex colors by uncommenting glEnableClientState(GL_COLOR_ARRAY) and glEnable(GL_BLEND), which should yield Figure 6-8 (center). And for Figure 6-8 (right), the Golden Gate Bridge is colored with a solid red. I shall let you, dear reader, figure out how to do this.

Using a single bitmap and colorizing it is a common practice to save memory. If you are doing some UI components in the OpenGL layer, consider using a single image, and colorize it using these techniques. You might ask why is it a solid red as opposed to merely being tinted red, allowing for some variation in colors. What is happening here is that the vertex's colors are being multiplied by the colors of each fragment. For the red, I've used the RGB triplet of 1.0,0.0,0.0. So when each fragment is being calculated in a channel-wise multiplication, the green and blue channels are going to be multiplied by 0, so they are completely filtered out, leaving just the red. If you wanted to let some of the other colors leak through, you would specify the vertices to lean toward a more neutral tone, with the desired tint color being a little higher than the others, such as 1.0,0.7,0.7.

Figure 6-8. *On the left, only the textures are displayed. In the center, they're blended with color, and for the one on the right they're solid red.*

You can also add translucency to textures quite easily. To enable this, I'll introduce a small simplifying factor here. You can colorize the textured face by using a single color by simply using `glColor4f()` and eliminate the need to create the vertex color array. Setting the alpha to less than 1.0 results in the see-through texture, as shown in Figure 6-9.

Figure 6-9. *The image on the left has an alpha of .5, while the figure on the right has an alpha of .75.*

Multitexturing

So now we've covered blending for colors and mixed mode with textures and colors, but what about combining two textures to make a third? Such a technique is called *multitexturing*. Multitexturing can be used for layering one texture on top of another while performing certain mathematical operations. More sophisticated applications include simple image processing. But let's go for the low-hanging fruit first.

Multitexturing requires the use of *texture combiners* and *texture units*. *Texture combiners* let you combine and manipulate textures that are bound to one of the hardware's texture units, the specific part of the graphics chip that wraps an image around an object. Before the iPhone 3GS, you had only two texture units to deal with, which was a limitation of the PowerVR MBX graphics chip from Imagination Technologies. When the 3GS came out, Apple switched to using the more powerful SGX chip, which increased that to a total of eight texture units. If you anticipate using combiners in a big way, you might want to verify the supported total by glGetIntegerv(GL_MAX_COMBINED_TEXTURE_IMAGE_UNITS, &numberTextureUnits), where numberTextureUnits is defined as a GLint.

To set up a pipeline to handle multitexturing, we need to tell OpenGL what textures to use and how to mix them together. The process isn't that much different (in theory at least) than defining the blend functions when dealing with the alpha and color blending operations previously. It does involve heavy use of the glTexEnvf() call, another one of OpenGL's wildly overloaded methods. (If you don't believe me, check out its official reference page on the OpenGL site.) This sets up the *texture environment* that defines each stage of the multitexturing process.

Figure 6-10 illustrates the combiner chain. Each combiner refers to the *previous* texture fragment (P0 or Pn) or the incoming fragment for the first combiner. It then takes a fragment from a "source" texture (called S0), combines it with P0, and hands it off to the next combiner if needed (called C1); then the cycle repeats.

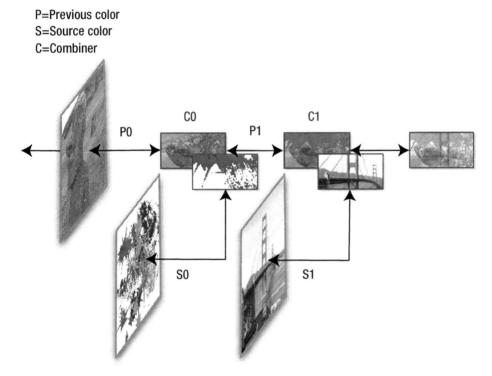

Figure 6-10. *The texture combiner chain*

The best way to tackle this topic is like any others: go to the code. In the following example, two textures are loaded together, bound to their respective texture units, and merged into a single output texture. Several kinds of methods used to combine the two images are tried with the results of each shown and examined in depth.

First, we revisit our old friend, `drawInRect()`. We're back to only a single texture, going up and down. The color support has also been stripped out. So, you should have something like Listing 6-4. And make sure that you are still loading a second texture.

Listing 6-4. *drawInRect() Revisited, Modified for Multitexture Support*

```
- (void)glkView:(GLKView *)view drawInRect:(CGRect)rect
{
    static const GLfloat squareVertices[] =
    {
        -0.5, -0.5, 0.0,
         0.5, -0.5, 0.0,
        -0.5,  0.5, 0.0,
         0.5,  0.5, 0.0
    };

    static  GLfloat textureCoords[] =
    {
        0.0, 0.0,
        1.0, 0.0,
        0.0, 1.0,
        1.0, 1.0
    };

    static float transY = 0.0;

    glMatrixMode(GL_PROJECTION);
    glLoadIdentity();

    [self setClipping];

    glClearColor(0.0, 0.0,0.0, 1.0);

    glClear(GL_COLOR_BUFFER_BIT);

    glMatrixMode(GL_MODELVIEW);
    glLoadIdentity();

    //Set up for using textures.

    glEnable(GL_TEXTURE_2D);
    glEnableClientState(GL_VERTEX_ARRAY);
    glVertexPointer(3, GL_FLOAT, 0, squareVertices);

    glEnableClientState(GL_TEXTURE_COORD_ARRAY);
    glClientActiveTexture(GL_TEXTURE0);                                 //1
    glTexCoordPointer(2, GL_FLOAT,0,textureCoords);

    glClientActiveTexture(GL_TEXTURE1);                                 //2
    glTexCoordPointer(2, GL_FLOAT,0,textureCoords);

    glLoadIdentity();
    glTranslatef(0.0, (GLfloat)(sinf(transY)/2.0), -2.5);
```

```
    [self multiTexture:m_Texture0.name tex1:m_Texture1.name];

    glDrawArrays(GL_TRIANGLE_STRIP, 0, 4);

    transY += 0.075f;
}
```

There is a new call here shown in lines 1 and 2, `glClientActiveTexture()`, which sets what texture unit to operate on. This is on the client side, not the hardware side of things, and indicates which texture unit is to receive the texture coordinate array. Don't get this confused with `glActiveTexture()`, used in Listing 6-5 below, that actually turns a specific texture unit on.

The other additional method we need is `multiTexture`, shown in Listing 6-5. This is a very simple default case. The fancy stuff comes later.

Listing 6-5. *Sets Up the Texture Combiners*

```
-(void)multiTexture:(GLuint)tex0 tex1:(GLuint)tex1
{
    GLfloat combineParameter=GL_MODULATE;                                      //1

    // Set up the first texture.

    glActiveTexture(GL_TEXTURE0);                                             //2
    glBindTexture(GL_TEXTURE_2D, tex0);                                       //3

    // Set up the second texture.

    glActiveTexture(GL_TEXTURE1);
    glBindTexture(GL_TEXTURE_2D, tex1);

    // Set the texture environment mode for this texture to combine.

    glTexEnvf(GL_TEXTURE_ENV, GL_TEXTURE_ENV_MODE, combineParameter);         //4
}
```

Here's what is going on:

- Line 1 specifies what the combiners should do. Table 6-2 lists all the possible values.

- `glActiveTexture()` makes active a specific hardware texture unit in line 2.

- Line 3 should not be a mystery, because you have seen it before. In this example, the first texture is bound to a specific hardware texture unit. The following two lines do the same for the second texture.

- Now tell the system what to do with the textures in line 4. Table 6-2 lists all the possible parameters. (In the table, P is previous, S is source, subscript a is alpha, and c is color and is used only when color and alpha have to be considered separately.)

Table 6-2. *Possible Values for* GL_TEXTURE_ENV_MODE

Texture Mode	Function
GL_ADD	$P_n + S_n$ (component-wise addition of the RGBA values from the two texture fragments, with S being source, P being the previous)
GL_BLEND	$P_n(1 - S_n) + S_n \times C$ (C is constant color set by GL_TEXTURE_ENV_COLOR)
GL_COMBINE	described below
GL_DECAL	$P_n \times (1 - S_{an}) + (S_{cn} \times S_{an})$
GL_MODULATE	$P_n \times S_n$
GL_REPLACE	Output color = S_n

Now compile and run. Your display should superficially resemble the results of Figure 6-11.

Figure 6-11. *Hedly is the "previous" texture on the left, while the Jackson Pollack-ish painting is the "source." When using* GL_MODULATE, *the results are on the right.*

Now it's time to play with other combiner settings. Try GL_ADD for the texture mode, followed by GL_BLEND and GL_DECAL. My results are shown in Figure 6-12. For addition, notice how the white part of the overlay texture is opaque. Because white is 1.0 for all three colors, it will always yield a 1.0 color so as to block out anything underneath. For the nonwhite shades, you should see a little of the Hedly texture poke through. GL_BLEND, as shown in Figure 6-12 (center), is not quite as obvious. Why cyan splats in place of the red? Simple. Say the red value is 1.0, its highest. Consider the equation for GL_BLEND:

$$\text{Output}= P_n(1 - S_n) + S_n \times C$$

The first section would be zero for red, because red's value of 1 is subtracted by the 1 in the equation, and by gosh, the second one would be too, providing that the default environment color of black is used. Consider the green channel. Assume that the background image has a value of .5 for green, the "previous" color, while keeping the splat color (the source) of solid red (so no blue or green in the splat). Now the first section of the equation becomes .5*(1.0-0.0), or .5. That is, the .5 value for green in the *previous* texture, Hedly, is multiplied against "1- minus-green" in the source texture. Because both the green and blue channels in the source's red splats would be 0.0, the combination of green and blue without any red gives a cyan shading, because cyan is the inverse of red. And if you look really closely at Figure 6-12 (center), you can just make out a piece of Hedly poking through. The same holds true for the magenta and yellow splats. In Figure 6-12 (right), GL_DECAL is used and can serve many of the same duties that decals for plastic models had, namely, the application of signs or symbols that would block out anything behind it. So for decals, typically the alpha channel would be set to 1.0 for the actual image part of the texture, while it would be 0.0 for any part that was not of the desired image. Typically the background would be black, and on your paint program you would have it generate an alpha channel based on luminosity or for the part of the image that has a nonzero color. In the case of the splat, because the background was white, I had to invert the colors first to turn it black, generate the mask, and merge it with the normal positive image. The image actually used is the rgb_splats_masked.256.color.png file you can find in the project download. Some alpha that is slightly less than 1 was generated for the green channel, and as a result, you can see a little part of Hedly showing through.

> **Note**   On older pre-iPhone 3GS/pre-iPod touch third-generation devices, Apple lists a number of caveats in its OpenGL ES programming guide. If you want to ensure your creation will work on earlier devices, you should check it out.

Figure 6-12. *On the left,* GL_ADD *was used,* GL_BLEND *was added for the center, and* GL_DECAL *was added on the right.*

One further task would be to animate the second texture. Add the following to `drawInRect()`:

```
for(i=0;i<8;i++)
{
        textureCoords2[i]+=.01;
}
```

Then make a duplicate of the original `textureCoords array`, and name it `textureCoords2`. The latter coordinates are specific to the second texture, so modify the second call to glTexCoordPointer() to use the new data. And finally, declare the index *i* somewhere. You should see texture 2 scrolling wildly on top of texture 1.

An effect like this could be used to animate rain or snow in a cartoonlike setting or a cloud layer surrounding a planet. The latter would be cool if you had two additional textures, one for the upper deck of clouds and one for the lower, moving at different rates.

As mentioned, the environment parameter `GL_COMBINE` needs an additional family of settings to get working, because it lets you operate on a much more precise level with the combiner equations. If you were to do nothing more than just using `GL_COMBINE`, it defaults to `GL_MODULATE`, so you'd see no difference between the two. Using `Arg0` and `Arg1` means the input sources are set up by using something like the following line, where `GL_SOURCE0_RGB` is the argument 0 or `Arg0`, referenced in Table 6-3:

`glTexEnvf(GL_TEXTURE_ENV, GL_SOURCE0_RGB, GL_TEXTURE);`

And similarly you'd use GL_SOURCE1_RGB for Arg1.

Table 6-3. *Possible Values for GL_COMBINE_RGB and GL_COMBINE_ALPHA Parameters*

GL_COMBINE_*	Function
GL_REPLACE	Arg0
GL_MODULATE	Arg0 * Arg1 *(the default)*
GL_ADD	Arg0 + Arg1
GL_ADD_SIGNED	Arg0 + Arg1-0.5
GL_INTERPOLATE	Arg0 * Arg2 + Arg1 * (1-Arg2)
GL_SUBTRACT	Arg0 – Arg1
GL_DOT3_RGB	4*(((Arg0red-.5)*(Arg1red-.5))+((Arg0green-.5)*(Arg1green-.5))+ ((Arg0blue-.5)*(Arg1blue-.5))) *(GL_COMBINE_RGB only)*
GL_DOT3_RGBA	Same as above, but with alpha added *(GL_COMBINE_RGBA only)*

Mapping with Bumps

You can do many extremely sophisticated things with textures; bump mapping is just one. So, what follows is a discussion of exactly what "bumps" are and why anyone should be concerned with mapping them.

As previously pointed out, much of the challenge in computer graphics is to make complicated-looking visuals using clever hacks behind the scenes. Bump mapping is just one of those tricks, and in OpenGL ES 1, it can be implemented with texture combiners.

Just as textures were "tricks" to layer complexity to a simple face, bump mapping is a technique to add a third dimension to the texture. It's used to generate a roughness to the overall surface of an object, giving some surprisingly realistic highlights when illuminated. It might be used to simulate waves on a lake, the surface of a tennis ball, or a planetary surface.

Roughness to an object's surface is perceived by the way it plays with both light and shadow. For example, consider a full moon vs. a gibbous moon, as shown in Figure 6-13. The moon is full when the sun is directly in front of it, and as a result, the surface is little more than varying shades of gray. No shadows whatsoever are visible. It's not much different than you looking at the ground facing away from the sun. Around the shadow of your head the surface looks flat. Now, if the light source is moved to the side of things, suddenly all sorts of details pop out. Figure 6-13 (right) shows a gibbous moon that has the sun toward the left, the moon's eastern limb. It's a completely different story, isn't it?

Figure 6-13. Relatively little detail shows on the left, while with oblique lighting, a lot more shows on the right.

Understanding how highlights and shadows work together is absolutely critical to the training of fine artists and illustrators.

Adding real surface displacement to replicate the entire lunar surface would likely require many gigabytes of data and is out of the question for the current generation of small handheld devices from both a memory and a CPU standpoint. Thus enters the rather elegant hack of bump mapping to the center stage.

If you remember in Chapter 4 on lighting, you had to add an array of "face normals" to the sphere model. Normals are merely vectors that are perpendicular to the face that show the direction the face is pointing. It is the angle of the normal to any of the light sources that largely determines just how bright or dark the face will be. And the more directly oriented the face is toward the light, the brighter it will be. So, what if you had a compact way to encode normals not on a face-by-face basis, because a model might have relatively few faces, but on, say, a pixel-by-pixel basis? And what if you could combine that encoded normal array with a real image texture and process it in a way that could brighten or darken a pixel from the image, based on the direction of incoming light?

This brings us back to the texture combiners. In Table 6-3, notice the last two combiner types: GL_DOT3_RGB and GL_DOT3_RGBA. Now, reach back, way back to your high-school geometry classes. Remember the dot product of two vectors? Both the dot products and cross products were those things that you scorned with the whine "Teacherrrrr?? Why do I need to know *this?*" Well, now you are going to get your answer.

The dot product is the length of a vector based on the angle of two other vectors. Still not following? Consider Figure 6-14 (left). The dot product is the "amount" of the normal vector that is aiming toward the light, and that value is used to directly illuminate the face. In Figure 6-14 (right), the face is at a right angle to the direction of the sun, so it is not illuminated.

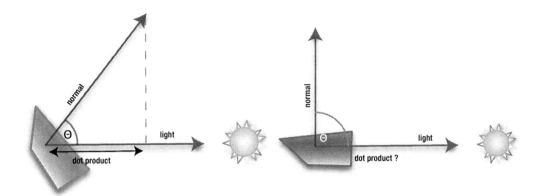

Figure 6-14. *On the left (left), the face is illuminated, which is not the case on the right (right).*

With this in mind, the "cheat" that bump mapping uses is as follows. Take the actual texture you want to use, and add a special second companion texture to it. This second texture encodes normal information in place of the RGB colors. So, instead of using floats that are 4 bytes each, it uses 1-byte values for the xyz of normal vectors that conveniently fit inside a single 4-byte pixel. Since the vectors usually don't have to be super accurate, the 8-bit resolution is just fine and is very memory efficient. So, these normals are generated in a way to map directly to the vertical features you want highlighted.

Because normals can have negative values as well as positive (negative when pointing away from the sun), the xyz values are centered in the range of 0 to 1. That is, -127 to +127 must be mapped to anywhere between 0 and 1. So, the "red" component, which is typically the x part of the vector, would be calculated as follows:

$$red = (x+1)/2.0$$

And of course this is similar for the green and blue bits.

Now look at the formula expressed in the GL_DOT3_RGB entry of Table 6-3. This takes the RGB triplet as the vector and returns its length. N is the normal vector, and L is the light vector, so the length is solved as follows:

$$length = 4 \times ((R_n - .5) \times (R_l - .5) + (G_n - .5) \times (G_l - .5) + (B_n - .5) \times (B_l - .5))$$

So if the face is aimed directly toward the light along the x-axis, the normal's red would be 1.0, and the light's red or x value would also be 1.0. The green and blue bits would be .5, which is the encoded form of 0. Plugging that into the earlier equation would look like this:

$$length = 4 \times ((1_n - .5) \times (1_l - .5) + (.5_n - .5) \times (.5_l - .5) + (.5_n - .5) \times (.5_l - .5))$$

$$length = 4 \times (.25 + 0 + 0) = 1.0$$

This is exactly what we'd expect. And if the normal is pointing up and away from the surface in the z direction, encoded in the blue byte, the answer should be 0 because the normals are largely aimed up away from the texture's X and Y planes. Figure 6-15 (left) shows a bit of our earth map, while Figure 6-15 (right) shows its corresponding normal map.

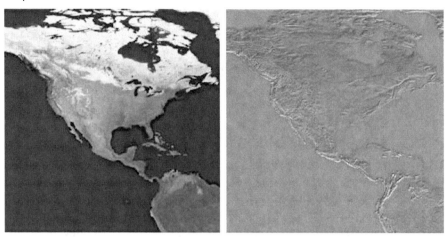

***Figure 6-15.** The left side is our image; the right is the matching normal map.*

And why is the normal map primarily purple? The straight-up vector pointing away from the earth's surface is encoded such that red=.5, green=.5, and blue=1. (Keep in mind that .5 is actually 0.)

When the texture combiner is set to the DOT3 mode, it uses the normal and a lighting vector to determine the intensity of each texel. That value is then used to modulate the color of the real image texture.

Now it's time to recycle the previous multitexture project. We'll need to add a second texture composed of the bump map, available from the Apress site, and change the way the combiners are set.

To the `viewDidLoad()` method, load the normal map for this example into m_Texture0, followed by the companion earth texture as m_Texture1. Then add the new routine, `MultiTextureBumpMap()`, as shown in Listing 6-6.

***Listing 6-6.** Setting Up the Combiners for Bump Mapping*

```
-(void)multiTextureBumpMap:(GLuint)tex0 tex1:(GLuint)tex1
{
    GLfloat x,y,z;
    static float lightAngle=0.0;

    lightAngle+=1.0;                                                    //1

    if(lightAngle>180)
        lightAngle=0;
```

```
// Set up the light vector.

x = sin(lightAngle * (3.14159 / 180.0));                              //2
y = 0.0;
z = cos(lightAngle * (3.14159 / 180.0));

// Half shifting to have a value between 0.0 and 1.0.

x = x * 0.5 + 0.5;                                                    //3
y = y * 0.5 + 0.5;
z = z * 0.5 + 0.5;

glColor4f(x, y, z, 1.0);                                              //4

//The color and normal map are combined.

glActiveTexture(GL_TEXTURE0);                                         //5
glBindTexture(GL_TEXTURE_2D, tex0);

glTexEnvf(GL_TEXTURE_ENV, GL_TEXTURE_ENV_MODE, GL_COMBINE);           //6
glTexEnvf(GL_TEXTURE_ENV, GL_COMBINE_RGB, GL_DOT3_RGB);              //7
glTexEnvf(GL_TEXTURE_ENV, GL_SRC0_RGB, GL_TEXTURE);                  //8
glTexEnvf(GL_TEXTURE_ENV, GL_SRC1_RGB, GL_PREVIOUS);                 //9

// Set up the Second Texture, and combine it with the result of the Dot3
combination.

glActiveTexture(GL_TEXTURE1);                                        //10
glBindTexture(GL_TEXTURE_2D, tex1);

glTexEnvf(GL_TEXTURE_ENV, GL_TEXTURE_ENV_MODE, GL_MODULATE);         //11

}
```

The preceding operation takes place using two *stages*. The first blends the bump map with the primary color, which is established using the glColor4f call. The second takes the results of that and combines it with the color image using our old friend GL_MODULATE.

So, let's examine it piece by piece:

- In line 1 we define lightAngle that will cycle between 0 and 180 degrees around the texture to show how the highlights look under varying lighting conditions.

- Calculate the xyz values of the light vector in lines 2ff.

- In line 3, the xyz components need to be scaled to match those of the bump map.

- Line 4 colors the fragments using the light vector components.

- Lines 5f set and bind the bump map first, which is tex0.

- GL_COMBINE in line 6 tells the system to expect a combining type to follow.

- In line 7, we specify that we're going to combine just the RGB values using GL_DOT3_RGB operations (GL_DOT3_RGBA includes the alpha but is not needed here).

- Here we set up "stage 0," the first of two stages. The source of the first bit of data is specified in line 8. This says to use the texture from the current texture unit (GL_TEXTURE0) as the source for the bump map assigned in line 5.

- Then line 9 tells it to blend with the previous color—in this case, that which was set via glColor() in line 4. For stage 0, GL_PREVIOUS is the same as GL_PRIMARY_COLOR, because there is no previous texture to use.

- Now set up stage 1 in line 10 and the following line. The argument, tex1, is the color image.

- Now all we want to do is combine the image with the bump map, which is what line 11 does.

Now all you have to do is to call the new method in place of multTexture() used in the previous exercise. My source texture is selected so that you can easily see the results. When started, the light should move from left to right and illuminate the edges of the land masses, as shown in Figure 6-16.

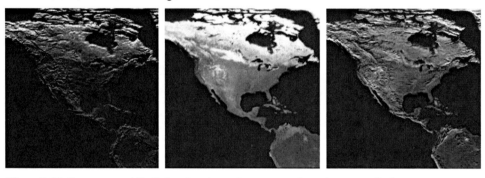

Figure 6-16. *Bump-mapped North America at morning, noon, and evening, respectively*

Looks pretty cool, eh? But can we apply this to a spinning sphere? Give it a shot and recycle the solar-system model from the end of the previous chapter. To make the fine detail of the bump map more easily seen, the sun is dropped in lieu of a somewhat larger image for the earth. So, we'll load the bump map, move the earth to the center of the scene, tweak the lighting, and add the combiner support.

So first off, add a new parameter to the init method of Planet.m for the bump map so that it looks like the following line, and call it where you generate the earth object:

```
-(id) init:(GLint)stacks slices:(GLint)slices radius:(GLfloat)radius
squash:(GLfloat)squash textureFile:(NSString *)textureFile bumpmapFile:(NSString
*)bumpmapFile
```

Underneath where you allocate the main image, add the following:

```
if(bumpmapFile!=nil)
        m_BumpMapInfo=[self loadTexture:bumpmapFile];
```

And to the header add this:

```
GLKTextureInfo  *m_BumpMapInfo;
```

Exchange the initGeometry() call in your solar-system view controller for Listing 6-7:

```
-(void)initGeometry
{
    m_Eyeposition[X_VALUE]=0.0;
    m_Eyeposition[Y_VALUE]=0.0;
    m_Eyeposition[Z_VALUE]=3.0;

    m_Earth=[[Planet alloc] init:50 slices:50 radius:1.0 squash:1.0
                textureFile:@"earth_light.png" bumpmapFile:@"earth_normal_hc.png"];
    [m_Earth setPositionX:0.0 Y:0.0 Z:0.0];
}
```

Meanwhile, use Listing 6-8 as the new execute() method to be placed in Planet.m and called from the bump mapping controller's executePlanet() routine. This mainly sets things up for the texture combiners and calls multiTextureBumpMap().

Listing 6-8. *The Modified Execute in Planet.m that Calls multiTextureBumpMap() for Bump Mapping*

```
-(bool)execute
{
    glMatrixMode(GL_MODELVIEW);
    glEnable(GL_CULL_FACE);
    glCullFace(GL_BACK);
    glEnable(GL_LIGHTING);

    glFrontFace(GL_CW);

    glEnable(GL_TEXTURE_2D);
    glEnableClientState(GL_VERTEX_ARRAY);
    glVertexPointer(3, GL_FLOAT, 0, m_VertexData);

    glEnableClientState(GL_TEXTURE_COORD_ARRAY);
    glClientActiveTexture(GL_TEXTURE0);

    glBindTexture(GL_TEXTURE_2D, m_TextureInfo.name);

    glTexCoordPointer(2, GL_FLOAT, 0, m_TexCoordsData);

    glClientActiveTexture(GL_TEXTURE1);
    glTexCoordPointer(2, GL_FLOAT,0,m_TexCoordsData);

    glMatrixMode(GL_MODELVIEW);

    glEnableClientState(GL_NORMAL_ARRAY);
    glNormalPointer(GL_FLOAT, 0, m_NormalData);
```

```
        glColorPointer(4, GL_UNSIGNED_BYTE, 0, m_ColorData);

        [self multiTextureBumpMap:m_BumpMapInfo.name tex1:m_TextureInfo.name];

        glDrawArrays(GL_TRIANGLE_STRIP, 0, (m_Slices+1)*2*(m_Stacks-1)+2);

    return true;
}
```

Make sure to copy over multiTextureBumpMap() from the previous exercise to Planet.m.

Now go to where you initialize the lights in your solar-system controller, and comment out the call to create the specular material. Bump mapping and specular reflections don't get along too well.

And to your solar-system's controller replace its current execute() and executePlanet() methods with listing 6-9. This dumps the sun, moves the earth into the center of things, and places the main light off to the left.

Listing 6-9. *The New Execute Routine that Places the Earth in the Center*

```
-(void)execute
{
        GLfloat posFill1[]={-8.0,0.0,5.0,1.0};
        GLfloat cyan[]={0.0,1.0,1.0,1.0};
        static GLfloat angle=0.0;
        GLfloat orbitalIncrement=.5;
        GLfloat sunPos[4]={0.0,0.0,0.0,1.0};

        glLightfv(SS_FILLLIGHT1,GL_POSITION,posFill1);

        glEnable(GL_DEPTH_TEST);

        glClearColor(0.0, 0.25f, 0.35f, 1.0);
        glClear(GL_COLOR_BUFFER_BIT);

        glPushMatrix();

        glTranslatef(-m_Eyeposition[X_VALUE],-m_Eyeposition[Y_VALUE],-
          m_Eyeposition[Z_VALUE]);
        glLightfv(SS_SUNLIGHT,GL_POSITION,sunPos);

        glEnable(SS_FILLLIGHT1);
        glDisable(SS_FILLLIGHT2);

        glPushMatrix();

        angle+=orbitalIncrement;

         [self executePlanet:m_Earth];

        glPopMatrix();

        glPopMatrix();
}
```

```
-(void)executePlanet:(Planet *)planet
{
        GLfloat posX, posY, posZ;
        static GLfloat angle=0.0;

        glPushMatrix();

        [planet getPositionX:&posX Y:&posY Z:&posZ];

        glTranslatef(posX,posY,posZ);

        glRotatef(angle,0.0,1.0,0.0);

        [planet execute];

        glPopMatrix();

        angle+=.4;
}
```

If you now see something like Figure 6-17, you may officially pat yourself on the back.

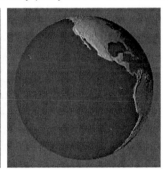

Figure 6-17. The bumpy Earth

OK, now for an experiment. Move the light's position so that it comes in from the right instead of the left. Figure 6-18 is the unexpected result. What's going on here? Now the mountains look like valleys.

Figure 6-18. Huh?

What's happening is that we are going where no combiner has gone before. By sticking in our own lighting, the effect of the simulated lighting as provided by the light vector is removed. With our light on the left, it just happens to look good mainly by luck. Bump mapping here works OK if the lighting of your scene is relatively static. It doesn't like multiple light sources. In fact, the pseudolighting effect specified via the light vector is ignored in lieu of the "real" light sources. Furthermore, if you turn off those sources, the light vector ignores any of the shading on the object altogether. In this case, you would see the entire planet lighten up and darken because that's what is happening to the texture itself, because it is merely a 2D surface. If part of it is lit, all is lit. So, what's a GL nerd to do? *Shaders my friend. Shaders.* And that is where OpenGL ES 2 and the iOS 5 extensions come into play; they are covered in Chapter 10.

Summary

In this chapter, you learned about the blending capabilities supplied by OpenGL ES 1. Blending has its own unique language as expressed through the blending functions and combiners. You've learned about translucency, how and when to apply it. Also covered were some of the neat tricks available by using both blending and textures for animation and bump mapping. In the next chapter, I'll start to apply some of these tricks and show others that can make for a more interesting 3D universe.

Chapter 7

Well-Rendered Miscellany

If we knew what it was we were doing, it would not be called research, would it?

—Albert Einstein

When starting this chapter, I tried to find a suitable quote about miscellany. Unfortunately, all I could find were collections of miscellaneous quotes. But the one by Albert Einstein is a real gem and can *almost* apply because you, dear reader, are conducting research—research in how to make richer, more involving and fun software. The products and tools that Apple releases are *fun* to use—to the point of almost being playful, charming, and wondrous. If vacuuming the house was as much fun as using an iPad, we'd all win awards from *Good Housekeeping* magazine.

In books like this, sometimes it's hard to make clean classifications of a particular topic. So, we just have to dump a lot things into a single chapter when they might not warrant a chapter of their own. So here I'm going to cover some classic presentation and rendering tricks, whether they can be applied to the solar-system project or not, that integrate UIKit elements with OpenGL windows and user interaction with components in your scenes.

Frame Buffer Objects

Usually referred to as FBOs, you can think of frame buffer objects as simply rendering surfaces. Up until now, you've been using one and you probably didn't know it; the EAGL context that your scene renders to is an FBO. What you probably didn't know is that you can have multiple screens at the same time. As before, we'll start off with the old standard, and then see where it can go from there.

Hedley Buffer Objects

You know the drill by this time: find the exercise from Chapter 5, with the original 2D textured square filled. This will serve as our basic framework as usual.

You'll have to create a separate object that encapsulates the new FBO. Call it FBOController and populate it with Listing 7-1 and Listing 7-2.

Listing 7-1. *The header for* FBOController.h

```
#import <Foundation/Foundation.h>
#import <UIKit/UIKit.h>
#import <GLKit/GLKit.h>

@interface FBOController : NSObject
{
    GLuint m_Texture;
    GLuint m_FBO1;
}

-(GLint)getFBOName;
-(GLuint)getTextureName;
-(id)initWidth:(float)width height:(float)height;

@end
```

Listing 7-2. *The main body of* FBController.m

```
#import <OpenGLES/ES1/gl.h>
#import <OpenGLES/ES1/glext.h>
#import "FBOController.h"


@implementation FBOController

-(id)initWidth:(float)width height:(float)height
{
    GLint originalFBO;
    GLuint depthBuffer;

    //Cache the original FBO, and restore it later.

    glGetIntegerv(GL_FRAMEBUFFER_BINDING_OES, &originalFBO);              //1

    glGenRenderbuffersOES(1, &depthBuffer);                              //2
    glBindRenderbufferOES(GL_RENDERBUFFER_OES, depthBuffer);

    glRenderbufferStorageOES(GL_RENDERBUFFER_OES,                        //3
    GL_DEPTH_COMPONENT16_OES, width, height);

    //Make the texture to render to.

    glGenTextures(1, &m_Texture);                                       //4
    glBindTexture(GL_TEXTURE_2D, m_Texture);
```

```
    glTexImage2D(GL_TEXTURE_2D, 0, GL_RGB, width, height, 0,
                        GL_RGB, GL_UNSIGNED_SHORT_5_6_5, 0);

    glTexParameterf(GL_TEXTURE_2D, GL_TEXTURE_MIN_FILTER, GL_LINEAR);
    glTexParameterf(GL_TEXTURE_2D, GL_TEXTURE_MAG_FILTER, GL_LINEAR);
    glTexParameterf(GL_TEXTURE_2D, GL_TEXTURE_WRAP_S, GL_CLAMP_TO_EDGE);
    glTexParameterf(GL_TEXTURE_2D, GL_TEXTURE_WRAP_T, GL_CLAMP_TO_EDGE);

    //Now create the actual FBO.

    glGenFramebuffersOES(1, &m_FBO1);                                    //5
    glBindFramebufferOES(GL_FRAMEBUFFER_OES, m_FBO1);

    // Attach the texture to the FBO.

    glFramebufferTexture2DOES(GL_FRAMEBUFFER_OES,                        //6
        GL_COLOR_ATTACHMENT0_OES, GL_TEXTURE_2D, m_Texture, 0);

    // Attach the depth buffer we created earlier to our FBO.

    glFramebufferRenderbufferOES(GL_FRAMEBUFFER_OES,                     //7
        GL_DEPTH_ATTACHMENT_OES, GL_RENDERBUFFER_OES, depthBuffer);

    // Check that our FBO creation was successful.

    glCheckFramebufferStatusOES(GL_FRAMEBUFFER_OES);                     //8

     GLuint uStatus = glCheckFramebufferStatusOES(GL_FRAMEBUFFER_OES);

     if(uStatus != GL_FRAMEBUFFER_COMPLETE_OES)
     {
         NSLog(@ "ERROR: Failed to initialise FBO");
         return 0;
     }

    glClear(GL_COLOR_BUFFER_BIT | GL_DEPTH_BUFFER_BIT);

    glBindFramebufferOES(GL_FRAMEBUFFER_OES, originalFBO);               //9

    return self;
}

-(GLint)getFBOName                                                       //10
{
    return m_FBO1;
}

-(GLuint)getTextureName                                                  //11
{
    return m_Texture;
}

@end
```

You should recognize the pattern here, because creating FBOs is a lot like many of the other OpenGL objects. So, let's break it down:

- FBOs, as with many of the OpenGL objects, use "names" as handles to uniquely identify them. In line 1, we're getting the original frame buffer object that serves as the main screen. The idea is to be a good neighbor and restore it at the very end. Otherwise, the wrong one could be used.

- Line 2 has us generating a name for our depth buffer. Then it is bound to the system as our current render buffer. If this is the first time that object has been bound, OpenGL will allocate it minus the image memory and then use that allocated memory in all subsequent bindings.

- In line 3 we actually allocated the memory for the buffer's image data. Since images require large blocks of memory, they should never be allocated until needed. That is why the bind and the allocation operations are usually kept separate.

- At this point in lines 4ff, we need to allocate a texture image and have it linked up to our frame buffer. This is the interface required to camouflage our FBO so it looks just like any other texture to OpenGL.

  Here we can also set up some of the normal texture settings for edge conditions and use bilinear filtering.

- Up until now we've merely created the depth buffer and image interface. In line 5, we actually create the frame buffer object and attach the previous bits to it.

- Line 6 attaches the texture first. Notice the use of `GL_COLOR_ATTACHMENT0_OES`.The texture bit actually holds the color information, so it is called the *color attachment.*

- In line 7, we do the same for the depth buffer, using `GL_DEPTH_ATTACHMENT_OES`. And remember that in OpenGL ES we have only three types of buffer attachments: depth, color, and stencil. The latter does things such as blocking rendering in a certain part of the screen. The adult version of OpenGL adds a fourth kind, `GL_DEPTH_STENCIL_ATTACHMENT`.

- Line 8 does a quick error check.

- As referenced earlier, we need to restore the original FBO for our main screen, in line 9.

- And finally, lines 10 and 11 provide some getters so we can use the new FBO.

So, that's merely creating an FBO. You'll see that it is a fairly no-frills piece of code, using the built-in functions available in both OpenGL ES 1 and 2. And yes, it does seem a little overly complicated, but it's easily wrapped with a helper function.

But we're still not quite done, because we now have to rejigger `drawInRect()` to use both FBOs.

To the end of the viewDidLoad() method, add the following lines:

```
m_FBOHeight=480;
m_FBOWidth=320;

m_FBOController=[[FBOController alloc]initWidth:m_FBOWidth height:m_FBOHeight];
```

Then modify the header as needed. The first line caches the original FBO so that it can be restored properly as needed.

Now add the new `drawInRect()` method shown in Listing 7-3.

Listing 7-3. *The new* `drawInRect()`, *renders to both FBOs*

```
- (void)glkView:(GLKView *)view drawInRect:(CGRect)rect
{
    static const GLfloat squareVertices[] =
    {
        -0.5, -0.5, 0.0,
        0.5, -0.5, 0.0,
        -0.5,  0.5, 0.0,
        0.5,  0.5, 0.0
    };

    static const GLfloat fboVertices[] =                                        //1
    {
        -0.5, -0.75, 0.0,
        0.5, -0.75, 0.0,
        -0.5,  0.75, 0.0,
        0.5,  0.75, 0.0
    };

    static  GLfloat textureCoords1[] =
    {
        0.0, 0.0,
        1.0, 0.0,
        0.0, 1.0,
        1.0, 1.0
    };

    static float transY = 0.0;
    static float rotZ = 0.0;
    static float z = -1.5;

    if(m_DefaultFBO==0)
        glGetIntegerv(GL_FRAMEBUFFER_BINDING_OES, &m_DefaultFBO);                //2

    glDisableClientState(GL_COLOR_ARRAY|GL_DEPTH_BUFFER_BIT);

    //Draw to the off-screen FBO first.

    glBindFramebufferOES(GL_FRAMEBUFFER_OES, [m_FBOController getFBOName]);       //3
```

```
    glClearColor(0.0, 0.0, 1.0, 1.0);
    glClear(GL_COLOR_BUFFER_BIT);

    glMatrixMode(GL_MODELVIEW);
    glLoadIdentity();

    glTranslatef(0.0, (GLfloat)(sinf(transY)/2.0), z);
    glRotatef(rotZ, 0, 0, 1.0);                                    //4

    glEnable(GL_TEXTURE_2D);
    glBindTexture(GL_TEXTURE_2D, m_Texture.name);

    glTexCoordPointer(2, GL_FLOAT,0,textureCoords1);
    glEnableClientState(GL_TEXTURE_COORD_ARRAY);

    glVertexPointer(3, GL_FLOAT, 0, squareVertices);
    glEnableClientState(GL_VERTEX_ARRAY);

    glDrawArrays(GL_TRIANGLE_STRIP, 0, 4);                         //5

    glBindFramebufferOES(GL_FRAMEBUFFER_OES, m_DefaultFBO);        //6
    glLoadIdentity();

    glTranslatef(0.0, (GLfloat)(sinf(transY)/2.0),z);

    glBindTexture(GL_TEXTURE_2D, [m_FBOController getTextureName]); //7


    glClearColor(1.0, 0.0, 0.0, 1.0);                             //8
    glClear(GL_COLOR_BUFFER_BIT);

    glTexCoordPointer(2, GL_FLOAT,0,textureCoords1);
    glEnableClientState(GL_TEXTURE_COORD_ARRAY);

    glVertexPointer(3, GL_FLOAT, 0, fboVertices);                 //9
    glEnableClientState(GL_VERTEX_ARRAY);

    glDrawArrays(GL_TRIANGLE_STRIP, 0, 4);

    transY += 0.075;
    rotZ+=1.0;
}
```

- In line 1, the vertices for the FBO are specified, not much different from those for the bouncing image.

- In line 2, we fetch and save the default FBO, the one used for the main display. And if you haven't done it yet, this should be declared as a GLint m_Default_FBO.

- Line 3 is where we actually tell OpenGL to use our new FBO using a bind method not unlike those used for basic texture mapping. Following that is the standard setup code to manage the transformations and so on.

- Line 4 adds a small rotation for some extra dynamic goodness.

- glDrawArray() at line 5 does just what it always does, but because the new FBO is bound to the system, its writes are redirected to that FBO instead of the main screen.

- Lines 6ff switch us over to the main FBO we've always used before. glLoadIdentity() erases any built-up transformations for the subview.

- glBindTexture() in line 7 is the heart of the magic. Instead of binding a "normal" texture as was done to the secondary FBO right after line 3, we now bind the FBO itself via its access texture. Anywhere textures can be used, our special FBO-texture can also be used.

- Notice that glClearColor in line 8 clears the background to red, while the secondary FBO shown earlier used blue. It's all the more blindingly nauseating to make the different objects stand out.

- Line 9 uses the new set of vertices. The original set drew a square for the textured block, but the new set draws a rectangle with the proportions of the normal screen so that it looks like a tiny and hyperactive version of the former. This is followed by the second glDrawArrays(), incrementing the rotation and translation values.

You should be able to run it and see it in all of its gaudy glory. If you intend to stare at it for an extended period of time, your doctor's permission will be necessary. Figure 7-1 (left) is the result.

Now, it's time to tweak. Put a second rotation of the main FBO this time around. Add it right before the second glTranslation() call, rotating in the same direction, and you should see Figure 7-1 (center). And what would you do to see Figure 7-1 (right)?

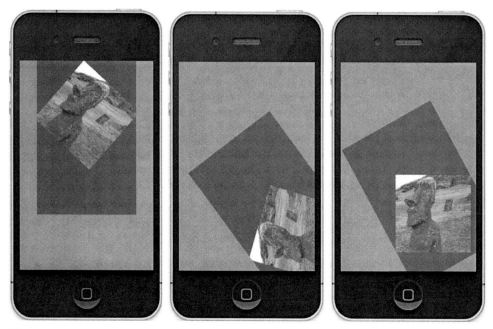

Figure 7-1. *On the left, just Hedly is spinning. Both Hedly and his window are now spinning counterclockwise in the middle. And on the right, the frame is spinning end over end.*

Sun Buffer Objects

There are a lot of fun and bizarre things you can do with this equivalent to having 3D superpowers. For example, you could simulate some animations on a little model of a TV set. You could show multiple views of the same data in a reflection of a puddle on the ground or the rearview mirror in a car. Better yet, put one OpenGL frame animating a scene on the sun in our solar-system simulator. It's not particularly realistic, but it's pretty cool.

Much of this is going to be left to the student this time around. I used Chapter 5's final projects for starters. You'll need to add the `FBController` object and initialize it in a different `drawInRect()` method taken from the previous exercise. The latter is in addition to the `execute()` method used in the solar system. I'll give you `drawInRect()`, as shown in Listing 7-4, and leave the rest up to you.

Listing 7-4. *Changes needed to* `drawInRect()`

```
- (void)glkView:(GLKView *)view drawInRect:(CGRect)rect
{
    static const GLfloat squareVertices[] =                              //1
    {
        -0.15f, -0.5, 0.0,
        -0.15f,  0.5, 0.0,
         0.15f, -0.5, 0.0,
         0.15f,  0.5, 0.0
    };
```

```
static  GLfloat textureCoords1[] =
{
    0.0, 0.0,
    0.0, 1.0,
    1.0, 0.0,
    1.0, 1.0
};

static const GLubyte squareColors[] = {
    255,   0, 255, 255,
    255, 255,   0, 255,
    0,   255, 255, 255,
    0,     0,   0,   0,
};

static float transY = 0.0;

glBindFramebufferOES(GL_FRAMEBUFFER_OES, [m_FBOController getFBOName]);

glPushMatrix();

glDisable(GL_LIGHTING);                                              //2

glClearColor(1.0, 1.0, 1.0, 1.0);
glClear(GL_COLOR_BUFFER_BIT|GL_DEPTH_BUFFER_BIT);

glMatrixMode(GL_MODELVIEW);
glLoadIdentity();

glTranslatef(0.0, (GLfloat)(sinf(transY)/2.0), -2.5);

glEnable(GL_TEXTURE_2D);
glBindTexture(GL_TEXTURE_2D, m_Hedly);

//  glColorPointer(4, GL_UNSIGNED_BYTE, 0, squareColors);            //3
//  glEnableClientState(GL_COLOR_ARRAY);

glTexCoordPointer(2, GL_FLOAT,0,textureCoords1);
glEnableClientState(GL_TEXTURE_COORD_ARRAY);

glVertexPointer(3, GL_FLOAT, 0, squareVertices);
glEnableClientState(GL_VERTEX_ARRAY);

glDrawArrays(GL_TRIANGLE_STRIP, 0, 4);

glPopMatrix();

glBindFramebufferOES(GL_FRAMEBUFFER_OES, m_DefaultFBO);

glEnable(GL_LIGHTING);
transY += 0.075;
}
```

This differs from the previous version of `drawInRect()` as follows:

- In line 1 we need to change the square dimensions of the "square" to compensate for the short but wide shape of the sun's texture geometry; otherwise, the image would be highly distorted.

- Line 2 disables the lighting so that the full image can be seen no matter what.

- Lines 3f were commented out to turn off the coloring, making the image of Hedly more visible.

I hope you get something like Figure 7-2, with Hedly bouncing up and down on the sun.

Figure 7-2. *Using an off-screen FBO to animate texture on another one*

Pretty slick, eh?

Lens Flare

We've all seen it. Those ghostly, glowing gossamer lights dancing around television scenes or invading an image whenever a camera is aimed toward the sun. This happens as the sun's light merrily bounces around to and fro in the camera's optics, causing numerous secondary images. These can be seen both as a bright broad haze and as many smaller artifacts. Figure 7-3a illustrates this with an image from the Apollo 14 moon landing mission in 1971. The flare obscures most of the lunar module. Even the iPhone has the similar issues, as demonstrated with Figure 7-3b. Even though the Hasselblad cameras that were used on the moon were the best in the world, we couldn't beat lens flare. Unfortunately, it has become one of the more common clichés in computer graphics, used as a tool that shouts "Hey! This is not a fake computer image, because it has *lens flare*!" However, lens flares do have their uses, especially in the arena of space simulations because the fake imagery frequently looks at the fake sun. In that case, both consciously and subconsciously, you'd expect some visual cue that you were looking at something very, very, very bright. It also helps give an extra sense of depth to the image. The flare is generated in the optics that are really near the user while the target is a bazillion miles away.

Figure 7-3. *On the left is a view on the moon from Apollo 14, and an iPhone 4 image is on the right.*

Depending on the specific optics and their various internal coatings, the flares can take many different forms, but they usually end up being just of bunch of ghostly polygons of varying sizes and hues. In the next exercise, we'll create a simple lens flare project that will illustrate using 2D images in a 3D environment. Because there is a lot of code for the setup, I will only highlight the key bits here. You will need to go to **www.apress.com** to get the full project.

Geometrically, lens flares are generally pretty simple because of their symmetry. They exhibit two main characteristics: all lens flares require a very bright light source, and they'll lie along a diagonal line going through the center of the screen, as shown in Figure 7-4.

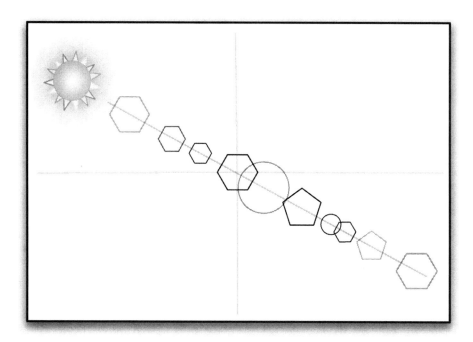

Figure 7-4. *Lens flares are caused by the inner reflections of a bright light source within a camera's lens.*

Since flare images are 2D, how do we put them in a 3D space? Going back to the original sample, the bouncy square was also 2D object. But displaying it relied on some defaults as to how the object was mapped to the screen. Here we get a little more specific.

Remember in Chapter 3, where I spoke of perspective vs. orthographic projections? The former is the way we perceive the dimensionality of objects; the latter is used when precise sizes and shapes are required, eliminating the distortion that perspective adds to the scene. So, when drawing 2D objects, you will generally want to ensure that their visual dimensions are untouched by any of the 3D-ness of the rest of your world.

When it comes to generating your lens flares, you will need a small collection of different shapes to represent some of the mechanics of the actual lens. The hexagonal or pentagonal images are those of the iris used to vary the intensity of the incoming light; see Figure 7-5. They will also exhibit different tints as a result of the various coatings used to protect the lenses or filter out unwanted wavelengths.

Figure 7-5. *A six-blade iris (image by Dave Fischer)*

The following steps are needed to generate the flare set:

1. Import the various images.

2. Detect where on the screen the source object is.

3. Create the imaginary vector that goes through the center of the screen so as to hold the individual pieces of art.

4. Add a dozen or more images, with random sizes, colors, and translucency, scattered up and down the vector.

5. Support touch dragging to test it in all different positions.

I started with the standard template and added support for touching and dragging the visuals. Following that, the sun image is loaded at startup and is drawn in `drawInRect()` at the current position of a user's finger, as demonstrated in Listing 7-5.

Listing 7-5. *The top-level* `drawInRect()`

```
- (void)glkView:(GLKView *)view drawInRect:(CGRect)rect
{
    GLfloat cx,cy;
    CGPoint centerRelative;
    CGRect frame = [[UIScreen mainScreen] bounds];

    glClearColor(0.0, 0.0, 0.0, 1.0);
    glClear(GL_COLOR_BUFFER_BIT);

    cx=(frame.size.width/2.0);                                    //1
```

```
    cy=(frame.size.height/2.0);

    centerRelative=CGPointMake(m_PointerLocation.x-cx,cy-m_PointerLocation.y);
                                                                          //2
    [[OpenGLCreateTexture getObject]renderTextureAt:centerRelative name:m_FlareSource
            size:3.0 r:1.0 g:1.0 b:1.0 a:1.0];
                                                                          //3
    [m_LensFlare execute:[[UIScreen mainScreen]applicationFrame]
source:m_PointerLocation];
}
```

I put the helper routines for creating and rendering a texture on their own module, renderTextureAt(), which is covered in Listing 7-6. However, there are three lines to take note of:

■ Lines 1ff get the center of the screen and creates the information needed to track the flare source (the sun) with the pointer.

■ In line 2, the flare's source object, usually the sun, is rendered.

■ Line 3 calls the helper routine that draws our 2D sun graphic in the sky.

Listing 7-6. *Rendering a 2D texture*

```
-(void)renderTextureAt:(CGPoint)position  name:(GLuint)name
        size:(GLfloat)size r:(GLfloat)r g:(GLfloat)g b:(GLfloat)b a:(GLfloat)a;    //1
{
    float scaledX,scaledY;
    GLfloat zoomBias=.1;
    GLfloat scaledSize;

    static const GLfloat squareVertices[] =
    {
        -1.0, -1.0, 0.0,
        1.0, -1.0, 0.0,
        -1.0,  1.0, 0.0,
        1.0,  1.0, 0.0,
    };

    static  GLfloat textureCoords[] =
    {
        0.0, 0.0,
        1.0, 0.0,
        0.0, 1.0,
        1.0, 1.0
    };

    CGRect frame = [[UIScreen mainScreen] bounds];
    float aspectRatio=frame.size.height/frame.size.width;

    scaledX=2.0*position.x/frame.size.width;                              //2
    scaledY=2.0*position.y/frame.size.height;

    glDisable(GL_DEPTH_TEST);                                             //3
```

```
        glDisable(GL_LIGHTING);

        glMatrixMode(GL_PROJECTION);                                    //4
        glPushMatrix();
        glLoadIdentity();

        glOrthof(-1,1,-1.0*aspectRatio,1.0*aspectRatio, -1, 1);        //5

        glMatrixMode(GL_MODELVIEW);                                     //6
        glLoadIdentity();

        glTranslatef(scaledX,scaledY,0);                               //7

        scaledSize=zoomBias*size;                                      //8

        glScalef(scaledSize,scaledSize, 1);                            //9

        glVertexPointer(3, GL_FLOAT, 0, squareVertices);
        glEnableClientState(GL_VERTEX_ARRAY);

        glEnable(GL_TEXTURE_2D);                                       //10
        glEnable(GL_BLEND);
        glBlendFunc(GL_ONE,GL_ONE_MINUS_SRC_COLOR);
        glBindTexture(GL_TEXTURE_2D,name);
        glTexCoordPointer(2, GL_FLOAT,0,textureCoords);
        glEnableClientState(GL_TEXTURE_COORD_ARRAY);

        glColor4f(r,g,b,a);                                            //11

        glDrawArrays(GL_TRIANGLE_STRIP, 0, 4);

        glMatrixMode(GL_PROJECTION);                                   //12
        glPopMatrix();

        glMatrixMode(GL_MODELVIEW);
        glPopMatrix();

        glEnable(GL_DEPTH_TEST);
        glEnable(GL_LIGHTING);
}
```

So, here is what's going on:

▓ In line 1, the *position* is the origin of the texture in pixels relative to the
  center, which is converted to normalized values later. The *size* is
  relative and needs to be played with to find the most appropriate. The
  final parameters are the colors and alpha. If you don't want any
  coloring, pass 1.0 for all of the values. Following this line, you'll
  recognize our old friends, the vertices and texture coordinates.

▓ Line 2 converts the pixel locations to relative values based on the width and height of the frame. The values are scaled by 2 because our viewport will be 2 units wide and high, going from -1 to 1 in each direction. These are the values eventually passed on to `glTranslatef()`.

▓ Next, turn off the any depth testing, just to be safe, along with the lighting, because the flares have to be calculated apart from the actual lighting in the scene.

▓ Since we're going to use orthographic projection, let's reset the `GL_PROJECTION` to the identity in line 4. Remember that any time to want to touch a specific matrix, you need to specify which one ahead of time. The `glPushMatrix()` method lets us tinker with the projection matrix without messing up anything prior in the chain of events.

▓ Line 5 is the heart of this routine. `glOrthof()` is a new call and sets up the orthographic matrix. In effect, it specifies a box. In this case, the box's width and depth go all from -1 to 1, while the height is scaled a little extra using the aspect ratio to compensate for it being a nonsquare display. This is why the `scaledX` and `scaledY` values were multiplied by 2.

▓ Next, set the identify matrix of the modelview, in lines 6f, followed by the call to `glTranslatef()` in line 7.

▓ Line 8 determines how to scale the collection of flares based on the field of view for our scene, followed by line 9 that performs the actual scaling. This is relative and depends on the magnification ranges you want to deal with. Right now, pinch-to-zoom is not implemented, so this stays constant. The `zoomBias` affects all the elements, which makes it easy to scale everything at once.

▓ Lines 10ff set up the blending function using the most common of the choices. This causes each of the reflections to blend in a very believable way, especially when they start stacking up in the center.

▓ Now set the color and draw the object.

▓ And again, be a good neighbor and pop the matrices so they won't affect anything else.

I created a flare object for the individual flares, and I created a `LensFlare` parent object to handle setting up the vector, contain each of the individual images, and place them when ready. The main loop from `LensFlare.mm` in Listing 7-7 should need very little explanation at this point. It merely calculates the start of the flare vector and then enumerates through the array to execute each entity.

Listing 7-7. The execute loop for the entire lens flare effect

```
-(void)execute:(CGRect)frame source:(CGPoint)source
{
    CGPoint position;
    NSEnumerator *e;
    Flare *object;

    static GLfloat deltaX=40,deltaY=40;
    static GLfloat offsetFromCenterX,offsetFromCenterY;
    static GLfloat startingOffsetFromCenterX,startingOffsetFromCenterY;

    int numElements;
    GLfloat cx,cy;

    static int counter=0;

    e=[m_Flares objectEnumerator];

    cx=(frame.size.width/2.0);
    cy=(frame.size.height/2.0);

    startingOffsetFromCenterX=cx-source.x;
    startingOffsetFromCenterY=source.y-cy;

    offsetFromCenterX=startingOffsetFromCenterX;
    offsetFromCenterY=startingOffsetFromCenterY;

    numElements=[m_Flares count];

    deltaX=2.0*startingOffsetFromCenterX;
    deltaY=2.0*startingOffsetFromCenterY;

    while (object = [e nextObject])
    {
        position=CGPointMake(offsetFromCenterX,offsetFromCenterY);


        [object renderFlareAt:position];

        offsetFromCenterX-=deltaX*[object getVectorPosition];
        offsetFromCenterY-=deltaY*[object getVectorPosition];
    }

    counter++;
}
```

Finally, each of the individual flare images must be loaded on initialization and added into an **NSArray**. A couple of lines follow:

```
[m_Flares addObject:[[Flare alloc]init:@"hexagon_blur.png"
        size:1.0   vectorPosition:(.05-ff)       r:1.0 g:0.73 b:0.30 a:.4]];
[m_Flares addObject:[[Flare alloc]init:@"glow.png"
        size:1.5   vectorPosition:(.055-ff)      r:1.0 g:0.73 b:0.50 a:.4]];
```

This demo has 24 such objects. Figure 7-6 shows the result.

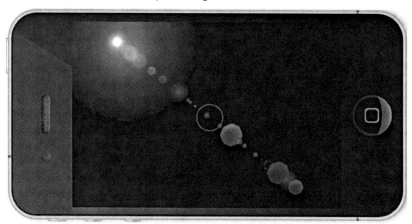

Figure 7-6. *Simple lens flare*

Unfortunately, there is one big gotcha in the lens flare biz. What happens if your light source goes behind something else? If it is a regular and known entity such as a round sphere in the center of the scene, it is pretty easy to figure out. But if it is a random object at a random place, it becomes much more difficult. Then what happens if the source is only partially eclipsed? Reflections will then dim and flicker out only when the entire object is hidden. The solution is left for you for the time being.

Stencils Reflective Surfaces

Another effect that is rapidly becoming a bit of a visual cliché, albeit still a cool one, is that of a mirrored surface underneath part or all of the scene. We Mac-heads see that every time we look at the Dock, for example, with the happy little icons dancing their jig-of-joy up and down, in effect saying "Look here! look here!" in their little squeaky voices. Underneath you will see a faint little reflection. It's the same for many third-party apps, of course, led by Apple's own designs and examples. See Figure 7-7.

Figure 7-7. *Reflections in Distant Suns. (Yes, it is a gratuitous plug.)*

Of course, Apple's examples were implemented in Core Graphics, but the principles are the same: it's a big fat hack! But so is most everything in graphics as we try to simulate the real world through whatever means necessary, and making a reflective surface of this type is no different.

This will introduce the next topic, which is about both stencils and reflections. Besides the "color" buffer (that is, the image buffer) and the depth buffer, OpenGL also has something called a *stencil buffer.*

In the pre-iOS5 days, creating a stencil buffer required another dozen-or-so lines of code. That has since been collapsed to only a single line, a mere trifle of code. In your viewDidLoad(), when the context is created, add:

```
view.drawableStencilFormat=GLKViewDrawableStencilFormat8;
```

The stencil format can be either 8 bits or none.

Next let's create the routines that will generate the actual stencil. Add Listing 7-8 to your view controller, and call `renderToStencil()` from your main draw loop.

Essentially, you render something to the stencil buffer as you would to any other, but in this case, any pixel and its value are used to determine how to render future images to the screen. The most common case is that any later image drawn to the stencil area will be rendered as it normally would, whereas anything outside of the stencil area is not rendered. These behaviors can be modified, of course, keeping with OpenGL's philosophy of making everything more flexible than the vast majority of engineers would use, let alone understand. Still, it can be very handy at times. We'll stay with the simple function for the time being.

Listing 7-8. *The stencil is generated like a normal screen object*

```
-(void)renderToStencil
{
    glEnable(GL_STENCIL_TEST);                           //1
    glStencilFunc(GL_ALWAYS,1, 0xffffffff);              //2

    glStencilOp(GL_REPLACE, GL_REPLACE, GL_REPLACE);     //3

    [self renderStage];                                  //4

    glStencilFunc(GL_EQUAL, 1, 0xffffffff);              //5
    glStencilOp(GL_KEEP, GL_KEEP, GL_KEEP);              //6
}
```

So, you establish your stencil the following way:

- Enable the stencil as done in line 1.

- Here in line 2 we specify the comparison function used whenever something is writing to the stencil buffer. Since we clear it each time through, it will be all zeros. The function GL_ALWAYS says that every write will pass the stencil test, which is what we want when constructing the stencil. The value of 1 is called the *reference* value. Since you can have any value from 0 to 255, it is possible to have a stencil behave differently based on the reference value supplied and how the stencil-op is set. The final value is a mask for the bit planes to access. Since we're not concerned about it, let's just turn them all on.

- Line 3 specifies what to do when a stencil test succeeds or fails. The first parameter pertains if the stencil test fails; the second, if the stencil passes but the depth test fails; and the third, if both succeed. Since we are living in 3D space here, having the stencil tests coupled to depth testing recognizes that there may be situations in which one overrules the other. Some of the subtleties in the use of the stencil buffer can get quite complicated. In this case, set all three to GL_REPLACE. Table 7-1 shows all the other permissible values.

▓ Line 4 calls our rendering function, pretty much as you would normally call it. In this case, it is writing both to the stencil buffer and to one of the color channels at the same time, so we can get a glint of sorts off of our new shiny stage or platform. Meanwhile, in the stencil buffer, the background will remain zeros, while the image will produce stencil pixels that are greater than 0, so it permits image data to write to it later.

▓ Lines 5 and 6 prepare the buffer now for normal use. Line 5 says that if the value in the currently addressed stencil pixel is 1, keep it unchanged as given in line 6. Otherwise, pass the fragment through to be processed as if the stencil buffer wasn't there (although it may still be ignored if it fails the depth test). So, any stencil pixel that is 0, the test will fail, and the incoming fragment will be locked out.

Table 7-1. *Possible values for* `glStencilOp()`

Op Type	Action
GL_KEEP	Keeps the current value.
GL_ZERO	Sets the stencil buffer value to 0.
GL_REPLACE	Sets the stencil buffer value to ref, as specified by glStencilFunc.
GL_INCR	Increments the current stencil buffer value. Clamps to the maximum representable unsigned value.
GL_INCR_WRAP	Increments the current stencil buffer value. Wraps stencil buffer value to zero when incrementing the maximum representable unsigned value.
GL_DECR	Decrements the current stencil buffer value. Clamps to 0.
GL_DECR_WRAP	Decrements the current stencil buffer value. Wraps stencil buffer value to the maximum representable unsigned value when decrementing a stencil buffer value of zero.
GL_INVERT	Bitwise inverts the current stencil buffer value.

As you can see, the stencil buffer is a very powerful instrument with a lot of subtlety. But any more extravagant use is reserved for future books as yet unnamed.

Now it's time for the `renderStage()` method, as shown in Listing 7-9.

Listing 7-9. *Rendering the reflective area to the stencil buffer only*

```
-(void)renderStage
{
    static const GLfloat flatSquareVertices[] =
    {
        -0.5,  0.0, -.5f,
```

```
        0.5,  0.0, -.5f,
       -0.5,  0.0,  0.5,
        0.5,  0.0,  0.5
};

static const GLubyte colors[] =
{
     255, 0,   0, 128,
     255,   0,   0, 255,
     0,   0,   0, 0,
     128,   0,   0, 128
};

glFrontFace(GL_CW);
glPushMatrix();
glTranslatef(0.0,-1.0,-3.0);
glScalef(2.5,1.5,2.0);

glVertexPointer(3, GL_FLOAT, 0, flatSquareVertices);
glEnableClientState(GL_VERTEX_ARRAY);

glColorPointer(4, GL_UNSIGNED_BYTE, 0, colors);

glDepthMask(GL_FALSE);                                      //1
glColorMask(GL_TRUE, GL_FALSE, GL_FALSE, GL_TRUE);          //2
glDrawArrays( GL_TRIANGLE_STRIP,0, 4);                      //3
glColorMask(GL_TRUE, GL_TRUE, GL_TRUE, GL_TRUE);            //4
glDepthMask(GL_TRUE);                                       //5

glPopMatrix();
}
```

- In line 1, writing to the depth buffer is disabled, and line 2 disables the green and blue color channels, so only the red one will be used. That is how the reflected area gets its little red highlight.

- Now we can draw the image to the stencil buffer in line 3.

- Lines 4 and 5 reset the masks.

At this point, the drawInRect() routine has to be modified, yet again. Yawn.... And if you can keep your peepers open, check out Listing 7-10 for the cruel and unvarnished truth. Sorry for repeating so much of the previous code, but it's much easier than saying "…and after the line about squirrel trebuchets add such-and-such a line…."

Listing 7-10. *The reflection drawInRect() method*

```
- (void)glkView:(GLKView *)view drawInRect:(CGRect)rect
{
     static GLfloat z=-3.0;
     static GLfloat spinX=0;
     static GLfloat spinY=0;
```

```
static const GLfloat cubeVertices[] =
{
        -0.5, 0.5, 0.5,
         0.5, 0.5, 0.5,
         0.5,-0.5, 0.5,
        -0.5,-0.5, 0.5,

        -0.5, 0.5,-0.5,
         0.5, 0.5,-0.5,
         0.5,-0.5,-0.5,
         0.5,-0.5,-0.5,
};

static const GLubyte cubeColors[] =
{
        255,   0,   0, 255,
          0, 255,   0, 255,
          0,   0,   0,   0,
          0,   0, 255, 255,

        255, 255,   0, 255,
          0, 255, 255, 255,
          0,   0,   0,   0,
        255,   0, 255, 255,
};

static const GLubyte tfan1[6 * 3] =
{
        1,0,3,
        1,3,2,
        1,2,6,
        1,6,5,
        1,5,4,
        1,4,0
};

static const GLubyte tfan2[6 * 3] =
{
        7,4,5,
        7,5,6,
        7,6,2,
        7,2,3,
        7,3,0,
        7,0,4
};

    static float transY = 0.0;

    glClearColor(0.0, 0.5, 0.7f, 1.0);
    glClear(GL_COLOR_BUFFER_BIT | GL_DEPTH_BUFFER_BIT | GL_STENCIL_BUFFER_BIT);      //1

    //Render to the stencil first.

    [self renderToStencil];                                                         //2
```

```
        glEnable(GL_CULL_FACE);
        glCullFace(GL_BACK);

        glMatrixMode(GL_MODELVIEW);
        glLoadIdentity();

    glPushMatrix();

    glEnable(GL_STENCIL_TEST);                                          //3
    glDisable(GL_DEPTH_TEST);

    glVertexPointer(3, GL_FLOAT, 0, cubeVertices);
    glEnableClientState(GL_VERTEX_ARRAY);
    glColorPointer(4, GL_UNSIGNED_BYTE, 0, cubeColors);
    glEnableClientState(GL_COLOR_ARRAY);

    glEnableClientState(GL_NORMAL_ARRAY);

    //Flip the image.

    glTranslatef(0.0,((GLfloat)(sinf(-transY)/2.0)-1.5),z);             //4
    glRotatef(spinY, 0.0, 1.0, 0.0);

    glScalef(1.0, -1.0, 1.0);                                           //5
    glFrontFace(GL_CW);

    glEnable(GL_BLEND);                                                 //6
    glBlendFunc(GL_ONE, GL_ONE_MINUS_SRC_COLOR);

    glDrawElements( GL_TRIANGLE_FAN, 6 * 3, GL_UNSIGNED_BYTE, tfan1);   //7
    glDrawElements( GL_TRIANGLE_FAN, 6 * 3, GL_UNSIGNED_BYTE, tfan2);


    glPopMatrix();

    glDisable(GL_BLEND);                                                //8
    glEnable(GL_DEPTH_TEST);
    glDisable(GL_STENCIL_TEST);

    //Do the main image.

    glPushMatrix();
    glScalef(1.0, 1.0, 1.0);                                            //9
    glFrontFace(GL_CCW);

    glTranslatef(0.0, (GLfloat)1.5*(sinf(transY)/2.0)+0.5,z);

    glRotatef(spinY, 0.0, 1.0, 0.0);

        glDrawElements( GL_TRIANGLE_FAN, 6 * 3, GL_UNSIGNED_BYTE, tfan1);
        glDrawElements( GL_TRIANGLE_FAN, 6 * 3, GL_UNSIGNED_BYTE, tfan2);
```

```
glPopMatrix();

spinY+=.25;
transY += 0.075;
}
```

And here's the breakdown:

- In line 1, `GL_STENCIL_BUFFER_BIT` is added to `glClear()`.

- Line 2 calls the new method `renderToStencil()`, which is back in Listing 7-9. This will actually create the stenciled region, poking the hole that we'll draw through next.

- Enable the stencil test in line 3.

- Here in lines 4 and 5 the reflection is drawn. First translate it down a little, subtracting 1.5, to ensure that it is below the real cube. And then it's a simple matter of "scaling" the y-axis to -1.0 to flip it upside-down. You will need to change the front face to clockwise at this point; otherwise, you'll see the back faces only.

- We want to make the lower image translucent instead of the full intensity, as we'd expect. In line 6f, blend is enabled and uses the most common blending function of `GL_ONE` and `GL_ONE_MINUS_SRC_COLOR` covered in Chapter 6.

- In lines 7ff we see that the inverted object is drawn exactly the same way as the original. When done, the blending is switched off in line 8 so that it doesn't affect the rendering of the primary cube. At the same time, stencil is switched off while depth test is switched back on.

- Since scale was touched to invert the image, in line 9 scale is reset to the default. The translation has been modified with a couple of other small values. This shifts it up a little bit just to get extra clearance for the inverted cube.

And now the test. Figure 7-8 is what you should see.

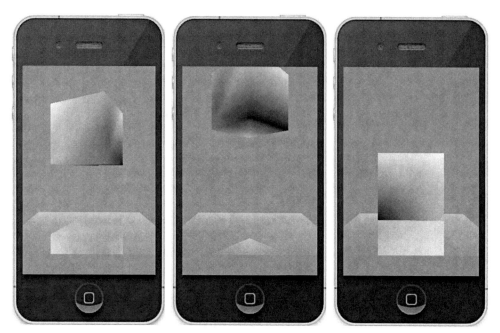

Figure 7-8. *Using stencils to create reflections*

Coming of the Shadows

Shadow casting has always been a bit of a black art in OpenGL, and it still is to a certain extent. However, with faster CPUs and GPUs, many tricks of the trade that were previously more the subject of a grad student's paper can finally step out of theory into the warm glow of real-world deployment. Rigorous solutions to shadow casting are still the domain of the non-real-time rendering that Hollywood employs, but basic shadows, under limited conditions, are available to full-motion rendering. With thanks to the various hardware manufacturers that have added both shadow and lighting support to their GPUs, our 3D universes look richer than ever before because few elements in computer graphics can add more realism than carefully managed shadows. (Ask any lighting director on a Hollywood movie.) And don't forget the per-pixel support via the use of shaders in OpenGL ES 2, which can let a programmer delicately shade every corner of every spooky castle in *Blow Up Everything 3*.

There are many ways to cast shadows, or at least shadow-looking things. Perhaps the simplest is to have a prerendered shadow texture: a bitmap that looks like a shadow on the ground, cast by your object, which is then moved around as it moves. It's cheap, fast, but extremely limited. On the other extreme is the full-blown render-everything-you-can-ever-see software that eats GPUs by the handful for lunch. In between the two, you'll find *shadow mapping*, *shadow volumes,* and *projection shadows*.

Shadow Mapping

At one time, one of the most popular forms of shadow casting was through the use of shadow mapping frequently employed in games. Although it is a bit of a bother to set up, not to mention describe, the theory is pretty simple...considering.

Shadow mapping requires two snapshots of the scene. One is from the light's point of view, and the other is from that of the camera's. When rendered from the light, the image will, by definition, see everything illuminated by itself. The color information is ignored, but the depth information is preserved, so we end up with a map of the visible fragments and their relative distances. Now take a shot from the camera's viewpoint. By comparing the two images, we can find out what bits the camera sees that the light cannot. Those bits are in shadow.

In practice, of course, it is a little more complicated than that.

Shadow Volumes

Shadow volumes are used for determining what part of your scene is illuminated and what is not by making very clever use of certain properties of the stencil buffer. What makes this technique so powerful is that it permits shadows to be cast across arbitrary geometric shapes as opposed to *projection shadows* (discussed later), which really works only for the simplified case of the shadow being thrown against a flat surface.

When a scene is rendered using the shadow volume technique, the stencil buffer will be left in a state in which any part of the resulting image that is shaded will have a corresponding stencil pixel that is greater than zero, while any part that is illuminated will have a zero. See Figure 7-9.

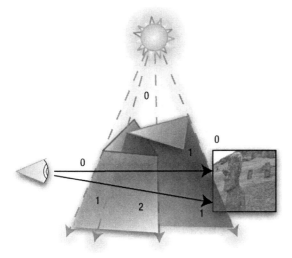

Figure 7-9. *Shadow volumes showing the corresponding values in the stencil buffer: 0 for any parts that are illuminated, >0 for regions in shadow*

This is done in three stages. The first pass is to render the image only with ambient light so that the shaded parts of the scene can still be visible. Next is the pass that writes only to the stencil buffer, and the final stage writes the normal image with full illumination. However, only the nonstenciled pixels can be written to the illuminated areas, while they're blocked from writing to the shaded parts, leaving just the original ambient pixels visible. In practice, this is a little more complicated.

Going back to the mysterious `glStencilOp()` function used in the reflectance exercise earlier, we can now make use of those weird `GL_INCR` and `GL_DECR` operations. `GL_INCR` can increase the count in a stencil pixel by one, and `GL_DECR` will reduce the count by one, both operations triggered under certain conditions.

The term *shadow volume* comes from the following example: imagine it's a foggy night. You take a bright light such as one of your car's headlights and shine it into the mist. Now do some shadow puppetry in the beam. You'll still see part of the beam going around your poorly done shadow of the state of Iowa and wander off into the distance. We're not interested in that part. What we want is the darkened part of the beam, which is the shadow that is cast by your hands. That is the shadow volume.

In your OpenGL scene, assume you have one light source and a few occluders. These cast shadows upon anything behind them, be it a sphere, cone, or bust of Woodrow Wilson. As you look from the side, you will see objects that are shaded and those that are illuminated. Now draw a vector from any fragment, illuminated or not, to your camera. If the fragment is illuminated, the vector must, by definition, travel through an even number of walls of your shadow volumes: one when it goes into the shaded volume and one when it comes out (of course, ignoring the special case for a vector on the edge of a scene that might not have to pass through any shaded regions). For a fragment inside one of the volumes, the vector will have to pass through an odd number of walls; the single extra wall that makes it odd comes from its own volume of residence. Got it? Wait, it gets better.

Now back to stencils. The shadow volumes are generated to look like any other geometry but are drawn only to the stencil, making them invisible since the color buffers are all switched off. The depth buffer is used so that the volume's walls will be rendered in the stencil only *if it is closer* than the real geometry. This trick lets the shadow trace the profiles of arbitrary objects without having to do complicated and fussy calculations of intersecting planes against spheres or Easter Island statues. It merely uses the depth buffer to do pixel-by-pixel tests to decide where shadow ends. So, when the volume is rendered to the stencil, each side of each "cone" of the shadow will affect the stencil in a different way. The side facing us will increment the value in the stencil buffer by one, while the other side will decrement it. So, any regions on the other side of the volume that are illuminated will match a part of the stencil mask in which all of the pixels are set to zero, because the vector must go through the same number of faces going in as going out. Any part that is in shade will have a corresponding stencil value of one.

Got that? That is why shadow volumes were never chosen for the exercise.

Blob Shadows

Blob shadows are a total cheat. It simply assumes that there is no real direct light source, so the object's shadow is little more than a blob underneath, as shown in Figure 7-10. As you can see, this won't work too well if our occluder (the shadow casting thing) is a giant man-eating burrito.

Figure 7-10. A blob shadow texture that is placed under all objects

Projection Shadows

Projection shadows are the "easiest" of the dynamic shadows algorithms to implement, but of course that also means they come with many restrictions, namely, that projection shadows work best when casting a shadow on a large flat surface, as shown in Figure 7-11. Also, shadows cannot be cast on arbitrary objects. As with the other approaches, the basic process is to take a snapshot of sorts from the light's point of view and one from the camera's. The light's view is squashed down flat on the plane, painted a suitable shadowy color (aka dark), followed by the occluder being rendered on top.

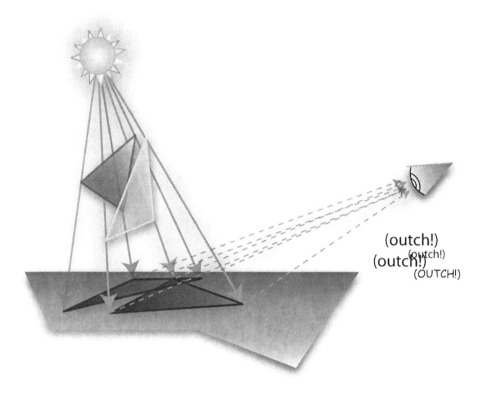

(outch!)
(outch!) (outch!)
(OUTCH!)

Figure 7-11. Projection of a shadow on a flat plane that is then "reprojected" out to poke the viewer's eye

The shaded area is calculated by using the intersection of the vectors and the plane, which travel from the light source by way of each of the vertices. Each point on the plane forms a "new" object that can then be transformed, as anything else on the plane would be. Listing 7-15 shows how this is coded.

Let's start again with the basic bouncy cube demo (even though much of it will be changed for the shadow code, it'll still serve as a working template), but we'll swap in new view controller code. Listing 7-11 covers some of the initialization parameters.

Listing 7-11. The initialization stuff to add to the view controller

```
- (void)viewDidLoad
{
        [super viewDidLoad];

//Normal wizard-produced code deleted for clarity.

        m_WorldRotationX=35.0;                                        //1
        m_WorldRotationY=0.0;
```

```
        m_SpinX=0.0;
        m_SpinY=0.0;
        m_SpinZ=0.0;

        m_WorldZ=-6.0;                                                    //2
        m_WorldY=-1.0;

        m_LightRadius=2.5;                                               //3

    [(EAGLView *)self.view setContext:context];
}
```

▨ In lines 1f, the world rotations are set up; 90° will have you looking
    straight down in the scene, while 0° will have you looking straight on
    the side.

▨ The world locations for the scene are established in lines 2f.
    Decreasing z will move the scene further away; increasing z moves it
    closer. Decreasing y will move it down on the screen, and increasing it
    will move it up.

▨ m_LightRadius in line 3 means the radius of the circle that the light
    moves above the scene.

The drawInRect() method is covered in Listing 7-12. The most immediate change you'll
notice is that the geometry and color arrays are nowhere to be found. Actually, I have
now moved them up to the top of the file as globally defined data. That made it a little
easier to break the rendering stuff into smaller bits. Interestingly enough, a lot of
OpenGL geometric descriptions are kept in .h files—really, really, really big .h files.
Apple actually recommends this approach for some tasks and uses it in its OpenGL
example that draws the infamous teapot. That file is more than 3,000 lines long.

Listing 7-12. The drawInRect() method for projected shadows

```
- (void)glkView:(GLKView *)view drawInRect:(CGRect)rect
{
    int lightsOnFlagTrigger=300;                                      //1
    bool lightsOnFlag=true;
    static int frameNumber=0;
    GLfloat minY=2.0;
    static GLfloat transY=0.0;


    m_TransY=(GLfloat)(sinf(transY)/2.0)+minY;                       //2

    glClear(GL_COLOR_BUFFER_BIT | GL_DEPTH_BUFFER_BIT);
    glClearColor(0.0, 0.0, 0.0, 1.0);

    glEnable(GL_DEPTH_TEST);

    [self updateLightPosition];                                      //3
```

```objc
glDisable( GL_LIGHTING );                                                    //4

glLoadIdentity();

glTranslatef(0.0,m_WorldY,m_WorldZ);                                         //5

[self drawPlatform:0.0 y:0.0 z:0.0];                                        //6

if(frameNumber>(lightsOnFlagTrigger/2))                                     //7
    lightsOnFlag=false;
else
    lightsOnFlag=true;

if(frameNumber>lightsOnFlagTrigger)
    frameNumber=0;

[self drawLight: GL_LIGHT0];                                                //8

glDisable( GL_DEPTH_TEST );                                                 //9

[self calculateShadowMatrix];                                              //10

if(lightsOnFlag)
    [self drawShadow];                                                     //11

glShadeModel( GL_SMOOTH );

glEnableClientState(GL_VERTEX_ARRAY);                                      //12
glVertexPointer( 3, GL_FLOAT, 0, m_CubeVertices );

glEnableClientState(GL_COLOR_ARRAY);
glColorPointer(4, GL_UNSIGNED_BYTE, 0, m_CubeColors);

glRotatef(m_WorldRotationX, 1.0, 0.0, 0.0);                                //13
glRotatef(m_WorldRotationY, 0.0, 1.0, 0.0);

glTranslatef(0.0,m_TransY, 0.0);                                           //14

glRotatef( m_SpinZ, 0.0, 0.0, 1.0 );                                       //15
glRotatef( m_SpinY, 0.0, 1.0, 0.0 );
glRotatef( m_SpinX, 1.0, 0.0, 0.0 );

glEnable( GL_DEPTH_TEST );                                                 //16
glFrontFace(GL_CCW);

glDrawElements( GL_TRIANGLE_FAN, 6 * 3, GL_UNSIGNED_BYTE, m_Tfan1);
glDrawElements( GL_TRIANGLE_FAN, 6 * 3, GL_UNSIGNED_BYTE, m_Tfan2);

glDisable(GL_BLEND);
glEnable(GL_LIGHTING);

transY+=.1;                                                                //17
frameNumber++;
```

```
    m_SpinX+=.4f;
    m_SpinY+=.6f;
    m_SpinZ+=.9f;

    return;
}
```

So, what's going on here? Well, sit a spell, and I'll tell you:

- Lines 1f are used to turn the light on and off so as to take before and after comparisons.

- Line 2 just generates the bounce factor. Since we need it twice, I pulled it out of the call to `glTranslate()` where it used to be.

- The light's position is updated at line 3 and is detailed later.

- In line 4, the lighting is turned off briefly because it can affect the way the shadows are rendered.

- Line 5 translates the scene to `mWorldY` and `mWorldZ` coordinates.

- The platform, or stage, is drawn in line 6.

- Lines 7ff toggle the light on and off every few seconds to show the scene with and without the shadow.

- In line 8, the `drawLight()` routine (Listing 7-13) is called to place a little floating ball in orbit around our scene.

- We need to disable the depth test when actually drawing the shadow, in line 9, otherwise, there will be all sorts of z contention that generates cool but useless flickering.

- Line 10 calls the routine to generate the shadow's matrix (detailed later), followed by line 11, which actually draws the shadow.

- Finally, we can start managing the occluder in line 12, the thing that actually causes the shadow to be thrown.

- Line 13 is used to aim our eye point down to center the scene since we are floating up above it.

- Now we get to the bouncy part—nothing really new in line 14.

- Lines 15ff add the extra spins. Note that the shadow generator also has the identical rotational code.

- Line 16 safely turns on the depth testing again, after which we can draw the two triangle fans as well.

- Lines 17ff handles some of the animation parameters, and then the buffer is updated to the screen.

OK, take a deep breath—we have more to cover. Listing 7-13 demonstrates the new drawLight() routine, while Listing 7-14 demonstrates drawPlatform(). The meat of the exercise is Listing 7-15, calculating the shadow's matrix, and Listing 7-16, drawing the shadow. Are you tingling yet? I know I am.

Listing 7-13. *The modified drawLight() routine*

```
-(void)drawLight:(int)lightNumber
{
    static GLbyte lampVertices[]={0,0,0};                            //1

    glDisableClientState(GL_COLOR_ARRAY);

    glEnable(GL_POINT_SMOOTH);                                       //2

    glPointSize(5.0);                                               //3
    glLightfv(lightNumber, GL_POSITION, iLightPos );               //4
    glPushMatrix();

    glRotatef(m_WorldRotationX, 1.0, 0.0, 0.0);                    //5
    glRotatef(m_WorldRotationY, 0.0, 1.0, 0.0);

    glTranslatef( iLightPosX, iLightPosY, iLightPosZ );            //6

    glColor4f( 1.0, 1.0, 0, 1.0);                                  //7
    glVertexPointer( 3, GL_BYTE, 0, lampVertices );                //8
    glDrawArrays(GL_POINTS, 0,1);

    glPopMatrix();

    glEnableClientState(GL_COLOR_ARRAY);
}
```

The preceding code will draw a round dot to the screen, showing where the light source is located at any moment.

■ Since we want only a single point to draw, we can specify a single vertex at the origin in line 1.

■ GL_POINT_SMOOTH is something new. It tells OpenGL that any points it draws should be round. Without this, the light would be rendered as a square.

■ Line 3 is another new call that tells the system that the point is to be 5 pixels across. The maximum size can vary on different devices but can typically go up to 64 or 128 pixels in diameter.

■ Now we can set the absolute position of the actual light here in line 4.

■ Lines 5ff rotate the lamp in world space, while line 6 translates it.

■ The color is set to yellow via line 7, while lines 8ff supply the vertex and then draw it via glDrawArrays().

But wait, there's more!

We need to add a floor or platform underneath the cube that the shadow will render up against, as shown in Listing 7-14.

***Listing 7-14.** The* `drawPlatform()` *routine that renders a floor beneath the cube*

```
-(void)drawPlatform:(float)x y:(float)y z:(float)z
{
    static const GLfloat platformVertices[] =                              //1
    {
        -1.0,-0.01,-1.0,
         1.0,-0.01,-1.0,
        -1.0,-0.01, 1.0,
         1.0,-0.01, 1.0
    };

    static const GLubyte platformColors[] =
    {
        128, 128, 128, 255,
        128,   0, 255, 255,
         64,  64,  64,   0,
        255,  64, 128, 255
    };

    GLfloat scale=1.5;                                                     //2

    glEnable( GL_DEPTH_TEST );
    glShadeModel( GL_SMOOTH );
    glDisable(GL_CULL_FACE);                                               //3
    glVertexPointer(3, GL_FLOAT, 0, platformVertices);
    glEnableClientState(GL_VERTEX_ARRAY);
    glColorPointer(4, GL_UNSIGNED_BYTE, 0, platformColors);
    glEnableClientState(GL_COLOR_ARRAY);

    glPushMatrix();

    glRotatef(m_WorldRotationX, 1.0, 0.0, 0.0);                            //4
    glRotatef(m_WorldRotationY, 0.0, 1.0, 0.0);

    glTranslatef(x,y,z);

    glScalef(scale,scale,scale);                                          //5

    glDrawArrays(GL_TRIANGLE_STRIP, 0, 4);

    glEnable(GL_CULL_FACE);

    glPopMatrix();
}
```

This merely draws the square base object that the shadow is projected against.

▓ Nothing special here in line 1, but instead of describing the square in the x-y plane as we've done before, it is in the x-z plane and y=0. Oh, wait! There is something special. Notice the y coordinates. Instead of being a sane value like 0.0, they are a slight negative value, of -0.01. That is a quick hack to fix a problem called "z fighting," in which pixels from co-planer objects may or may not share the same depth value. The result is two faces flickering at one moment; face A is the frontmost, and the next, the pixels of face B, now think they are frontmost. *(Note that it shows only on hardware. It will look fine in the simulator.)* If you look hard enough in almost any real-time 3D software, you will likely see some z's fighting in the background. Figure 7-12.

In this case, the fix is to drop the y of the platform down just a tad, to be below the shadow. This fix doesn't always work, because it depends on the environment, the scale of things you're dealing with, and so on. Another workaround is to use the call `glPolygonOffset()`. But that again is no assurance of success. Sometimes you just have to try to see what works.

▓ Since the platform's coordinates are normalized, we need to scale them up a bit to make it usable, as in line 2.

▓ Line 3 turns off face culling. The reason is that since the platform is a single square and we could go under it easily enough, we need to see both sides of the same faces.

▓ Line 4 is the same here as elsewhere; it merely rotates the platform into world space.

▓ Line 5 does the actual scaling; place it as the first transformation to be executed. (Remember, the transformation stack can be thought of as a FIFO: the first transformation in is the first to be executed. If the scaling was after another transformation, it would scale things off-center from the desired result.)

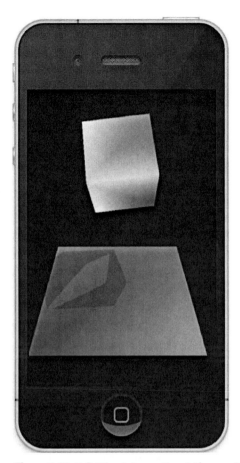

Figure 7-12. *Z-fighting between the platform and the shadow*

Now we get to the real fun stuff, actually calculating and drawing the shadow. Listing 7-15 shows how the matrix is generated, while Listing 7-16 draws the squashed shadow.

Listing 7-15. *Calculating the shadow matrix*

```
-(void)calculateShadowMatrix
{
    GLfloat shadowMat_local[16] =
    {
         iLightPosY, 0.0,         0.0,        0.0,
        -iLightPosX, 0.0, -iLightPosZ,      -1.0,
                0.0,      0.0, iLightPosY,        0.0,
                0.0,      0.0,        0.0, iLightPosY
    };
```

```
    for ( int i=0;i<16;i++ )
    {
        iShadowMat[i] = shadowMat_local[i];
    }
}
```

This is actually a simplified version of the more generalized matrix given by the following:

```
[ dotp-l[0]*p[0],           -l[1]*p[0],      -l[2]*p[0],     -l[3]*p[0],
        -l[0]*p[1], dotp-l[1]*p[1],      -l[2]*p[1],      -l[3]*p[1],
        -l[0]*p[2],      -l[1]*p[2], dotp-l[2]*p[2],      -l[3]*p[2],
        -l[0]*p[3],      -l[1]*p[3],      -l[2]*p[3], dotp-l[3]*p[3] ]
```

dotp is the dot-product between the light vector and the normal to the plane, l is the position of the light, and p is the plane (the "platform" in my code). Since our platform is in the x/z plane, the plane equation looks like p=[0,1,0,0], or otherwise, p[0]=p[2]=p[3]=0. This means most of the terms in the matrix get zeroed out. Once the matrix is generated, multiplying it by the existing Modelview matrix maps the points to your local space along with everything else.

Listing 7-16. *The tweaked* drawShadow() *routine*

```
- (void)drawShadow
{
    glPushMatrix();

    glRotatef(m_WorldRotationX, 1.0, 0.0, 0.0);                        //1
    glRotatef(m_WorldRotationY, 0.0, 1.0, 0.0);

    glMultMatrixf( iShadowMat );                                       //2

    //Place the shadows.

    glTranslatef(0.0,m_TransY, 0.0);                                   //3

    glRotatef( m_SpinZ, 0.0, 0.0, 1.0 );                              //4
    glRotatef( m_SpinY, 0.0, 1.0, 0.0 );
    glRotatef( m_SpinX, 1.0, 0.0, 0.0 );

    //Draw them.

    glDisableClientState(GL_COLOR_ARRAY);

    glEnable(GL_BLEND);                                                //5
    glBlendFunc(GL_ZERO,GL_ONE_MINUS_SRC_ALPHA);

    glColor4f( 0.0, 0.0, 0.0, .3 );                                    //6

    glEnableClientState(GL_VERTEX_ARRAY);
    glVertexPointer( 3, GL_FLOAT, 0, m_CubeVertices );                 //7

    glDrawElements( GL_TRIANGLE_FAN, 6 * 3, GL_UNSIGNED_BYTE, m_Tfan1);
    glDrawElements( GL_TRIANGLE_FAN, 6 * 3, GL_UNSIGNED_BYTE, m_Tfan2);
```

```
//  glLineWidth(3.0);                                                    //8
//  glDrawElements( GL_LINES, 6 * 3, GL_UNSIGNED_BYTE, m_Tfan1);
//  glDrawElements( GL_LINES, 6 * 3, GL_UNSIGNED_BYTE, m_Tfan2);

    glDisable(GL_BLEND);

    glPopMatrix();
}
```

- First rotate everything to world space, just as we have done before in line 1.

- Line 2 multiplies the shadow matrix with the current Modelview matrix.

- Lines 3 and 4ff perform the same transformations and rotations on the shadow as on the actual cube.

- Next we can add a little blending to the shadow in lines 5ff and 6. The alpha value is set to .3. The higher the value, the darker the shadow, with it being solid black, of course, when the alpha is at 1.0.

- In lines 7ff we render the geometry just as with the actual cube, except now it's distorted to look like it's stretched out along the surface.

Now it's time to update the light's position, as in Listing 7-17.

Listing 7-17. *Updating the light's position*

```
- (void)updateLightPosition
{
    iLightAngle += (GLfloat)1.0;                    //in degrees

    iLightPosX   = m_LightRadius * cos( iLightAngle/57.29 );
    iLightPosY   = 4.0;
    iLightPosZ   = m_LightRadius * sin( iLightAngle/57.29  );

    iLightPos[0] = iLightPosX;
    iLightPos[1] = iLightPosY;
    iLightPos[2] = iLightPosZ;
}
```

This updates the light's position one degree each refresh. The y-value is fixed, so the light traces its little orbit in the x/z plane. In addition to all of the previous, make sure to add the standard setClipping() routine we've used in the past and call it from viewDidLoad().

And to top it off, Listing 7-18 is the header for this project.

Listing 7-18. *The header for the shadow casting exercise*

```
#import <UIKit/UIKit.h>
#import <GLKit/GLKit.h>
#import <OpenGLES/EAGL.h>
```

```
#import <OpenGLES/ES1/gl.h>
#import <OpenGLES/ES1/glext.h>
#import <OpenGLES/ES2/gl.h>
#import <OpenGLES/ES2/glext.h>

@interface ShadowCastingViewController : GLKViewController
{
    EAGLContext *context;
    GLuint program;

    GLfloat m_WorldRotationX;
    GLfloat m_WorldRotationY;

    GLfloat m_LightRadius;

    /** Angle of the light. */
    GLfloat iLightAngle;

    /** X coordinate of the light */
    GLfloat iLightPosX;

    /** Y coordinate of the light */
    GLfloat iLightPosY;
    GLfloat iLightPosZ;
    GLfloat iLightPos[4];

    GLfloat m_WorldZ;
    GLfloat m_WorldY;

    GLfloat m_TransY;
    GLfloat m_SpinX;
    GLfloat m_SpinY;
    GLfloat m_SpinZ;

    GLfloat iShadowMat[16];
}

@property (readonly, nonatomic, getter=isAnimating) BOOL animating;
@property (nonatomic) NSInteger animationFrameInterval;

-(void)drawPlatform:(float)x y:(float)y z:(float)z;
-(void)drawLight:(int)lightNumber;
-(void)updateLightPosition;
-(void)drawShadow;
-(void)calculateShadowMatrix;
-(void)setClipping;
-(void)startAnimation;
-(void)stopAnimation;
-(void)viewDidLoad;
-(void)viewDidUnload;
-(void)applicationWillResignActive:(NSNotification *)notification;
-(void)applicationDidBecomeActive:(NSNotification *)notification;
-(void)applicationWillTerminate:(NSNotification *)notification;
-(void)dealloc;
-(void)didReceiveMemoryWarning;
```

```
-(void)viewWillAppear:(BOOL)animated;
-(void)viewWillDisappear:(BOOL)animated;
```

@end

After it's compiled, do you see something like Figure 7-13 (the final image is left to you, dear reader, to generate).

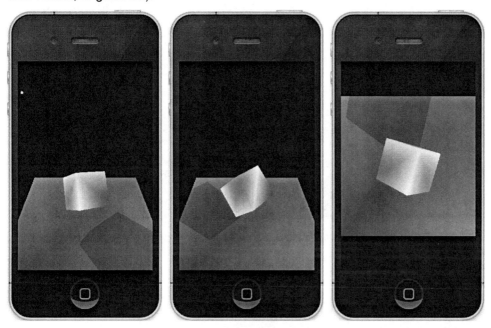

Figure 7-13. *The left and middle images are from the side; the rightmost image is looking down from above.*

And as with our other exercises, tweaking is mandatory.

It's one thing to see the nice dark shadow, but it's another thing to actually see how the shadow is composed. Go to `drawShadow()` and replace the calls to `glDrawElements()` with the following:

```
glLineWidth(3.0);
glDrawElements( GL_LINES, 6 * 3, GL_UNSIGNED_BYTE, m_Tfan1);
glDrawElements( GL_LINES, 6 * 3, GL_UNSIGNED_BYTE, m_Tfan2);
```

`glLineWidth(3.0)` is a new call, and when lines are drawn, this specifies how wide they should be, with 1.0 being the default. Figure 7-14 now shows the flattened image in wireframe mode.

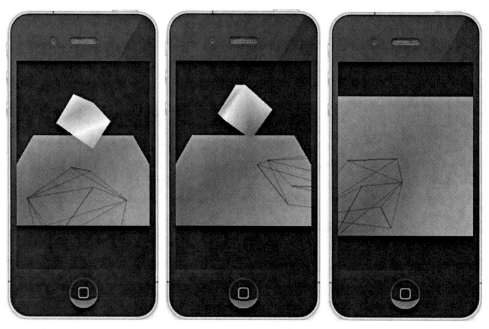

Figure 7-14. Showing the shadow in wireframe mode. The cube has been removed in the rightmost image to show the wireframe more clearly.

You can also have multiple lights. Figure 7-15 shows two side-by-side lights.

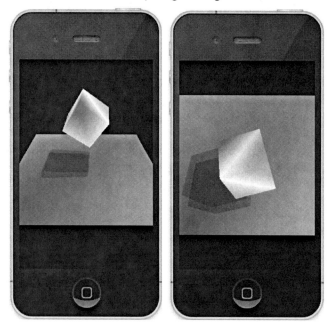

Figure 7-15. The cube with multiple lights

In all of these images, the background is black. Change the coloring of the background and run. What's going on in Figure 7-16?

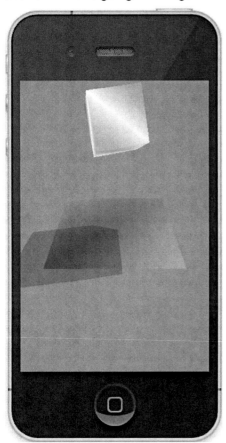

Figure 7-16. *Surprise! The shadow is not clipped to the platform.*

What's happening here is that we were cheating when it comes to clipping the shadow against the platform. With the background black, the part of the shadow that rendered off the platform was invisible. But now as the background is brightened, you can see the full shadow. What happens if you need a light background in the first place? Use stencils to clip around the platform, blanking out any extra part of the shadow that we don't need, similarly to the earlier reflection exercise.

Summary

In this chapter, we covered a number of extra tricks to add more realism to an OpenGL ES scene. First were frame buffer objects that let you draw to multiple OpenGL frames and merge them together. Next came lens flares that can add visual drama to outdoor scenes, followed by reflections and stencils that are heavily used by Apple in a lot of its UI design. We ended with one of the many ways shadows can be cast against a background using shadow projection. Next, some of these tricks will be applied to our little solar-system project.

Putting It All Together

A single lifetime, even though entirely devoted to the sky, would not be enough for the investigation of so vast a subject.

—Seneca, Roman philosopher

Well, now we've made it all the way up to Chapter 8. This is when we can take what was learned from the exercises up to this point and slap it together into a more complete solar-system model. And afterward, I hope you will say, "Wow! That's kinda cool!"

This chapter will be very code heavy, because the model requires both a number of new routines and modifications to existing projects. So, as with Chapter 7 I'll be breaking with the style of the previous chapters and will not present entire code files because of their length or to avoid repetition; therefore, you are encouraged to fetch the full projects, as well as some data files, from the Apress site to ensure that you have fully functional examples. A few new tricks will also be tossed in for good measure such as how to integrate the standard iPhone UIKit and the use of quaternions. Note that although a lot of the following code is based on previous exercises, there are likely some small tweaks needed to integrate it into the larger package, so unfortunately this won't simply be a cut-and-paste situation.

But What About a Retina Display?

Yes, I know, everything looks better on a Retina display, so let's tell OpenGL how to handle the higher resolution before we do anything else. Oh, wait. We don't have to do that anymore. Pre-iOS 5, it was necessary to tell the OpenGL view object how to size itself using the setContentScaleFactor instance variable. It would be 1.0 for the old-school displays, or 2.0 for Retina. Under the GLKit, that kind of housekeeping is no longer needed. However, you will still need to grab the actual dimensions of the view when it comes time to set the glViewPort() when setting the viewing frustum, as follows, remembering that the view here is actually the GLKView subclassed from the UIView.

```
glViewport(0, 0, view.drawableWidth, view.drawableHeight);
```

Using the "drawable" fields is recommended by Apple, although the more traditional way, using the frame of the mainScreen, should still be valid if you are creating a display to be the size of the screen.

Revisiting the Solar System

Go back to Chapter 5 and get the solar-system model that was used as the final project. The Chapter 7 model was used as a surface for displaying dynamic textures on 3D objects, but that won't be used here in that way.

So, the first thing to tackle is resizing our models to make a slightly more realistic presentation. As of right now, it looks like the earth is about a third the size of the sun and only a few thousand miles (or furlongs if you care) away. Considering that it is a pleasant fall day here in Northern California and the earth is anything but a burnt cinder, I bet the model is wrong. Well, let's make it right. This will be done in the initGeometry() method in your solar-system controller. And while we're at it, the type of m_Eyeposition will be changed to upgrade it to a slightly more objectified object customized for 3D operations. The new routine is in Listing 8-1. Make sure to add a texture for the sun's surface while you are at it; otherwise, nasty things might happen.

Listing 8-1. Resizing the objects for the solar system

```
-(void)initGeometry
{
    //Let 1.0=1 million miles.
    // The sun's radius=.4.
    // The earth's radius=.04 (10x larger to make it easier to see).

    m_Eyeposition.x=0;
    m_Eyeposition.y=0;
    m_Eyeposition.z=93.25;

    m_Earth=[[Planet alloc] init:48 slices:48 radius:0.04
            squash:1.0 textureFile:@"earth_light.png"];

    [m_Earth setPositionX:0.0 Y:0.0 Z:93.0];

    m_Sun=[[Planet alloc] init:48 slices:48 radius:0.4
            squash:1.0 textureFile:@"sun_surface.png"];
}
```

m_Eyeposition is now defined as a new GLKVector3 object.

> **Note** The new iOS5 vector classes are very well thought out, because they use unions to support xyz values, rgb, stp (for texture coordinates), and the ever popular array format, float v[3]. Similar conventions are used for the other container classes as well.

The scale of our model is set at 1 unit=1 million miles (1.7m kilometers or 8.3m furlongs). The sun has a radius of 400,000 miles, or .4 in these units. That means earth's radius would be .004, but I've increased it by 10 times, to .04, to make it a little easier to deal with. Because earth's default position is along the +Z-axis, let's put the eye position right behind the earth, only a quarter million miles away, at "93.25." And in `the execute method for the solar-system object`, remove `glRotatef()` so that the earth will now stay fixed. That makes things a lot simpler for the time being. Make sure to modify the headers as needed. Go to your friend, `setClipping()`, and change the field of view from 50 degrees to 30; also, set zFar=2000 (to handle future objects). You should ultimately get something that looks like Figure 8-1. Because the sun is actually behind the earth from our viewpoint, I cranked up the specular lighting for SS_FILLLIGHT1.

Figure 8-1. *Our home on a tiny screen*

"All well and good, code-boy!" you must be muttering under your breath. "But now we're stuck in space!" True enough, so that means the next step is to add a navigational element. And that means (cue dramatic music) we'll be adding *quaternions*.

What Are These Quaternion Things Anyway?

On October 16, 1843, in Dublin, Irish mathematician Sir William Hamilton was taking a stroll by the Royal Canal when he had a sudden flash of mathematical inspiration. He'd been working on ways to meaningfully multiply and divide two points in space and suddenly saw the formula for quaternions in his mind: $i^2 = j^2 = k^2 = ijk = -1$. Impressive, huh?

He was so excited that he couldn't resist the temptation to carve it into the stonework of the Brougham Bridge he had just come to (no doubt nestled in between lesser graffiti like "Eamon loves Fiona, 1839" or "Patrick O'Callahan rulz!"). Radically new ways to look at physics and geometry descended directly from this insight. For example, the classic Maxwell's equations in electromagnetic theory were described entirely through the use of quaternions. As newer methods of dealing with similar situations came about, quaternions were shunted aside until the late 20th century, when they found a significant role in 3D computer graphics, in navigation of the Apollo spacecraft to the moon, and in other areas that rely heavily on rotations in space. Because of their compact nature, they could describe a direction vector, and hence a 3D rotation, more efficiently than the standard 3x3 matrix. Not only that, but they provided much superior means of concatenating a series of rotations on top of each other. So, what does this mean?

In Chapter 2, we covered the traditional 3D transformation math using matrices. If you wanted to rotate an object 32° around the z-axis, you would instruct OpenGL ES to perform a rotation via the command `glRotation(32,0,0,1)`. Similar commands would be executed for the x- and y-axes as well. But what if you wanted a funky sort of rotation that an airplane might make when banking to the left? How would that be described in the `glRotatef()` format? Using the more traditional way, you would generate separate matrices for the three rotations and then multiply them in order of *yaw* (rotation around the Y-axis), *pitch* (rotation around the X-axis), and *roll* around the Z-axis. That's a lot of math to aim toward one direction. But if this is for a flight simulator, your banking motion will constantly update to new rolls and headings, incrementally. That would mean you'd have to calculate the three matrices each time for the deltas of your trajectory since the last frame and not absolute values from some starting point.

In the early days of computers, when floating-point calculations were expensive and shortcuts were regularly invoked for performance reasons, round-off errors were common and would likely build up over time, causing the current matrices to be "out of square." However, quaternions were brought to the rescue because they had a couple of very compelling properties. The first is that a quaternion can represent a rotation of an object in space roughly equivalent to how `glRotatef()` works but by using fractional axis values. It's not a direct one-to-one correlation, because you still need to go about some of that math stuff to convert attitudes to and from a quaternion. The second and more important property derives from the fact that an arc on a sphere can be described by two quaternions, one at each endpoint. And any point between them on the arc can also be described by a quaternion merely by interpolating the distance from one endpoint to the other by using spherical geometry, as shown in Figure 8-2. That is, if you were going through an arc of 60°, you could find an intermediate quaternion, say, 20° from the starting point by tracing a third of the way along the arc. In the next frame, if you were to jump to 20.1°, you merely add a teeny-tiny more of that arc to your *current* quaternion instead of having to go through the tedious process of generating the three matrices each time and multiplying them together. This process is called *slerping,* where *slerp* stands for *spherical linear interpolation*. Because an axis/angle pair does not rely on a cumulative summation of all previous ones like when using matrices but on an instantaneous value, there is no error buildup as a result of the former.

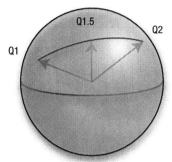

Figure 8-2. *An intermediate quaternion; Q1.5 on a sphere can be interpolated from two others, Q1 and Q2.*

Slerp is used to provide those smooth animations of a viewpoint's "camera" when going from one point to another. It can be part of a flight simulator, a space simulator, or the view from a chase car for a racing game. And naturally they are used in real flight guidance systems as well.

So, now with that bit of background, we're going to use quaternions to help move the earth around.

Moving Things in 3D

Since we are not animating the earth currently, there needs to be a way to move it around so we can investigate it from all ends. With that in mind, since the earth is our target of interest, we'll set up a situation in which the eye point will effectively hover over the earth directed by pinch and drag gestures.

The first step is to add gesture recognizers, which have been available on the iPad from day one but available on the other devices only since iOS 4.

> **Note**   For a "real" application, you might consider whether the convenience of gesture recognizers is worth cutting off the first-generation iOS users who are limited to iOS 3.*x*.

If you are new enough to iOS programming, you might not have come across gesture recognizers. In brief, they handle the tedium of determining what kind of touch gesture the user has made, something the developer had to do early on. It could get plenty messy, especially when taking care of rotation gestures. Swipe, tap, pinch, and pan gestures are also handled. However, they did leave out momentum swipes, the kind of action that can keep a list scrolling for a while after you've lifted your finger.

Here we'll need only the pinch and pan gestures. To your view controller's viewDidLoad() method, add Listing 8-2.

Listing 8-2. *Allocating the gesture recognizers*

```
UIPinchGestureRecognizer *pinchGesture =
    [[UIPinchGestureRecognizer alloc]initWithTarget:self
      action:@selector(handlePinchGesture:)];

    [self.view addGestureRecognizer:pinchGesture];

    UIPanGestureRecognizer *panGesture =
    [[UIPanGestureRecognizer alloc]initWithTarget:self
      action:@selector(handlePanGesture:)];
    [self.view addGestureRecognizer:panGesture];
```

Next we need to add the two handlers, handlePanGesture() and handlePinchGesture(), shown in Listing 8-3.

Listing 8-3. *The Two Handlers for the Gesture Recognizers*

```
- (IBAction)handlePanGesture:(UIPanGestureRecognizer *)sender
{
    static CGPoint prevLocation;
    CGPoint translate = [sender translationInView:self.view];

    UIGestureRecognizerState state;

    state=sender.state;

    if(state==UIGestureRecognizerStateBegan)
    {
        prevLocation=translate;
        [m_SolarSystem lookAtTarget];
    }
    else if(state==UIGestureRecognizerStateChanged)
    {
        CGPoint currlocation =translate;

        m_PointerLocation=CGPointMake(currlocation.x, currlocation.y);

        [self setHoverPosition:0 location:currlocation prevLocation:prevLocation];

        prevLocation=currlocation;
    }
}
```

```
- (IBAction)handlePinchGesture:(UIGestureRecognizer *)sender
{
    static float startFOV=0.0;
    CGFloat factor = [(UIPinchGestureRecognizer *)sender scale];
    UIGestureRecognizerState state;

    state=sender.state;

    if(state==UIGestureRecognizerStateBegan)
    {
        startFOV=[m_SolarSystem getFieldOfView];
    }
    else if(state==UIGestureRecognizerStateChanged)
    {
        float minFOV=5.0;
        float maxFOV=75.0;
        float currentFOV;

        currentFOV=startFOV*factor;

        if((currentFOV>=minFOV) && (currentFOV<=maxFOV))
            [m_SolarSystem setFieldOfView:currentFOV];
    }
}
```

handlePanGesture() calculates the difference in the touch location from the previous call as a finger is dragged across the screen. It feeds those differences to setHoverPosition(), which will then move your eye point to a new position over the earth. Add CGPoint m_PointerLocation to the header.

The other handler, handlePinchGesture(), handles pinches. The UIPinchGestureRecognizer() returns a simple magnification value starting with 1.0 when the gesture begins. As the gesture continues, the state changes to UIGestureRecognizerStateChanged, and the scale value increases for an expanding pinch to indicate a zoom-in operation or decreases when the person is zooming out. Here it is necessary to cache the starting field of view of the display, because each scale value is cumulative vs. a delta from the previous event. That way, we're scaling up the original value each time as opposed to rescaling the field of view, which would be done if we only had the deltas to play with. Otherwise, our FOV would jump in successively larger jumps. Also, notice that I did place limits to the range of values of the FOV, from 5° to 75°.

It is now necessary to add to your solar-system handler the instance variable float m_FieldOfView, along with the accessor methods in Listing 8-4, and initialize it to 30°.

Listing 8-4. *Accessors for* m_FieldOfView *in the Solar-System Controller*

```
-(float)getFieldOfView
{
    return m_FieldOfView;
}
```

```
-(void)setFieldOfView:(float)fov
{
    m_FieldOfView=fov;

    [self setClipping];
}
```

Then move setClipping() from the view controller to the solar-system controller, and swap out the autovariable fieldOfView for m_FieldOfView, making sure to initialize it to something like 30° at program startup and to call setClipping() at object creation, as used to be done in the view controller. Reinitializing the projection matrix is now necessary, because setClipping() will be called repeatedly during the pinch-to-zoom operations, and we don't want them to build on each other. Otherwise, the view quickly gets wacky.

Finally, you need to add two stubs, which will prevent a crash should you accidentally do a drag operation. This will be filled in for the next task. To your view controller, add:

```
-(void)setHoverPosition:(unsigned)nFlags location:(CGPoint)location
        prevLocation:(CGPoint)prevLocation
{

}
```

To the solar-system controller, add:

```
-(void)lookAtTarget
{


}
```

If all works as designed, you should be able to zoom in and out from the earth model, as shown in Figure 8-3.

Figure 8-3. *Zooming in and out using pinch gestures*

Now we're going to do the rotation support, which includes those quaternion things. To the solar-system controller, add Listing 8-5 (and you can also get rid of the lookAtTarget() stub). The helper function getPosition() for m_Earth is added in Listing 8-7, so don't fret if you get the red dots-of-doom from 8-5.

Listing 8-5. *New helper routines for the solar-system controller*

```
-(GLKVector3)getTargetLocation
{
    return [m_Earth getPosition];
}

-(void)lookAtTarget
{
    GLKVector3 targetLocation=[m_Earth getPosition];
```

```
        gluLookAt(m_Eyeposition.x,m_Eyeposition.y,m_Eyeposition.z,
                targetLocation.x,targetLocation.y,targetLocation.z,
                0.0,1.0,0.0);
}

-(GLKVector3)getEyeposition
{
    return m_Eyeposition;
}

-(void)setEyeposition:(GLKVector3)loc
{
    m_Eyeposition=loc;

}
```

In normal OpenGL, I've mentioned the existence of a utility library called GLUT. Unfortunately, there is no complete GLUT library for iOS as of this writing, so I've had to create my own where I stuff most any basic 3D utility method. With that in mind, create a new object called miniglu.mm (the "mm" suffix lets the Objective C compiler understand straight C code mixed with ObjC), add the the contents of Listing 8-6, and add static GLKQuaternion m_Quaternion to the top of the file. And make sure to add miniglu.h where needed.

This is kept as generic-C because GLUT is meant to be as portable as possible.

Listing 8-6*. Two routines for miniGLU.mm*

```
void gluLookAt(GLfloat eyex, GLfloat eyey, GLfloat eyez,
                GLfloat centerx, GLfloat centery, GLfloat centerz,
                GLfloat upx, GLfloat upy, GLfloat upz)
{
    GLKVector3 up;                                                      //1
    GLKVector3 from,to;
    GLKVector3 lookat;
    GLKVector3 axis;
    float angle;

    lookat.x=centerx;                                                   //2
    lookat.y=centery;
    lookat.z=centerz;

    from.x=eyex;
    from.y=eyey;
    from.z=eyez;

    to.x=lookat.x;
    to.y=lookat.y;
    to.z=lookat.z;

    up.x=upx;
    up.y=upy;
    up.z=upz;
```

```
    GLKVector3 temp = GLKVector3Subtract(to,from);                         //3
    GLKVector3 n=GLKVector3Normalize(temp);

    temp = GLKVector3CrossProduct(n,up);
    GLKVector3 v=GLKVector3Normalize(temp);

    GLKVector3 u = GLKVector3CrossProduct(v,n);

    m_Quaternion=                                                          //4

GLKQuaternionMakeWithMatrix3(GLKMatrix3MakeWithRows(v,u,GLKVector3Negate(n)));

    axis=GLKQuaternionAxis(m_Quaternion);
    angle=GLKQuaternionAngle(m_Quaternion);

    glRotatef(angle*57.29, axis.x, axis.y, axis.z);                       //5
}

GLKQuaternion gluGetOrientation()
{
    return m_Quaternion;
}
```

Before we continue, `gluLookAt()` will need some, er, a lot of explanation. `gluLookAt()` does exactly what its name implies. You pass it the location of your eye point, the thing you want to look at, and an up vector to specify roll angles. Naturally, straight up would be equal to no roll whatsoever. But you still need to supply it.

Let's take a closer look:

■ As referenced earlier, we need to grab points or vectors to fully describe our position in space and that of the target, as in lines 1ff. The up vector is local to your eye point, and it is typically just a unit vector pointing up the y-axis. You could modify this if you wanted to do banking rolls.

■ In lines 2ff, the terms passed through in discrete values are mapped to `GLKVector3` objects. Why instead of vectors in? The official GLUT libraries don't use vector objects, so this matches the existing standard.

■ Lines 3ff generate three new vectors, two using cross products. This ensures everything is both normalized and the axis squared.

■ Some examples of `gluLookAt()` generate a matrix. Here, quaternions are used instead. In line 4, the quaternion is created by our new vectors and is used to get the axis/angle parameters that `glRotatef()` likes to use, as in line 5. Note that the resulting quaternion is cached via a global that can be picked up later if the instantaneous attitude is needed via `gluGetOrientation()`. It's clumsy, but it works. In real life, you probably wouldn't want to do this, because it assumes only a single viewpoint in your entire world. In reality, you might want to have more than one—if, for example, you wanted two simultaneous displays showing your object from two different vantage points.

Now you can make some tweaks to Planet.mm. Since we're using the new vector/point objects, the instance variable, m_Pos, will be converted from a simple array to a GLKVector3 type. Listing 8-7 shows those changes, and remember to change its definition in the header as well and the initialization line in the initialization routine.

Listing 8-7. *Some small helper functions for* Planet.mm

```
-(GLKVector3)getPosition
{
    return m_Pos;
}

-(void)setPosition:(GLKVector3)position
{
    m_Pos=position;
}

-(void)getPositionX:(GLfloat *)x Y:(GLfloat *)y Z:(GLfloat *)z
{
        *x=m_Pos.x;
        *y=m_Pos.y;
        *z=m_Pos.z;
}

-(void)setPositionX:(GLfloat)x Y:(GLfloat)y Z:(GLfloat)z
{
        m_Pos.x=x;
        m_Pos.y=y;
        m_Pos.z=z;
}
```

Next is the heart of this hover stuff. Replace the stub for setHoverPostion() in the **view controller** with the code from Listing 8-8 and add miniglu.h.

Listing 8-8. *Adding the view's rotation code*

```
-(void)setHoverPosition:(unsigned)nFlags location:(CGPoint)location
prevLocation:(CGPoint)prevLocation
{
    int dx;
    int dy;
    GLKQuaternion orientation,tempQ;
    GLKVector3 offset,objectLoc,vpLoc;
    GLKVector3 offsetv=GLKVector3Make(0.0,0.0,0.0);

    float reference=300;
    float scale=4.0;
    GLKMatrix3 matrix3;

    CGRect frame = [[UIScreen mainScreen] bounds];

    glMatrixMode(GL_MODELVIEW);
    glLoadIdentity();
```

```
        orientation=gluGetOrientation();                              //1

        vpLoc=[m_SolarSystem getEyeposition];                         //2

        objectLoc=[m_SolarSystem getTargetLocation];                  //3

        offset.x=(objectLoc.x-vpLoc.x);
        offset.y=(objectLoc.y-vpLoc.y);
        offset.z=(objectLoc.z-vpLoc.z);

        offsetv.z=GLKVector3Distance(objectLoc,vpLoc);                //4

        dx=location.x-prevLocation.x;                                 //5
        dy=location.y-prevLocation.y;

        float multiplier;

        multiplier=frame.size.width/reference;

        glMatrixMode(GL_MODELVIEW);

        float c,s;
        float rad=scale*multiplier*dy/reference;

        s=sinf(rad*.5);                                               //6
        c=cosf(rad*.5);

        tempQ=GLKQuaternionMake(s,0.0,0.0,c);            //Rotate around the X-axis.
        orientation=GLKQuaternionMultiply(tempQ,orientation);

        rad=scale*multiplier*dx/reference;

        s=sinf(rad*.5);
        c=cosf(rad*.5);

        tempQ=GLKQuaternionMake(0.0,s,0.0,c);           //Rotate around the Y-axis.
        orientation=GLKQuaternionMultiply(tempQ,orientation);

        matrix3=GLKMatrix3MakeWithQuaternion(orientation);

        matrix3=GLKMatrix3Transpose(matrix3);                         //7
        offsetv=GLKMatrix3MultiplyVector3(matrix3, offsetv);

        vpLoc.x=objectLoc.x+offsetv.x;                                //8
        vpLoc.y=objectLoc.y+offsetv.y;
        vpLoc.z=objectLoc.z+offsetv.z;

        [m_SolarSystem setEyeposition:vpLoc];

        [m_SolarSystem lookAtTarget];                                 //9
}
```

So, what's going on here?

▓ First we get the cached quaternion from miniGLU, in line 1, along with the viewpoint's xyz location from the solar-system object in line 2. Since that hasn't been added yet, feel free to add that now. It is simply a getter for the already existing m_Eyeposition object in the solar-system controller.

▓ Line 3 gets the target's location. In this case, the target is merely earth. With that in hand, we need to find the offset of our eye point from the earth's center and then calculate that distance, as in line 4.

▓ Line 5 takes the screen coordinates of the previous and current positions, so we know just how much we moved since the last time.

▓ Lines 6ff create a fractional rotation for each new position of the touch. Using the actual orientation quaternion (recovered in line 1) ensures that the new orientation from each touch position is preserved, representing the cumulative rotations of the eye point. The three values of scale, multiplier, and reference are all arbitrary. Scale is fixed and was used for some fine-tuning to ensure things moved at just the right speed that ideally will match that of your finger. The multiplier is handy for orientation changes because it is a scaling factor that is based on the screen's current width and a reference value that is also arbitrary.

Those are then multiplied against the x and y deltas and passed into the quaternion that is used to generate the final matrix, as in line 7.

▓ Line 7 takes the new matrix and multiplies it against the offset vector to transform it to the new position, while lines 8ff actually perform the translation to the new position and updates the solar-system controller.

▓ And finally, earth is reentered in line 9.

Ready? Ha-ha! Not quite. In initLighting(), ensure that glShadeModel() is set to GL_SMOOTH, check that the fill light 2 is disabled, and, most importantly, delete the line that attenuates the sunlight.

And of course, make sure to modify the headers as needed, but you probably already know that. We hope you will now be able to move the earth around at will. You should see something akin to Figure 8-4. And notice that you should see the sun, albeit much smaller now, pop in and out.

Figure 8-4. *The hover mode lets you rotate the arth at will.*

So, that's part one of today's exercise. Remember those lens flare things from Chapter 7? Now we can put them to use.

Adding Some Flare

From Chapter 7, grab the four source files from the lens flare exercise, and add them to your project along with the artwork. This will require some substantial updates to your main execute method in the solar-system controller, mainly for managing the lens flare object in terms of both positioning and highlighting.

Something like a lens flare effect has all sorts of small issues that will be addressed. Namely, if the flare's source object, in the case the sun, goes behind the earth, the flare itself should vanish. Also note that it won't vanish immediately but will actually fade out. There are a couple of new utility routines that need to be added before the flare itself can be rendered.

For starters, though, you'll need to allocate both the lens flare object and a new texture object for rendering the sun. Add the following two lines to the `init` routine of the solar-system controller:

```
m_LensFlare=[[LensFlare alloc]init];

m_FlareSource= m_FlareSource=[[OpenGLCreateTexture
getObject]loadTexture:@"gimp_sun3.png"];
```

Now is the time to dump any image utilities over into their own routine. I've created OpenGLCreateTexture for this and have moved loadTexture() from the solar-system controller to here. This will help support the above call. The .png file can be whatever you want that will replace the current 3D sun model. What we want this for is to draw a flat bitmap of the sun where the spherical model would normally render as it has done in the past. The reason is that we can finely control the look of our star to make it resemble more closely how the eye might perceive this. The stark yellow ball, while technically more accurate, just doesn't look right because any optical receptor to this would add all sorts of various distortions, reflections, and highlights (lens flares, for example). Shaders could be employed that mathematically model the optics of the eye, for example, but that's a lot of work for a fuzzy ball-like-thing for the time being. You can download my own artwork from the Apress site if you choose. Or just copy something to suit your own tastes. Figure 8-5 is what I am using with translucent background. Interesting enough, this image fools my own eyes enough to make my brain think that I am actually looking at something too bright, because it causes all sorts of eyestrain when I stare at it.

This uses a technique called *billboarding*, which takes a flat 2D texture and keeps it aimed toward the viewer no matter what where they are. It permits complex and fairly random organic objects (things called *trees* I think) to be easily depicted while using only simple textures. As your viewpoint changes, the billboard objects rotate to compensate.

Figure 8-5. *The sun image used to give a more authentic-looking glow*

Add the following to the interface definition for the **solar-system controller**:

```
LensFlare *m_LensFlare;
GLKTextureInfo *m_FlareSource;
```

Next, move the **createTexture** module created in Chapter 7 over, and add it to this project in its own file, such as OpenGLCreateTexture.mm. This way, texture generation is no longer confined to the planet object but accessible by anyone. When done, add the contents of Listing 8-9 for a more flexible rendering routine. What this does is draw a rectangular texture to the screen in orthographic mode. This means they would be unaffected by perspective. That way, you can draw textures near the viewpoint or way in the background behind other stuff and still count on them being the same size no matter what. Something like this is very handy when drawing text labels, for example, to the screen. Since OpenGL has no native text support, any labels must be drawn as any other texture. Also, UI elements can be drawn to the GL layer as well using these techniques.

Listing 8-9. *A more flexible 2D texture renderer to support the addition of lens flares*

```
-(void)renderTextureAt:(CGPoint)position  name:(GLuint)name
       size:(GLfloat)size r:(GLfloat)r g:(GLfloat)g b:(GLfloat)b a:(GLfloat)a;       //1
{

    float scaledX,scaledY;
    GLfloat zoomBias=.1;
    GLfloat scaledSize;

    static const GLfloat squareVertices[] =
    {
       -1.0f, -1.0f, 0.0,
        1.0f, -1.0f, 0.0,
       -1.0f,  1.0f, 0.0,
        1.0f,  1.0f, 0.0,
    };

    static  GLfloat textureCoords[] =
    {
        0.0, 0.0,
        1.0, 0.0,
        0.0, 1.0,
        1.0, 1.0
    };

    CGRect frame = [[UIScreen mainScreen] bounds];
    float aspectRatio=frame.size.height/frame.size.width;

    scaledX=2.0*position.x/frame.size.width;
    scaledY=(2.0*position.y/frame.size.height)*aspectRatio;

    glDisable(GL_DEPTH_TEST);
    glDisable(GL_LIGHTING);                                                          //2

    glDisable(GL_CULL_FACE);
    glDisableClientState(GL_COLOR_ARRAY);

    glMatrixMode(GL_PROJECTION);
    glPushMatrix();
    glLoadIdentity();

    glOrthof(-1,1,-1.0*aspectRatio,1.0*aspectRatio, -1, 1);                          //3

    glMatrixMode(GL_MODELVIEW);
    glPushMatrix();
    glLoadIdentity();
```

```
        glTranslatef(scaledX,scaledY,0);

        scaledSize=zoomBias*size;

        glScalef(scaledSize,scaledSize, 1);

        glVertexPointer(3, GL_FLOAT, 0, squareVertices);
        glEnableClientState(GL_VERTEX_ARRAY);

        glEnable(GL_TEXTURE_2D);
        glEnable(GL_BLEND);
            glBlendFunc(GL_ONE,GL_ONE_MINUS_SRC_COLOR);
        glBindTexture(GL_TEXTURE_2D,name);
        glTexCoordPointer(2, GL_FLOAT,0,textureCoords);
        glEnableClientState(GL_TEXTURE_COORD_ARRAY);

        glColor4f(r,g,b,a);

        glDrawArrays(GL_TRIANGLE_STRIP, 0, 4);

        glMatrixMode(GL_PROJECTION);
        glPopMatrix();

        glMatrixMode(GL_MODELVIEW);
        glPopMatrix();

        glEnable(GL_DEPTH_TEST);
        glEnable(GL_LIGHTING);
}
```

A few notes are needed for this:

 ▨ What this routine does, as evidenced by its parameter list in line 1, is
   to draw a texture to a specific screen-relative position. The name
   parameter is merely its OpenGL ES handle. The color values can be
   used to tint the image in whatever way you want. Otherwise, most of
   the code resembles the original bouncy square demo from the first
   chapter, with some exceptions, of course.

 ▨ Lines 2ff turn off the lighting, because we don't want it to affect our
   images at this level. Likewise, face culling is switched off to ensure
   that this block is actually rendered just in case another routine
   specified the windingness to be different from what we have here. And
   to be safe, ensure that the color array client state is disabled.

▨ glOrthof() in line 3 is a new routine that changes the projection matrix otherwise set up in setClipping(). Here you establish a viewing volume with the six sides similar to setting the viewing frustum elsewhere. However, the zNear and zFar planes are a bit different. In orthographic projection mode, the depth of your space is mapped linearly, so a z of .5 is going to interpreted a lot differently than a similar z value when in perspective mode. So, mixing the two can have unexpected results if you are relying on depth buffering to manage proper z-culling. If you want to ensure your 2D object is always visible, then set zNear to 0 and the depth value to 0.

Setting ortho's windows from -1 to 1 means that any 2D objects drawn to the screen will use normalized coordinates, instead of traditional screen coordinates. So something placed at 0,0 will be exactly in the center of the screen. renderTextureAt() uses values based on actual pixel positioning, but those are converted to the normalized ortho coordinates when actually going out to the screen.

> **Note**   In this routine, a lot of necessary state calls are made all to ensure that the image will render as expected, but they come with a fairly high overhead. You want to change the state as little as possible if speed is critical. This illustrates one of the issues with a state machine such as OpenGL, because it holds a particular state until explicitly changed elsewhere. That means you shouldn't expect a state to be what you really need, forcing lengthy and frequently redundant code blocks to ensure you get what you want. A lot of optimizing tricks can be employed to minimize state changes. One easy way would be to batch the texture calls together as much as possible and then call the state routines only once for each batch operation.

Both the lens flare manager, which I call LensFlare.mm, and the individual flare object need to be modified. To the execute method of LensFlare.mm I've added two new parameters. execute() should now look like this:

```
-(void)execute:(CGRect)frame source:(CGPoint)source scale:(float)scale
alpha:(float)alpha
```

scale sizes the various individual flare objects, and alpha sets their translucency. These get passed on to the actual flare object when called. The flare's own execute routine is actually called renderFlareAt() and should look like this:

```
-(void)renderFlareAt:(CGPoint)position  scale:(float)scale alpha:(float)alpha
{
    [[OpenGLCreateTexture getObject]renderTextureAt:position
    name:m_Name size:m_Size*scale  r:m_Red*alpha g:m_Green*alpha b:m_Blue*alpha a:alpha];
}
```

And from the lens flare object, ensure that `renderFlareAt()` is called with the new parameters.

Another three helper routines we need are `gluGetScreenLocation()`, `gluProject()`, and `gluMultMatrixVector3f()`, which will return the screen coordinates of a specified 3D point by mimicking exactly what is happening inside OpenGL. With this we can get the screen location of the sun needed to aim the flare in the proper direction. One end will lead right to the sun, while the other will mirror that. To achieve this, add Listing 8-10 to miniGLU.

Listing 8-10. *Gets the screen coordinates of a given 3D location*

```
GLint gluProject(GLfloat objx, GLfloat objy, GLfloat objz,
                         const GLfloat modelMatrix[16],
                         const GLfloat projMatrix[16],
                         const GLint viewport[4],
                         GLfloat *winx, GLfloat *winy, GLfloat *winz)
{
    float in[4];
    float out[4];

    in[0]=objx;                                                      //1
    in[1]=objy;
    in[2]=objz;
    in[3]=1.0;

    gluMultMatrixVector3f (modelMatrix, in, out);                    //2

    gluMultMatrixVector3f (projMatrix, out, in);

    if (in[3] == 0.0)
        in[3]=1;

    in[0] /= in[3];
    in[1] /= in[3];
    in[2] /= in[3];

    /* Map x, y and z to range 0-1 */

    in[0] = in[0] * 0.5 + 0.5;                                       //3
    in[1] = in[1] * 0.5 + 0.5;
    in[2] = in[2] * 0.5 + 0.5;

    /* Map x,y to viewport */
    in[0] = in[0] * viewport[2] + viewport[0];
    in[1] = in[1] * viewport[3] + viewport[1];

    *winx=in[0];
    *winy=in[1];
    *winz=in[3];

    return(GL_TRUE);
}
```

```
void gluGetScreenLocation(GLfloat xa,GLfloat ya,GLfloat za,GLfloat *sx, GLfloat
*sy,GLfloat *sz)
{
        GLfloat mvmatrix[16];
        GLfloat projmatrix[16];
        GLfloat x,y,z;
        GLint viewport[4];

        glGetIntegerv(GL_VIEWPORT,viewport);                                    //4
        glGetFloatv(GL_MODELVIEW_MATRIX,mvmatrix);
        glGetFloatv(GL_PROJECTION_MATRIX,projmatrix);

        gluProject(xa,ya,za,mvmatrix,projmatrix,viewport,&x,&y,&z);

        y=viewport[3]-y;                                                        //5

        *sx=x;
        *sy=y;

        if(sz!=NULL)
            *sz=z;

        float scale=[[UIScreen mainScreen] scale];                             //6

        *sx/=scale;
        *sy/=scale;
}

void gluMultMatrixVector3f(const GLfloat matrix[16], const GLfloat in[4],GLfloat out[4])
{
        int i;

        for (i=0; i<4; i++)
        {
                out[i] =
                in[0] * matrix[0*4+i] +
                in[1] * matrix[1*4+i] +
                in[2] * matrix[2*4+i] +
                in[3] * matrix[3*4+i];
        }
}
```

In gluProject() we supply the needed matrices along with the desired xyz coordinates we're investigating, and it returns the screen xyz (yes, z) of the point's projected location.

▓ Lines 1ff map the object coordinates to an array that will then be multiplied by the modelMatrix (supplied as one of the arguments).

- The multiplication is done via another GLUT helper routine at lines 2ff. First the projection matrix and then the model matrix operate on our object's xyz coordinates. (Remember, the first transform in the list is the last to be executed.) Note that the first call to gluMultMatrixVector3f() passes the "in" array, followed by the "out," while the second one passes the two arrays in reverse order. There's nothing clever here—the second instance reverses the use of the two just to recycle the existing arrays.

- In lines 3ff, the resulting values of the earlier calculations are normalized and then mapped against the screen's dimensions, giving us the final values.

- We'd likely never to have to call gluProject() directly; instead, the caller is gluGetScreenLocation(), which merely gets the needed matrices in lines 4ff, passes them on to gluProject(), and retrieves the screen coordinates. Because of the inversion of the Y-axis that OpenGL ES does, we need to uninvert it in line 5.

- And one final tweak comes courtesy of the Retina display, in line 6. The de facto screen dimensions on the iPhone are 320x480. What the scale value is used for is to scale up any screen coordinates to handle the higher resolution. Scale would be 1 on any pre-Retina devices, while it would be 2 otherwise.

The execute() routine in the SolarSystemController must be modified quite a bit to manage the calling and placement of the lens flare, while along with an executePlanet() adds some new parameters to actually identify where the flare should be located on the screen. Both are given in Listing 8-11.

Listing 8-11. *The modified execute() and executePlanet() methods*

```
-(void)execute
{
    float earth_sx,earth_sy,earth_sz,earth_sr;
    float sun_sx,sun_sy,sun_sz,sun_sr;
    GLfloat paleYellow[]={1.0,1.0,0.3,1.0};
    GLfloat white[]={1.0,1.0,1.0,1.0};
    GLfloat cyan[]={0.0,1.0,1.0,1.0};
    GLfloat     black[]={0.0,0.0,0.0,0.0};
    GLfloat sunPos[4]={0.0,0.0,0.0,1.0};

    [self setClipping];

    glMatrixMode(GL_MODELVIEW);
    glShadeModel(GL_SMOOTH);
    glEnable(GL_LIGHTING);
    glEnable(GL_BLEND);
    glBlendFunc(GL_SRC_ALPHA, GL_ONE_MINUS_SRC_ALPHA);
```

```
    glPushMatrix();

    glTranslatef(-m_Eyeposition.x,-m_Eyeposition.y,-m_Eyeposition.z);          //1

     glLightfv(SS_SUNLIGHT,GL_POSITION,sunPos);
    glEnable(SS_SUNLIGHT);

      glMaterialfv(GL_FRONT_AND_BACK, GL_EMISSION, paleYellow);

       [self executePlanet:m_Sun sx:&sun_sx sy:&sun_sy sz:&sun_sz           //2
            screenRadius:&sun_sr render:FALSE];

      glMaterialfv(GL_FRONT_AND_BACK, GL_EMISSION, black);

    glPopMatrix();

    if((m_LensFlare!=NULL) && (sun_sz>0))                                    //3
    {
        float sunWidth=75;                                                   //4

        sunWidth*=(sun_sr/5.0);

        [[OpenGLCreateTexture getObject]renderTextureInRect:                 //5
        CGRectMake(sun_sx-sunWidth/2.0, sun_sy-sunWidth/2.0,sunWidth,sunWidth)
        name:m_FlareSource.name depth:-10 r:1.0 g:1.0 b:1.0 a:1.0];
    }

    glEnable(SS_FILLLIGHT2);

    glMatrixMode(GL_MODELVIEW);
    glPushMatrix();

    glTranslatef(-m_Eyeposition.x,-m_Eyeposition.y,-m_Eyeposition.z);          //6

    glMaterialfv(GL_FRONT_AND_BACK, GL_DIFFUSE, cyan);
    glMaterialfv(GL_FRONT_AND_BACK, GL_SPECULAR, white);

    [self executePlanet:m_Earth sx:&earth_sx sy:&earth_sy sz:&earth_sz       //7
        screenRadius:&earth_sr render:TRUE];

    glPopMatrix();


    if((m_LensFlare!=NULL) && (sun_sz>0))                                    //8
    {
        float scale=1.0;
        CGRect frame = [[UIScreen mainScreen] bounds];
        float delX=frame.size.width/2.0-sun_sx;
        float delY=frame.size.height/2.0-sun_sy;
        float grazeDist=earth_sr+sun_sr;
        float percentVisible=1.0;
        float vanishDist=earth_sr-sun_sr;
```

```
        float distanceBetweenBodies=sqrt(delX*delX+delY*delY);

        if((distanceBetweenBodies>vanishDist) && (distanceBetweenBodies<grazeDist))
        {
            percentVisible=(distanceBetweenBodies-vanishDist)/(2.0*sun_sr);

            if(percentVisible>1.3)                                              //9
                percentVisible=1.3;
            else if(percentVisible<0.2)
                percentVisible=1.3;
        }
        else if(distanceBetweenBodies>grazeDist)
        {
            percentVisible=1.0;
        }
        else
        {
            percentVisible=0.0;
        }

        scale=STANDARD_FOV/m_FieldOfView;

        if(percentVisible>0.0)
        [m_LensFlare execute:[[UIScreen mainScreen]applicationFrame]           //10
        source:CGPointMake(sun_sx,sun_sy) scale:scale alpha:percentVisible];
    }
}
                                                                               //11
-(void)executePlanet:(Planet *)planet sx:(float *)sx sy:(float *)sy sz:(float *)sz
        screenRadius:(float *)screenRadius render:(BOOL)render
{
    static GLfloat angle=0.0;
    GLKVector3 planetPos;
    float temp;
    float distance;
    CGRect frame = [[UIScreen mainScreen] bounds];

    glPushMatrix();

    planetPos=[planet getPosition];

    glTranslatef(planetPos.x,planetPos.y,planetPos.z);

    if(render)
        [planet execute];                                                      //12

    distance=GLKVector3Distance(m_Eyeposition, planetPos);
    temp=(0.5*frame.size.width)/tanf(GLKMathDegreesToRadians(m_FieldOfView)/2.0);
    *screenRadius=temp*[planet getRadius]/distance;
```

```
gluGetScreenLocation(planetPos.x,-planetPos.y,planetPos.z,sx,sy,sz);        //13

glPopMatrix();

angle+=.5;
}
```

In addition to the previous, add the following to the header:

```
#define STANDARD_FOV                    30.0                //in degrees
```

OK, now for the chalk talk:

- You'll notice that two identical `glTranslatef()` calls are made. The first one in line 1 sets things up for line 2 results. But we need to pop it off the stack when our custom sun image is rendered in line 4. It needs to be called again in line 6, when the earth is drawn to the screen.

- In line 2 it looks like we're rendering the sun. But not really. This is to extract the location on the main screen that the sun would actually draw to. The last parameter, `render`, will have the routine just return the screen location and expected radius but not actually draw the sun.

- Line 3 decides whether we should draw the new sun if a lens flare object has been created and if the sun is likely to be visible based on its z-coordinate. If z is negative, then it is behind us, so we can skip it altogether.

- Lines 4f figure out how large to render the new texture. Naturally we can't use just the radius, because the texture is considerably larger to handle the main image plus the glow. The various values used are rather arbitrary in calculating the `sunWidth, but they balance out nicely.`

- The call to `renderTextureInRect()` in line 5 makes sure that the sun's rect is centered by subtracting half of `sunWidth` from the screen x and screen y locations.

  As a side effect of the way this is drawn, depth cueing doesn't work very well, so z-buffering cannot be used. By drawing it as the first item, we are assured that the closer objects will properly write over any part of the image as needed.

- Line 6 is a repeat of the first line, but this time used to render the earth in line 7. Got that? Note that we get the earth's screen x and y values, along with the radius as we did for the sun earlier.

▒ Then we come down to where the flare is actually rendered starting with lines 8ff. Most of the code here largely handles one basic effect: what happens when the sun goes behind the earth. Naturally, the lens flare will vanish, but it won't pop in or out instantly because the sun has a finite diameter. So, values such as the grazeDist and vanishDist tell us when the sun first intersects the earth, starting the dimming process, and when it is finally covered completely, blanking out the flare images. Using the earth's screen x and y values as well as those for the sun, it becomes an easy matter to specify a fade function.

▒ Lines 9ff actually determine the brightness of the flares. percentVisible is "full" brightness at 1.0 but can actually be a little more, because it multiplies the colors of the flare by this number. Since not all colors would be maxed out at 1.0, I can actually go a little higher. But why? When the sun goes behind the earth, one might expect the final beams of light to be refracted by the atmosphere just a tad, magnifying the brightness for one short and, in this case, barely visible flash. (You get extra credit if you want to make it one of the fabled green flashes.)

▒ The flare's execute method is called in line 10. The sun's screen x and screen y values serve as the sourceLocation parameter that causes the lens flare.

▒ We also need an updated executePlanet() to return the new values used to place the sun and the flare images, as in line 11.

▒ One of the enhancements is in line 12, where we can block the actual rendering of the body if all we're interested in are their screen parameters.

▒ And finally (it's about time, eh?), we have the call to the new gluGetScreenLocation helper function, line 13, in miniGLU.mm, covered earlier.

To the planet object, add a getter routine for the radius that, in this case, is identical to the m_Scale variable:

```
-(float)getRadius
{
    return m_Scale;
}
```

That should do it. I am sure you'll be able to compile with no errors or warnings, because you're just that good. And because you are just that good, you will likely be rewarded with the images in Figure 8-6. And feel free to play with ambient light and specular lighting as I have done. The effect might not be very realistic, but it looks very nice.

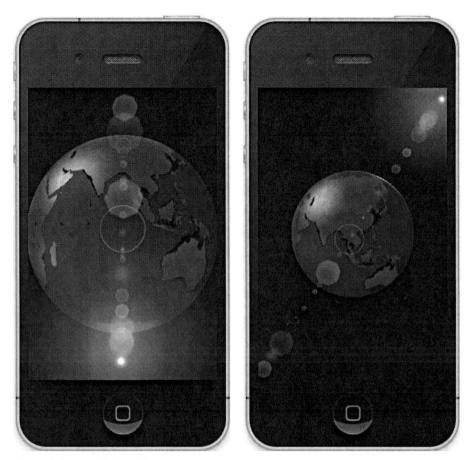

Figure 8-6. Look, Ma! Lens flare!

Seeing Stars

Of course, no solar-system model would be complete without some nice stars in the background, would it? Up to this point all of the examples have been small enough to print their entirety here in the text, but now that will change just a bit as we add a simple star field in the background. The difference is largely in the database required that you will need to fetch from the Apress web site, because it will contain just over 500 stars down to a magnitude of 4.0 as well as an additional database containing constellation outlines and names for a number of the more prominent groupings.

> **Note**   A star's magnitude is its apparent brightness; the larger the value, the dimmer the star is. The brightest star in the sky is Sirius, at a visual magnitude of -1.46. The dimmest stars visible to the naked eye are about magnitude 6.5. Binoculars top out at about 10th magnitude, while the Hubble Space Telescope reaches way out to magnitude 31.5. Each whole number is a difference of about 2.5 times in actual brightness, so a star of magnitude 3 is about 2.5 times brighter than one that is magnitude 4.

Besides the triangular faces that OpenGL ES uses for creating solid models, you can also specify that each vertex of your model be rendered as a point image of a given magnitude and size. This proves a natural fit for our own little star field. Since this will eventually be paired up with a number of constellation outlines, let's create a new object that will support both kinds of data, as shown in Listings 8-12a and 8-12b. And while you're at it, ensure you have OpenGLOutlines.h and .mm from the site.

Listing 8-12a. The Constellation Collection header

```
#import <Foundation/Foundation.h>
#import "OpenGLOutlines.h"
#import "OpenGLStars.h"

@interface OpenGLConstellations : NSObject
{
    OpenGLOutlines *m_Outlines;
    OpenGLStars *m_Stars;

}

-(void)execute:(BOOL)constOutlinesOn names:(BOOL)constNamesOn;

@end
```

Listing 8-12b. The Constellation Collection body

```
#import "OpenGLConstellations.h"

@implementation OpenGLConstellations

- (id)init
{
    self = [super init];

    if (self)
    {
        m_Outlines=[[OpenGLOutlines alloc]init];
        m_Stars=[[OpenGLStars alloc]init];
    }

    return self;
}
```

```
-(void)execute:(BOOL)constOutlinesOn names:(BOOL)constNamesOn
{
    [m_Outlines execute: constOutlinesOn showNames: constNamesOn];
    [m_Stars execute];
}

@end
```

Not much to that one. So, let's go on to the star object itself, as shown in Listings 8-13a, 8-13b, and 8-13c. This will use a method of data "interleaving" that Apple recommends for the purpose of increasing performance.

Listing 8-13a. *The Star Container header*

```
#import <Foundation/Foundation.h>
#import <OpenGLES/ES1/gl.h>
#import <OpenGLES/ES1/glext.h>

struct starData                                                    //1
{
    GLfloat x;
    GLfloat y;
    GLfloat z;
    GLfloat mag;
    GLfloat r,g,b,a;
    GLint hdnum;
};

@interface OpenGLStars : NSObject
{
    struct starData *m_Data;
    int m_TotalStars;
}

-(void)execute;
-(void)init:(NSString *)filename;
-(id)init;

@end
```

Listing 8-13b. *The Star Container body*

```
#import "OpenGLUtils.h"
#import "OpenGLSolarSystem.h"
#import "OpenGLStars.h"
#import "miniGLU.h"

@implementation OpenGLStars

- (id)init
{
    self = [super init];
```

```
    if (self)
    {
        [self init:@"stars"];
    }

    return self;
}

-(void)init:(NSString *)filename
{
    NSArray *fatData;
    NSDictionary *dict;
    NSNumber *ra,*dec;
    starData *sd;
    float mag;
    float x,y,z;
    int i,j;

    m_TotalStars=0;

    NSString *thePath = [[NSBundle mainBundle]  pathForResource:filename
    ofType:@"plist"];

    fatData = [[NSArray alloc] initWithContentsOfFile:thePath];          //2

    m_TotalStars=[fatData count];

    m_Data=(struct starData *)malloc([fatData count]*sizeof(struct starData));

    for(i=0;i<m_TotalStars;i++)
    {
        dict=(NSDictionary *)[fatData objectAtIndex:i];

        ra=(NSNumber *)[dict objectForKey:@"ra"];                        //3
        dec=(NSNumber *)[dict objectForKey:@"dec"];

        [[OpenGLUtils getObject]sphereToRectTheta:[ra floatValue]/DEGREES_PER_RADIAN
        phi:[dec floatValue]/DEGREES_PER_RADIAN radius:STANDARD_RADIUS
        xprime:&x yprime:&y zprime:&z];

        //Create nice compressed data array.

        sd=(struct starData *)&m_Data[i];

        sd->x=x;
        sd->y=y;
        sd->z=z;
        sd->mag=[[dict objectForKey:@"mag"]floatValue];

        mag=1.0-sd->mag/4.0;                                            //4
```

```
        if(mag<.2)
            mag=.2;
        else if(mag>1.0)
            mag=1.0;

        sd->r=sd->g=sd->b=mag;

        sd->a=1.0;
        sd->hdnum=[[dict objectForKey:@"hdnum"]longValue];
    }
}

-(void)execute
{
    int len;
    GLfloat pointSize[2];

    glDisable(GL_LIGHTING);                                              //5
    glDisable(GL_TEXTURE_2D);
    glDisable(GL_DEPTH_TEST);

    glEnableClientState(GL_VERTEX_ARRAY);
    glEnableClientState(GL_COLOR_ARRAY);

    glMatrixMode(GL_MODELVIEW);
    glBlendFunc(GL_ONE, GL_ONE_MINUS_DST_ALPHA);
    glEnable(GL_BLEND);

    len=sizeof(struct starData);

    glColorPointer(4, GL_FLOAT, len, &m_Data->r);                       //6
    glVertexPointer(3,GL_FLOAT,len,m_Data);

    glGetFloatv(GL_SMOOTH_POINT_SIZE_RANGE,pointSize);                  //7
    glEnable(GL_POINT_SMOOTH);
    glPointSize(3.0);

    glDrawArrays(GL_POINTS,len,m_TotalStars);                          //8

    glDisableClientState(GL_VERTEX_ARRAY);
    glDisableClientState(GL_COLOR_ARRAY);
    glEnable(GL_DEPTH_TEST);
    glEnable(GL_LIGHTING);
}

@end
```

The stars are initially stored as a plist. That's not very efficient but works well for a small dataset. In Distant Suns, my stars are stored in a tightly packed binary file, which is nice for my 300,000-star database.

▓ In line 1 of Listing 8-13a, we define a structure for each star. Its position is in rectangular coordinates since that is what OpenGL expects, followed by a magnitude, colors, and something called the *hdnum*. The magnitude value in this structure is normalized and used in the RGBA fields. Because stars can actually be different colors—red giants and yellow dwarfs, for example—these values could encode their true shades were we going to do that.

The `hdnum` is the identifier for stars in the "Henry Draper Catalog," which covers most stars down to about magnitude 10. As with the colors, it is not used here except for possible testing and debugging.

▓ Next we jump to Listing 8-13b where we read in the data from the plist in line 2.

▓ Lines 3ff fetch the locations of each star and, using a helper function (Listing 8-14), convert the spherical coordinates to rectangular.

▓ Line 4 and the following lines take in the actual magnitude value and convert it to a normalized shade of gray, clamping the values from .2 to 1.0 and ensuring that the dimmest stars will still be visible.

▓ Now on to the execute method where lines 5ff disable stuff that might otherwise interfere with our renderings. The depth test is turned off to minimize interference of the points with the constellation outlines. We could have left z-buffering on and drawn the constellations lines a little bit behind the stars but at a slight loss of performance.

▓ The calls to set the color and vertex pointers in lines 6f make use of the `stride` parameter. Since the colors are in a format that OpenGL already understands (the RGBA quadruplet in floats), there is no need to have to extract them into their own array. So, all we need to do is to pass a pointer to the address of the first component (which happens to be red) and a value that tells the system how large the structure is so it knows where to pick up each successive color or vertex element in the case of vertex data.

▓ Lines 7ff tell the system how to render the points, both size and style. Size is specified by `glPointSize()` with a value of 3.0 pixels, which seems to work for both the standard and Retina displays. We can also have points that are either square or rounded. Since I don't know of any square stars last I checked, we can use rounded points by enabling `GL_POINT_SMOOTH` capabilities. And if we really want really nicely anti-aliased points, then blending needs to be activated for those to work. Figure 8-7 shows the difference between the three styles.

Note   If you want to draw really big stars, there is a limit to the maximum size that varies from machine to machine. You can check the size range using the `glGetFloatv()` call, in line 7. The simulator shows a range from .1 to 511 pixels, while the iPad 1 shows it as 1 to 511. Note that single pixel points are almost impossible to see on the Retina display.

Figure 8-7. *From left to right, a close-up on an 8-pixel-wide unsmoothed point, with smoothing, and with smoothing and blending*

▨ In line 8 we can finally draw the stars, followed by just some basic cleanup stuff.

I decided to add a utilities object, because the project gets a little more complicated. Create OpenGLUtils as a singleton, and add the contents of Listing 14.

Listing 8-14. *A helper function to convert spherical coordinates to rectangular added to* OpenGLUtils

```
#import "OpenGLSolarSystem.h"
#import "OpenGLUtils.h"

static OpenGLUtils *m_Singleton;

@implementation OpenGLUtils

+(OpenGLUtils *)getObject
{
        @synchronized(self)
        {
                if(m_Singleton==nil)
                {
                        [[self alloc]init];
                }
        }

        return m_Singleton;
}
```

```
+(id)allocWithZone:(NSZone *)zone
{
    @synchronized(self)
        {
        if (m_Singleton == nil)
            {
            m_Singleton = [super allocWithZone:zone];

            return m_Singleton;  // Assignment and return on first alUI.
        }
    }
    return nil; //On subsequent allocation attempts, return nil.
}

-(void)sphereToRectTheta:(float)theta phi:(float)phi radius:(float)radius
                xprime:(float *)xprime   yprime:(float *)yprime zprime:(float *)zprime
{
    float cos_theta,sin_theta,cos_phi,sin_phi;

    phi=RADIANS_PER_90_DEGREES-phi;        /* phi is to be measured starting from the z-
axis. */

    sin_theta=sin(theta);
    cos_theta=cos(theta);

    sin_phi=sin(phi);
    cos_phi=cos(phi);

    *xprime=(float)(radius*cos_theta*sin_phi);
    *yprime=(float)(radius*cos_phi);
    *zprime=(float)-1.0*(radius*sin_theta*sin_phi);
}

@end
```

Now we can go ahead and concentrate on drawing outlines for some of the major constellations. As with the stars, you need to fetch the data file, `outlines.plist` from Apress. First we'll cover the rendering of the names to the screen.

Unfortunately, for all that OpenGL gives us, text support is not one of them. Thus, it is up to us, the long-suffering engineers, to implement our own text manager. There are three ways to do this. The first is to write text out as a collection of vectors, but that's a poor solution because it looks terrible along with being a CPU hog. The second is to generate a texture for each text string, while the third is to generate a "font atlas" (also known as *sprite sheets*). Font atlases are used to contain multiple related images on a single bitmap, with each image plucked out as needed. For text, this would have all possible characters jammed together along with reference data specifying the location of each character. The second way, generating a texture, is easier to implement, but font atlases are far more flexible, because it will let you put up arbitrary lines of text. I vote for the easy one. With this in mind, I can introduce you to the `OpenGLText` manager in Listings 8-15a and 8-15b.

Listing 8-15a. *The header for creating a label texture*

```
#import <Foundation/Foundation.h>

@interface OpenGLText : NSObject
{
        GLuint m_Name;
        NSUInteger m_Width;
        NSUInteger m_Height;
        GLfloat m_MaxS;
        GLfloat m_MaxT;
}

-(id)initWithText:(NSString*)string size:(CGSize)size
alignment:(UITextAlignment)alignment font:(UIFont*)font;
-(void)renderAtPoint:(CGPoint)point depth:(CGFloat)depth red:(float)red
green:(float)green blue:(float)blue alpha:(float)alpha;

-(void)drawAtPoint:(CGPoint)point depth:(GLfloat)depth red:(GLfloat)red
green:(GLfloat)green blue:(GLfloat)blue alpha:(GLfloat)alpha tname:(GLuint)tname;

@end
```

Listing 8-15b. *The body for creating a label texture*

```
#import "OpenGLSolarSystem.h"
#import "OpenGLText.h"
#import "OpenGLCreateTexture.h"

@implementation OpenGLText

-(id)initWithText:(NSString*)string size:(CGSize)size
alignment:(UITextAlignment)alignment font:(UIFont*)font                          //1
{
    NSUInteger width;
    NSUInteger height;
    NSUInteger i;
    CGContextRef context;
    void* data;
    CGColorSpaceRef  colorSpace;
    GLint saveName;

     glEnable(GL_TEXTURE_2D);

     width = size.width;

     if((width != 1) && (width & (width - 1)))                                    //2
     {
         i = 1;

         while(i < width)
               i *= 2;
```

```
        width = i;
    }
    height = size.height;

    if((height != 1) && (height & (height - 1)))
    {
        i = 1;

        while(i < height)
            i *= 2;

        height = i;
    }

    colorSpace = CGColorSpaceCreateDeviceGray();                    //3

    data = calloc(height, width);                                  //4

    context = CGBitmapContextCreate(data, width, height, 8, width, colorSpace,
                            kCGImageAlphaNone);

    CGColorSpaceRelease(colorSpace);

    CGContextSetGrayFillColor(context, 1.0, 1.0);                  //5

    UIGraphicsPushContext(context);                                //6

    [string drawInRect:CGRectMake(0, 0, size.width, size.height) withFont:font
    lineBreakMode:UILineBreakModeWordWrap alignment:alignment];

    UIGraphicsPopContext();

    glGenTextures(1, &m_Name);                                     //7
    glGetIntegerv(GL_TEXTURE_BINDING_2D, &saveName);

    glBindTexture(GL_TEXTURE_2D, m_Name);
    glTexParameteri(GL_TEXTURE_2D,GL_TEXTURE_MIN_FILTER,GL_LINEAR);
    glTexParameteri(GL_TEXTURE_2D,GL_TEXTURE_MAG_FILTER,GL_LINEAR);

    glTexImage2D(GL_TEXTURE_2D, 0, GL_LUMINANCE, width, height, 0,   //8
                GL_LUMINANCE,  GL_UNSIGNED_BYTE, data);

    glBindTexture(GL_TEXTURE_2D, saveName);                        //9

    m_Width=width;
    m_Height=height;
    m_MaxS=size.width/(float)width;
    m_MaxT=size.height/(float)height;

    CGContextRelease(context);
    free(data);

    return self;
}
```

```
-(void)renderAtPoint:(CGPoint)point depth:(CGFloat)depth red:(float)red
green:(float)green

blue:(float)blue alpha:(float)alpha
{

    float scale;

    int boxRect[4];

    glBindTexture(GL_TEXTURE_2D,m_Name);

    glEnable(GL_BLEND);
    glBlendFunc(GL_ONE,GL_ONE_MINUS_SRC_ALPHA);

    glDisable(GL_DEPTH_TEST);
    glEnable(GL_TEXTURE_2D);
    glDisable(GL_LIGHTING);

    glColor4f(red, green, blue, alpha);

    boxRect[0]=0;
    boxRect[1]=0;
    boxRect[2]=m_Width;
    boxRect[3]=m_Height;

    scale=[[UIScreen mainScreen] scale];                                    //10

    glTexParameteriv(GL_TEXTURE_2D, GL_TEXTURE_CROP_RECT_OES,(GLint *)boxRect);  //11

    glDrawTexfOES(point.x*scale, (480-point.y)*scale, depth, m_Width,m_Height);  //12

    glDisable(GL_TEXTURE_2D);
    glEnable(GL_DEPTH_TEST);
    glDisable(GL_BLEND);
    glEnable(GL_LIGHTING);
}

@end
```

Here's what is happening:

▨ The parameters in line 1 include the string, its size as determined by using the ever-so-handy sizeWithFont() method of NSString, the alignment, and the UIFont.

▨ Here in lines 2ff, the size of the desired texture is upped to be power-of-two (POT) needed for older devices. You can check the APPLE_texture_2D_limited_npot extension. If it exists, any size textures will work.

▨ We need to first use CoreGraphics to generate a bitmap with the desired text, in line 3, and then convert it to an OpenGL ES texture. Lines 4ff now allocate memory for the actual data and then create a new bitmap context with the data block.

- Setting the fill color in line 5 ensures that the filled text characters are visible.

- Lines 6ff push the new context on the stack, write the text to that context, and then pop it back off.

- Now the OpenGL texture is created in the standard way with lines 7ff preparing the way and line 8 actually generating texture itself. Note that to be a good neighbor, the new texture's name is only temporarily bound, and the previously bound texture is restored in line 9.

Jumping down to `renderAtPoint()`, the only other method in this object, we use a slightly different and more simple form of drawing a texture to the screen with `glDrawTexfOES()`. While Apple supports this, remember that the `OES` suffix says that there is no guarantee that this call will be available on other OpenGL ES implantations, so use at your own risk. Moreover, you can't do any transformations on it either.

- `glDrawTexfOES()` doesn't recognize the `contentScaleFactor` used to get OpenGL ES to recognize a high-resolution Retina display. So, we must scale things up manually in line 10.

- `glDrawTexfOES()` brings in a new texture parameter in line 11, `GL_TEXTURE_CROP_RECT_OES using the supplied boxRect`. This lets you clip only part of the texture to use for display. Here we're saying that we want the entire content.

- And finally the label is drawn to the buffer. Notice how the scale factor is used in both x and y in line 12.

Now for the loader/renderer for the outlines themselves. Because of the length of the rest of the code and because a lot of it resembles the star module, only excerpts will be used here to highlight the noteworthy parts.

When read from the plist, the data for each constellation's outline is converted to an array of floats that OpenGL will understand and then store back in the original dictionaries as an `NSData` object. That way, the original data is kept around if need be while being easily linked with the OpenGL representation of the same data, as shown in Listing 8-16, also in `OpenGLOutlines`.

Listing 8-16. *Allocating the vertex buffers*

```
coordArray=[dict objectForKey:@"coordinates"];
numpoints=[coordArray count];
numbytes=numpoints*3*sizeof(GLfloat);

data=(GLfloat *)malloc(numbytes);

for(j=0;j<numpoints;j++)
{

    coords=[coordArray objectAtIndex:j];

    ra=(NSNumber *)[coords objectForKey:@"ra"];
    dec=(NSNumber *)[coords objectForKey:@"dec"];
```

```
[[OpenGLUtils getObject]sphereToRectTheta:15.0*[ra floatValue]/DEGREES_PER_RADIAN
    phi:[dec floatValue]/DEGREES_PER_RADIAN radius:STANDARD_RADIUS
    xprime:&x yprime:&y zprime:&z];

index=j*3;

data[index+0]=x;
data[index+1]=y;
data[index+2]=z;
}
```

```
nsdata=[[NSData alloc]initWithBytes:data length:numbytes];
```

```
[dict setObject:nsdata forKey:@"binarydata"];
```

As with point sizes, OpenGL will likewise let you vary the width of the lines using
`glLineWidth()`, which takes a `GLfloat` as a parameter. `glLineWidth()` doesn't know
about Retina scaling, so if you want to have the lines look the same across platforms,
make sure to double the width when appropriate.

One final thing to add: allocation and invocation. In the solar-system controller, allocate
the constellation object, the container for the stars, lines and names, and invoke it. (I'll
let you figure out when and where.) The Boolean parameters switch on the particular
displayable, needed for when the UI is added:

```
[m_Constellations execute:TRUE names:m_TRUE];
```

Now we're ready to see something. With a little luck and perseverance, you might have
something that looks like Figure 8-8.

Figure 8-8. *Our one-planet solar system*

Cool, eh? And of course, if you don't see the above, recheck all of your code, and feel free to cheat by just getting the entire project from Apress. Of course it's missing the clouds, but those will be handled a little later.

At this stage, a small problem arises as OpenGL ES shows off a slightly uglier side of things. Examine the lines closely on your emulator or on a non-Retina device. They don't look particularly good, do they? Anti-aliasing of lines was something the OpenGL ES standards committee apparently felt they could leave out, even though it is standard in the desktop libraries.

> **Note**   The simulator can generate anti-aliased lines, but not so when run on real hardware.

Why? Beats me. But the smooth lines we take for granted on desktops are absent on the handhelds. The Retina display makes anti-aliasing pretty much moot simply because of its resolution. However, on non-Retina devices, including the iPad (as of this writing), it still looks pretty rough. There are a couple of workarounds, one more of a hack than the other. The first and more hacky of the two, dumps the normal OpenGL lines support and substitutes really long and thin textured objects, because they can be smoothed out. A nice side effect is that (with a little extra work) you can get dotted lines as well. The less hacky version, but a lot easier to do, is to use a feature found in iOS 4 and after: multisampled anti-aliasing (MSAA to its friends).

Multisampling as a means toward anti-aliasing requires the addition of a special multisample frame buffer object. Your image is initially written to the special buffer in a resolution that is higher than your final display. It is then "resolved" into a smaller buffer, with the final pixels representing blended versions of the originals. Typically the multisampling buffer is four times larger than the final one; that is, each of the final pixels is generally a weighted average of the four pixels in the former (not unlike texture filtering covered in Chapter 5). This is also called full-screen anti-aliasing, because that is exactly what it does. The benefits are a smoother image; the drawbacks include a performance hit and extra memory used for the off-screen buffer. Figure 8-9 (left) shows one of our lines with no MSAA, while Figure 8-9 (right) shows it with MSAA turned on.

Figure 8-9. Multisample anti-aliasing, before (left) and after (right)

Another nice addition in iOS5's GLKit is support for MSAA that is built into GLKView. Previously, it took about 40 lines of code, but now all you need to do is to add the following to viewDidLoad() in your view controller:

```
view.drawableMultisample=GLKViewDrawableMultisample4X;
```

Adding a UI

Of course, any app that doesn't have a means to interact with it is usually called a *demo*. But here our little demo will in fact gain both a simple user-interface and HUD graphics.

When it comes to adding UI elements to your OpenGL app, I have some very good news. Because the `GLKView` is a subclass of `UIView`, you can treat it like any other view object. This means you can create and add any other UIView object, hence practically any UIKit controls, as subviews to your 3D scene. This also means you have full access to animation properties of the views as well, to create a truly fluid interface. Figure 8-10 shows a quick UI I added to the example to turn on and off various objects along with an animated sweep that goes across the screen. The buttons are UIButtons with custom imagery, the text is a UILabel, and the green lines sweep across the screen like some sort of radar sequence.

And surprisingly, the performance generally holds up. So, it has two things going for it. The downside is that it will lock you even more into the iOS universe. Considering that OpenGL ES is an industry standard, you might want to consider the implications of mixing the standard with nonstandard objects. In fact, many authors eschew any Objective-C and iOS-specific stuff as much as they can, rolling their own UI within the OpenGL world. That way, ports to other devices can be reduced to days, instead of months.

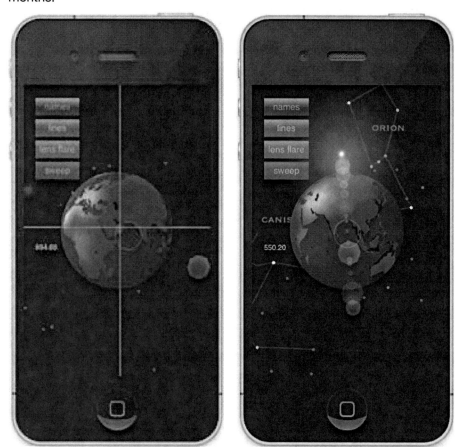

Figure 8-10. *Adding interface elements to the solar system*

In Distant Suns I have a date/time widget on the left side of the screen that lets users very quickly advance forward or backward in time (Figure 8-11). That was completely rendered in the OpenGL layer, largely to see whether I could do it. It looks and works very well, while the bottom and top toolbars are standard issue UIKit models.

Figure 8-11. *Distant Suns with custom date wheel on the left side yet with a standard UIKit toolbar at the same time*

Early on, Apple did caution about mixing the two worlds for performance reasons, in particular when the practice was to use an `NSTimer` to drive the rendering loop. With the addition of `CADisplayLink` with iOS 3.1, things got much better. There are a number of other best practices to keep in mind:

- Disable any OpenGL rendering loops if the view is hidden or the app is pushed to the background.

- Disable any OpenGL view if performing full-screen core animations.

- The simpler the dialog windows, the less of a performance hit on the OpenGL graphics.

- Use transparency sparingly, in particular if your OpenGL view is on top.

See? Sometimes the easy way can be the best way.

Summary

In this chapter, we took many of the tricks learned in previous chapters and combined them into a more complete and more attractive solar-system model. A one-planet solar system is not that impressive as it stands. So, I'll leave it up to you, dear reader, to add the moon, add some other planets, and get the earth to revolve around the sun.

Furthermore, we covered several other topics and tricks in past that I couldn't get around to adding to the project. For example, FBOs could be used to insert a secondary view of the earth from a different angle in the screen.

However, we did add lens flare, point and line objects, made the application support high-res Retina displays, and covered full-screen anti-aliasing and the mixing of both OpenGL views and standard iOS controls.

In the next chapter, we'll look into optimization tricks and using Apple's own tools to find bottlenecks in OpenGL ES applications.

Chapter 10

OpenGL ES 2, Shaders, and...

Her angel's face, As the great eye of heaven shined bright, And made a sunshine in the shady place.

—Edmund Spenser

There are two different versions of the OpenGL ES graphics library on your iOS devices. This book has largely dealt with the higher-level one, known as OpenGL ES 1, sometimes referred to as 1.1 or 1.*x*. The second version is a rather confusingly named OpenGL ES 2. The first one is by far the easier of the two; it comes with all sorts of helper libraries doing much of the 3D mathematics and all of the lighting, coloring, and shading on your behalf. ES 2 eschews all of those niceties and is sometimes referred to as the "programmable function" version (vs. ES 1's "fixed function" design, which is generally sneered at by the true pixel-jockeys who prefer more control over their imagery, usually for immersive 3D game environments where every little visual footnote is emphasized). For that, OpenGL ES 2 was released.

In this chapter, we'll just touch ever so briefly on shaders, just enough to give you a general feel for them. Afterward, I'll go into some more of the GLKit goodness not covered in previous chapters.

Version 1 is relatively close to the desktop variety of OpenGL, making porting applications, particularly vintage ones, a little less painful than having a badger gnaw your face off. The things that were left out were done so to keep the footprint small on limited-resource devices and to ensure performance was as good as could be.

Version 2 defenestrated compatibility altogether and concentrated on performance and flexibility-oriented features aimed primarily at entertainment-oriented software. Among the things left out were `glRotatef()`, `glTranslatef()`, matrix stack operations, and so on. But what we got in return are some delightful little morsels such as a programmable pipeline via the use of *shaders*. And the loss of the transformation methods have been replaced with the new iOS5 GLKit math libraries, so the learning curve is just a little less steep now.

As to be expected, version 2 is way too large to cover in a single chapter, so what follows is a general overview that should give you a good feel for the topic and whether it is something you'd want to tackle at some point.

Shaded Pipelines

If you have had a passing familiarity with OpenGL or Direct3D, the mere mention of the term *shaders* might give you the shivers. They seem like a mysterious talisman belonging to the innermost circles of graphics priesthood.

Not so.

The "fixed function" pipeline of version 1 refers to the lighting and coloring of the vertices and fragments. For example, you are permitted to have up to eight lights, and each light has various properties. The lights illuminate surfaces, each with their own properties called *materials*. Combining the two, we get a fairly nice, but constrained, general-purpose lighting model. But what if you wanted to do something different? What if you wanted to have a surface fade to transparency depending on its relative illumination? The darker, the more transparent? What if you wanted to accurately model shadows of, say, the rings of Saturn, thrown upon its cloud decks, or the pale luminescent light you get right before sunrise? All of those would be next to impossible given the limitations of the fixed-function model, especially the final one, because the lighting equations are quite complicated once you start taking into consideration the effect of moisture in the atmosphere, backscattering, and so on. Well, a programmable pipeline that lets you model those precise equations without using any tricks such as texture combiners is exactly what version 2 gives us.

Back to Where We Started

Let's go back to the very first example given in Chapter 1, the two cubes. You have already tweaked one of the shaders and lived to tell about it, but now we can go a little deeper.

The pipeline architecture of ES 2 permits you to have different access points in the geometric processing, as shown in Figure 10-1. The first hands you each vertex along with the various attributes (for example, xyz coordinates, colors, and opacity). This is called the *vertex shader*, and you have already played with one in the first chapter. At this point, it is up to you to determine what this vertex should look like and how it should be rendered with the supplied attributes and the state of your 3D world. When done, the vertex is handed back to the hardware, rasterized with the data you calculated, and passed on as 2D fragments to your fragment shader. It is here where you can combine the textures as needed, do any final processing, and hand it back to eventually be rendered in the frame buffer.

If this sounds like a lot of work for each fragment of each object in your scene roaring along at 60 fps, you are right. But fundamentally, shaders are small programs that are actually loaded and run on the graphics hardware itself and, as a result, are very, very fast.

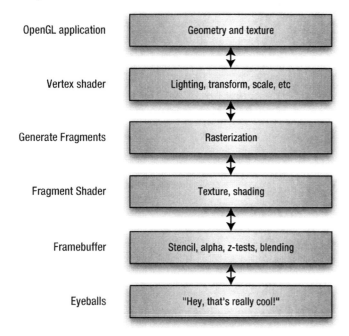

Figure 10-1. *Overview of OpenGL ES 2 architecture*

Shader Structure

Both vertex and fragment shaders are similar in structure and look a little like a small C program. The entry point is always called `main()` as in C (and Objective-C), while the syntax is likewise very C-ish.

The shader language, called GLSL (not to be confused with its Direct3d counterpart, HLSL), contains a rich set of built-in functions that belong to one of three main categories:

- Math operations oriented toward graphics processing such as matrix, vector, trig, derivative, and logic functions

- Texture sampling

- Small helper utilities such as modulo, comparisons, and valuators

Values are passed to and from shaders in the following types:

- Uniforms, which are values passed from the calling program. These might include the matrices for transformations or projection. They are available in both the vertex and fragment shaders, and they must be declared as the same type in each place.

- Varying variables (yes, it is a dumb-sounding name), which are variables defined in the vertex shader that are passed on to the fragment shader.

Variables may be defined as the usual numeric primitives or as graphics-oriented types based on vectors and matrices, as shown in Table 10-1.

Table 10-1. *Variable Types Allowed by GLSL*

Class	Type	Description
Primitives	float, int, bool	You really don't need me to define these now, do you?
Vectors	int, ivec2, ivec3, ivec4, float, vec2, vec3, vec4, bool, bvec2, bvec3, bvec4	Float, int, and bools are "one-dimensional vectors." Boolean vectors hold only bool values in their components.
Matrices	mat2, mat3, mat4	Nope, no Boolean matrices here.

In addition to these types, you can supply modifiers to define the precision of int- and float-based types. These can be `highp` (24 bit), `mediump` (16 bit), or `lowp` (10 bit), with `highp` being the default. All transformations must be done in `highp`, while colors need only `mediump`. (It beats me why there is no precision qualifier for bools, though.)

Any basic types can be declared as constant variables, such as `const float x=1.0`.

Structures are also allowed and look just like their C counterparts.

Restrictions

Since shaders reside on the GPU, they naturally have a number of restrictions to them, limiting their complexity. They may be limited by "instruction count," number of uniforms permitted (typically 128), number of temporary variables, and depth of loop nesting. Unfortunately, on OpenGL ES, there is no real way to fetch these limits from the hardware, so you can only be aware that they exist and keep your shaders as small as possible.

There are also differences between the vertex and fragment shaders. For example, `highp` support is optional, whereas it is mandatory on the vertex shader. Bah.

Back to the Spinning Cubes

So, now let's jump back to the original example of the dueling cubes and break down how a basic OpenGL ES 2 program is structured. As you'll see, the process of generating a shader is not unlike generating most any other application. You have your basic compile, link, and load sequence. Listing 10-1 demonstrates the first part of that process, compiling the thing. In Apple's example, all of these steps are placed in a view controller, but they can go anywhere.

Listing 10-1. *Compiling a Shader*

```
- (BOOL)compileShader:(GLuint *)shader                                          //1
        type:(GLenum)type file:(NSString *)file
{
    GLint status;
    const GLchar *source;

    source = (GLchar *)[[NSString stringWithContentsOfFile:file
                         encoding:NSUTF8StringEncoding error:nil] UTF8String];

    if (!source)
    {
        NSLog(@"Failed to load vertex shader");
        return NO;
    }

    *shader = glCreateShader(type);                                             //2

    glShaderSource(*shader, 1, &source, NULL);                                  //3
    glCompileShader(*shader);                                                   //4

#if defined(DEBUG)

    GLint logLength;
    glGetShaderiv(*shader, GL_INFO_LOG_LENGTH, &logLength);                     //5

    if (logLength > 0)
    {
        GLchar *log = (GLchar *)malloc(logLength);
        glGetShaderInfoLog(*shader, logLength, &logLength, log);                //6
        NSLog(@"Shader compile log:\n%s", log);
        free(log);
    }

#endif

    glGetShaderiv(*shader, GL_COMPILE_STATUS, &status);                         //7

    if (status == 0)
    {
        glDeleteShader(*shader);                                                //8
        return NO;
    }
```

```
        return YES;
}
```

When you get away from all of the error handling code, the process boils down to creating a shader, passing in the source, and compiling.

- In the argument list of line 1, an address is passed to receive the newly generated shader's. handle. A type value is also supplied, which can be either GL_VERTEX_SHADER or GL_FRAGMENT_SHADER. And finally a file name is specified. You don't need to supply a shader from a file, because others may actually specify the shader as static strings defined inside the body of the code.

- In line 2, glCreateShader() generates an empty shader object and returns its handle.

- Line 3 passes the source of the shader to the newly created object, because its real job is to contain the text strings used to define the shader.

- Next we compile the thing in line 4.

- Now we should check the compilation status. Since there is no means to debug shaders when on the GPU, a nice error management system has been provided that can send back fairly detailed strings to the calling program. Line 5 gets the length of the string, while 6 gets the actual contents. For example, in Shader.vsh, I supplied a variable that was never defined and received the following:

  ```
  ERROR: 0:19: Use of undeclared identifier 'normalX'
  ```

- But instead of using a string to determine what to do, you can also get a numerical error of either GL_TRUE if the compile was actually successful or GL_FALSE if otherwise, as shown in line 7. And if not, delete the shader, as in line 8.

The next step in the process is to link the program, as shown in Listing 10-2. glLinkProgram() is the only call of any significance, with the rest being error handling.

Listing 10-2. Linking the Newly Created Shader Program

```
- (BOOL)linkProgram:(GLuint)prog
{
    GLint status;
    glLinkProgram(prog);

#if defined(DEBUG)
    GLint logLength;

    glGetProgramiv(prog, GL_INFO_LOG_LENGTH, &logLength);
```

```
    if (logLength > 0)
    {
        GLchar *log = (GLchar *)malloc(logLength);
        glGetProgramInfoLog(prog, logLength, &logLength, log);
        NSLog(@"Program link log:\n%s", log);
        free(log);
    }
#endif

    glGetProgramiv(prog, GL_LINK_STATUS, &status);

    if (status == 0)
    {
        return NO;
    }

    return YES;
}
```

After linking, it is customary to "validate" the program. Validation is a way for the OpenGL implementors to return information about any aspects of your code, such as recommended improvements. You would use this primarily during the development process, as shown in Listing 10-3. And as before, it is largely error handling.

Listing 10-3. Program Validation

```
- (BOOL)validateProgram:(GLuint)prog
{
    GLint logLength, status;

    glValidateProgram(prog);
    glGetProgramiv(prog, GL_INFO_LOG_LENGTH, &logLength);

    if (logLength > 0)
    {
        GLchar *log = (GLchar *)malloc(logLength);
        glGetProgramInfoLog(prog, logLength, &logLength, log);
        NSLog(@"Program validate log:\n%s", log);
        free(log);
    }

    glGetProgramiv(prog, GL_VALIDATE_STATUS, &status);

    if (status == 0)
    {
        return NO;
    }

    return YES;
}
```

The final routine, loadShaders(), as shown in Listing 10-4, ties together the three routines from earlier and binds our attributes and parameters to the program. That way, we can pass an array of vertex information or parameters and specify their names on both sides of the fence.

Listing 10-4. Loading the Shaders and Resolving Parameters

```
- (BOOL)loadShaders
{
    GLuint vertShader, fragShader;
    NSString *vertShaderPathname, *fragShaderPathname;

    _program = glCreateProgram();                                          //1

    vertShaderPathname = [[NSBundle mainBundle]
                          pathForResource:@"Shader" ofType:@"vsh"];

    if (![self compileShader:&vertShader                                   //2
                   type:GL_VERTEX_SHADER file:vertShaderPathname])
    {
        NSLog(@"Failed to compile vertex shader");
        return NO;
    }

    fragShaderPathname = [[NSBundle mainBundle] pathForResource:@"Shader"
    ofType:@"fsh"];

    if (![self compileShader:&fragShader
                   type:GL_FRAGMENT_SHADER file:fragShaderPathname])
    {
        NSLog(@"Failed to compile fragment shader");
        return NO;
    }

    glAttachShader(_program, vertShader);                                  //3
    glAttachShader(_program, fragShader);

    glBindAttribLocation(_program, ATTRIB_VERTEX, "position");            //4
    glBindAttribLocation(_program, ATTRIB_NORMAL, "normal");

    if (![self linkProgram:_program])                                     //5
    {
        NSLog(@"Failed to link program: %d", _program);

        if (vertShader)
        {
            glDeleteShader(vertShader);
            vertShader = 0;
        }

        if (fragShader)
        {
            glDeleteShader(fragShader);
            fragShader = 0;
        }
```

```
    if (_program)
    {
        glDeleteProgram(_program);
        _program = 0;
    }

    return NO;
}

uniforms[UNIFORM_MODELVIEWPROJECTION_MATRIX] =                           //6
    glGetUniformLocation(_program, "modelViewProjectionMatrix");

uniforms[UNIFORM_NORMAL_MATRIX] =
    glGetUniformLocation(_program, "normalMatrix");

if (vertShader)                                                          //7
{
    glDetachShader(_program, vertShader);
    glDeleteShader(vertShader);
}

if (fragShader)
{
    glDetachShader(_program, fragShader);
    glDeleteShader(fragShader);
}

    return YES;
}
```

Here's what's happening:

- Line 1 generates a program handle and creates an empty program object. You keep this handle around and use it to specify which program you want to use for a specific piece of geometry, because you can have multiple programs and swap them back and forth as needed.

- Now the shaders are compiled in lines 2ff.

- Lines 3f bind the specific shader to the new program object. Each program object must have one vertex and one fragment shader.

- In lines 4ff, we bind whatever attributes we want to the program. In the actual vertex shader code, you can see attributes by those names defined for use:

```
attribute vec4 position;
attribute vec3 normal;
```

  The names can be nearly anything you want; there is nothing special about the use of position or normal.

- Line 5 links both shaders.

▨ Besides binding the attributes to named entities in the shaders, you can also do the same with uniforms, as demonstrated in lines 6 and 7. Remember that uniforms are merely values passed from the calling program. (They differ from attributes in that attributes are mapped one-to-one with each vertex.) In this case, we are supplying two matrices and naming them `modelViewProjectionMatrix` and `normalMatrix`. Looking again in the vertex shader, you can see the following:

```
uniform mat4 modelViewProjectionMatrix;
uniform mat3 normalMatrix;
```

▨ Lines 7ff support a memory optimization quark. Once linked, the shader code is copied into the program, so the shader objects as we have them are no longer needed. Since they use reference counts, `glDetachShader()` serves to decrease the count by one, and, of course, when 0, they can be safely deleted.

▨ As a side effect, if you change the shader in anyway, it will have to be relinked before the changes take effect. And in case you may have to relink things, the driver may hold onto some cached information to use later. Otherwise, the detach/delete process can aid the driver in reusing the cached memory.

As you can see, the actual calls required are pretty minimal, but Apple's demo includes all of the error handling as well, which is why it was retained.

Now with that out of the way, we can look at the two shaders. Listing 10-5 is the vertex shader, `Shader.vsh`. Note that the shaders pairs share the same prefix, with the vertex shader having a suffix of `vsh` while the fragment shader uses `fsh`.

Listing 10-5. *The Demo's Vertex Shader*

```
attribute vec4 position;                                                 //1
attribute vec3 normal;

varying lowp vec4 colorVarying;                                          //2

uniform mat4 modelViewProjectionMatrix;                                  //3
uniform mat3 normalMatrix;

void main()
{
    vec3 normalDirection = normalize(normalMatrix * normal);             //4
    vec3 lightPosition = vec3(0.0, 0.0, 1.0);                            //5
    vec4 diffuseColor = vec4(0.4, 0.4, 1.0, 1.0);                        //6

    float nDotVP = max(0.0, dot(eyeNormal, normalize(lightPosition)));   //7

    colorVarying = diffuseColor * nDotVP;                                //8

    gl_Position = modelViewProjectionMatrix * position;                  //9
}
```

Here's a closer look:

- Lines 1f declare the attributes that we specified in the calling code. Remember that attributes are arrays of data mapping directly to each vertex and are available only in the vertex shader.

- In line 2, a varying vector variable is declared. This will be used to pass color information down to the fragment shader.

- Lines 3f declare two uniforms that were originally specified in `loadShaders()` earlier.

- In Line 4, the normal is multiplied by the `normalMatrix`. You can't use the Modelview matrix in this case, because normals do not need to be translated, and any scaling done in the Modelview would distort the normal. As it turns out, you can use the inverse and transposed Modelview matrix for the normals. With that in hand, the result is normalized.

- Lines 5 supplies the position of the light, while line 6 supplies the default color. Normally you wouldn't embed that data inside a shader, but it is likely done this way just as a convenience.

- Now, in line 7, the dot product of the normal (now called `eyeNormal`) and the position of the light is taken to produce the angle between the two. The `max()` function ensures that the return value is clamped to be >=0 to handle any negative values.

- Now by simply multiplying the dot product by the diffuse color, as shown in line 7, we get the luminosity of a face relative to the local position of the light. The closer the normal aims toward the light, the brighter it should be. As it aims away from the light, it will get darker, finally going to 0.

- `gl_Position` is a predefined varying in GLSL and is used to pass the transformed vertex's position back to the driver.

The fragment shader in this example is the most basic there is. It simply passes the color info from the vertex shader through and untouched. `gl_FragColor` is another predefined varying, and it is here where any final calculations would be made, as shown in Listing 10-6.

Listing 10-6. *The Simplest Fragment Shader*

```
varying lowp vec4 colorVarying;

void main()
{
    gl_FragColor = colorVarying;
}
```

Now we're ready to use our shaders, which turn out to be surprisingly straightforward. First, `glUseProgram()` sets the current program, followed by the `glUniform*` functions that pass the values from your app to the shaders on the card. The attributes are usually supplied at the same time as the geometry, via the use of calls such as `glVertexAtttribPointer()`.

One additional note regarding this example is to be found in its `setupGL()` method. This was briefly touched upon in Chapter 1 but now is a good time to take a little closer look at how the data is actually passed to the GPU in an OpenGL ES 2 program. Vertex array objects (VAOs), not to be confused with vertex buffer objects, represent a collection of information that describes a specific state of your scene. As with other objects, creating/using VAOs follows the same path: generate a unique ID, bind it, fill it up, and then unbind it until needed. Many VAOs can be generated that haul about the pointers of the geometry and attributes different aspects of your world. In the cube example, consider Listing 10-7. After the VAO ID is generated and bound as the current VAO, a vertex buffer object is created for the interleaved geometric data. Afterward, the VAO is notified about how the VBO data is organized, and in this case, just the position and normals are addressed.

Listing 10-7. *Creating the Vertex Array Object*

```
glGenVertexArraysOES (1, &_vertexArray);
glBindVertexArrayOES(_vertexArray);

glGenBuffers(1, &_vertexBuffer);
glBindBuffer(GL_ARRAY_BUFFER, _vertexBuffer);
glBufferData(GL_ARRAY_BUFFER, sizeof(gCubeVertexData), gCubeVertexData,
GL_STATIC_DRAW);

glEnableVertexAttribArray(GLKVertexAttribPosition);
glVertexAttribPointer(GLKVertexAttribPosition, 3, GL_FLOAT, GL_FALSE, 24,
BUFFER_OFFSET(0));
glEnableVertexAttribArray(GLKVertexAttribNormal);
glVertexAttribPointer(GLKVertexAttribNormal, 3, GL_FLOAT, GL_FALSE, 24,
BUFFER_OFFSET(12));

glBindVertexArrayOES(0);
```

When it comes time to draw, the VAO handle is set to be the current one, and the normal `glDrawArray()` routine is called.

Earth at Night

Let's start with our earth model and see how shaders can be used to make it more interesting. You're familiar with the image used for the earth's surface, as shown in Figure 10-2 (left), but you may have also seen a similar image of the earth at night, as shown in Figure 10-2 (right). What would be neat is if we could show the night texture on the dark side of the earth, instead of just a dark version of the regular texture map.

Figure 10-2. *The daytime earth (left) vs. the nighttime earth (right)*

Under OpenGL 1.1, this would be very tricky to accomplish if at all. The algorithm should be relatively simple: render two spheres of exactly the same dimensions. One has the night image, and the other has the day image. Vary the daylight-side alpha channel of the texture of the day-side earth based on the illumination. When illumination reaches 0, it is completely transparent, and the night portion shows through. However, under OpenGL ES 2, you can code the shaders very easily to match the algorithm almost exactly.

So, I started with the cube template from Apple and dumped the cube stuff and added `Planet.mm` and `Planet.h` files. `setupGL()` was changed to Listing 10-8. Notice the loading of the two textures and two shader programs.

Listing 10-8. *Setting Up to Show Earth at Night*

```
- (void)setupGL
{
    int planetSize=20;

    [EAGLContext setCurrentContext:self.context];

    [self loadShaders:&m_NightsideProgram shaderName:@"nightside"];
    [self loadShaders:&m_DaysideProgram shaderName:@"dayside"];

    float aspect = fabsf(self.view.bounds.size.width / self.view.bounds.size.height);
    m_ProjectionMatrix = GLKMatrix4MakePerspective(GLKMathDegreesToRadians(65.0f),
    aspect, 0.1f, 100.0f);
```

```
    glEnable(GL_DEPTH_TEST);

    m_EyePosition=GLKVector3Make(0.0,0.0,65.0);

    m_WorldModelViewMatrix=GLKMatrix4MakeTranslation(-m_EyePosition.x,-m_EyePosition.y,-
    m_EyePosition.z);

    m_Sphere=[[Planet alloc] init:planetSize slices:planetSize radius:10.0f squash:1.0f
    textureFile:NULL];
    [m_Sphere setPositionX:0.0 Y:0.0 Z:0.0];

    m_EarthDayTexture=[self loadTexture:@"earth_light.png"];
    m_EarthNightTexture=[self loadTexture:@"earth_night.png"];

    m_LightPosition=GLKVector3Make(100.0, 10,100.0);     //behind the earth

}
```

In loadShaders() I merely added one more attribute, namely, texCoord, or the texture
coordinates. These are recovered in the fragment shader:

```
    glBindAttribLocation(*program, ATTRIB_VERTEX, "position");
    glBindAttribLocation(*program, ATTRIB_NORMAL, "normal");
    glBindAttribLocation(*program, GLKVertexAttribTexCoord0, "texCoord");
```

I also pass the light's position as a *uniform*, instead of hard-coding it in the vertex
shader. This is set up in a couple of steps:

   ▓ First, add it to the shader: uniform vec3 lightPosition;.

   ▓ Then in loadShaders(), you fetch its "location" using
      glGetUniformLocation(). That merely returns a unique ID for this
      session that is then used when setting or getting data from the shader.

   ▓ The light's position can then be set by using this:

```
 glUniform3fv(uniforms[UNIFORM_LIGHT_POSITION],1,m_LightPosition.v);
```

Then change the call to add two parameters so that it can be called with different shader
names, and add a pointer to a progam handle. And remember to change the code to
support the parameters instead of the temp variables:

```
    - (BOOL)loadShaders:(GLuint *)program  shaderName:(NSString *)shaderName
```

Now in Listing 10-9, both sides of the earth are drawn, with the night side going first,
while the daylight side goes second. The programs are swapped as needed.

Listing 10-9. *The* drawInRect() *Method to Handle This Situation*

```
- (void)glkView:(GLKView *)view drawInRect:(CGRect)rect
{
    GLfloat gray=0.0;
    static int frame=0;
```

```
glClearColor(gray,gray,gray, 1.0f);
glClear(GL_COLOR_BUFFER_BIT | GL_DEPTH_BUFFER_BIT);

//nightside

[self useProgram:m_NightsideProgram];

[m_Sphere setBlendMode:PLANET_BLEND_MODE_SOLID];
[m_Sphere execute:m_EarthNightTexture.name];

//dayside

[self useProgram:m_DaylightProgram];

[m_Sphere setBlendMode:PLANET_BLEND_MODE_FADE];
[m_Sphere execute:m_EarthDayTexture.name];

//atmosphere

glCullFace(GL_FRONT);
glEnable(GL_CULL_FACE);
glFrontFace(GL_CW);

frame++;
}
```

On the day side of the earth, I use the program m_DaysideProgram, while on the night side, I use another one, called m_NightsideProgram. Both use the identical vertex shader, as shown in Listing 10-10.

Listing 10-10. *The Vertex Shader for Both the Day and Night Sides of the Earth*

```
attribute vec4 position;
attribute vec3 normal;
attribute vec2 texCoord;                                          //1

varying vec2 v_texCoord;

varying lowp vec4 colorVarying;

uniform mat4 modelViewProjectionMatrix;
uniform mat3 normalMatrix;
uniform vec3 lightPosition;                                       //2

void main()
{
    v_texCoord=texCoord;                                         //3

    vec3 eyeNormal = normalize(normalMatrix * normal);
    vec4 diffuseColor = vec4(1.0, 1.0, 1.0, 1.0);
```

```
        float nDotVP = max(0.0, dot(normalDirection, normalize(lightPosition)));

        colorVarying = diffuseColor * nDotVP;

        gl_Position = modelViewProjectionMatrix * position;
}
```

This is almost identical to Apple's template, but we've added a couple of things:

▩ Line 1 serves to pass an additional attribute, namely, the texture coordinates for each vertex. This is then passed straight through to the fragment shader via line 3 using the **v_texCoord** varying.

▩ In line 2 is the new uniform you may recall in the view controller's code that holds the position of the light.

Listing 10-11 shows the fragment shader for the daylight side of the earth, while Listing 10-12 does the same but for the night side.

Listing 10-11. *The Fragment Shader for the Daylight Side of the Earth*

```
varying lowp vec4 colorVarying;                                         //1

precision mediump float;
varying vec2 v_texCoord;                                                //2
uniform sampler2D s_texture;                                            //3

void main()
{
    gl_FragColor = texture2D( s_texture, v_texCoord )*colorVarying;     //4
}
```

You can see how simple these are for such beautiful results:

▩ Line 1 picks up the varying variable, **colorVarying**, from the vertex shader.

▩ Line 2 does the same for the texture coordinates, followed by line 3 that has the texture. The **sampler2D**, as shown in line 3, is a built-in uniform variable that points out which texture unit is being used.

▩ Finally, in line 4, the built-in function **texture2D** extracts the value from the texture referenced by **s_texture** at the coordinates of **v_texCoord**. That value is then multiplied by **colorVarying**, the "real" color of the fragment. The less the **colorVarying** is, the darker the color becomes.

Listing 10-12 shows how to do the night side of the earth.

Listing 10-12. *Rendering the Night Side*

```
varying lowp vec4 colorVarying;

precision mediump float;
varying vec2 v_texCoord;
uniform sampler2D s_texture;
```

```
void main()
{
    vec4 newColor;

    newColor=1.0-colorVarying;                                          //1

    gl_FragColor = texture2D( s_texture, v_texCoord )*newColor;         //2
}
```

Here in line 1, we're merely taking the opposite of what was in the day-side shader. As the color increases because of the sun, the dark-side texture fades to nothing. This might be overkill, because the night-side texture would be washed out by the other, but the lights are just a little too visible after the terminator for my taste.

There's one final thing to do, and that is to modify your planet object so as to be drawable with a vertex array object. Yes, it's yet another interminable listing, as shown in Listing 10-13. The data must first be packed into more efficient interleaved form, referenced in Chapter 9. Afterward, a VAO is generated as a wrapper of sorts.

Listing 10-13. *Creating a VAO for the Planet*

```
-(void)createInterleavedData
{
    int i;
    GLfloat *vtxPtr;
    GLfloat *norPtr;
    GLfloat *colPtr;
    GLfloat *textPtr;
    int xyzSize;
    int nxyzSize;
    int rgbaSize;
    int textSize;

    struct VAOInterleaved *startData;

    int structSize=sizeof(struct VAOInterleaved);
    long allocSize=structSize*m_NumVertices;

    m_InterleavedData=(struct VAOInterleaved *)malloc(allocSize);        //1

    startData=m_InterleavedData;

    vtxPtr=m_VertexData;
    norPtr=m_NormalData;
    colPtr=m_ColorData;
    textPtr=m_TexCoordsData;

    xyzSize=sizeof(GLfloat)*NUM_XYZ_ELS;
    nxyzSize=sizeof(GLfloat)*NUM_NXYZ_ELS;
    rgbaSize=sizeof(GLfloat)*NUM_RGBA_ELS;
    textSize=sizeof(GLfloat)*NUM_ST_ELS;

    for(i=0;i<m_NumVertices;i++)                                         //2
    {
```

```
            memcpy(&startData->xyz,vtxPtr,xyzSize);      //geometry
            memcpy(&startData->nxyz,norPtr,nxyzSize);    //normals
            memcpy(&startData->rgba,colPtr,rgbaSize);    //colors
            memcpy(&startData->st,textPtr,textSize);     //texture coords

            startData++;

            vtxPtr+=NUM_XYZ_ELS;
            norPtr+=NUM_NXYZ_ELS;
            colPtr+=NUM_RGBA_ELS;
            textPtr+=NUM_ST_ELS;
        }
}


-(void)createVAO
{
    GLuint numBytesPerXYZ,numBytesPerNXYZ,numBytesPerRGBA;
    GLuint structSize=sizeof(struct VAOInterleaved);

    [self createInterleavedData];

    //note that the context is set in the in the parent object

    glGenVertexArraysOES(1, &m_VertexArrayName);
    glBindVertexArrayOES(m_VertexArrayName);

    numBytesPerXYZ=sizeof(GL_FLOAT)*NUM_XYZ_ELS;
    numBytesPerNXYZ=sizeof(GL_FLOAT)*NUM_NXYZ_ELS;
    numBytesPerRGBA=sizeof(GL_FLOAT)*NUM_RGBA_ELS;

    glGenBuffers(1, &m_VertexBufferName);
    glBindBuffer(GL_ARRAY_BUFFER, m_VertexBufferName);
            glBufferData(GL_ARRAY_BUFFER, sizeof(struct VAOInterleaved)*m_NumVertices,
        m_InterleavedData, GL_STATIC_DRAW);


    glEnableVertexAttribArray(GLKVertexAttribNormal);
    glVertexAttribPointer(GLKVertexAttribNormal, NUM_NXYZ_ELS, GL_FLOAT, GL_FALSE,
        structSize, BUFFER_OFFSET(numBytesPerXYZ));

    glEnableVertexAttribArray(GLKVertexAttribColor);
    glVertexAttribPointer(GLKVertexAttribColor, NUM_RGBA_ELS, GL_FLOAT,
        GL_FALSE, structSize, BUFFER_OFFSET(numBytesPerNXYZ+numBytesPerXYZ));

    glEnableVertexAttribArray(GLKVertexAttribTexCoord0);

    glVertexAttribPointer(GLKVertexAttribTexCoord0,NUM_ST_ELS, GL_FLOAT,  GL_FALSE,
        structSize,
        BUFFER_OFFSET(numBytesPerNXYZ+numBytesPerXYZ+numBytesPerRGBA));
}
```

▨ In line 1 allocate an array of structures to carry each of the components. Here the structure is defined in `Planet.h` :

```
struct VAOInterleaved
    {
        GLfloat xyz[NUM_XYZ_ELS];
        GLfloat nxyz[NUM_NXYZ_ELS];
        GLfloat rgba[NUM_RGBA_ELS];
        GLfloat st[NUM_ST_ELS];
    };
```

▨ Lines 2ff scan through all the data and copy it to the interleaved array.

▨ Down in the next method, the VAO is created. Much like the earlier example for the cubes, the only new elements are the addition of the texture coordinates and the RGBA color data to the mix.

Now with that out of the way, check the results in Figure 10-3.

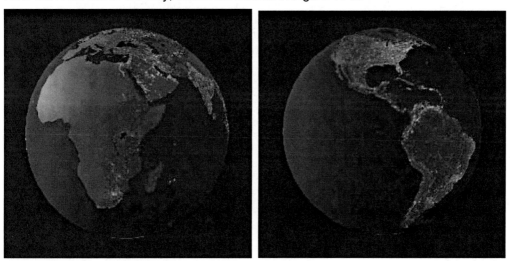

Figure 10-3. *Illuminating the darkness one texel at a time*

But What About Specular Reflections?

Just as any other shiny thing (and the earth is shiny in the blue parts), you might expect to see some sort of reflections of the sun in the water. Well, you'd be right. Figure 10-4 shows a real image of the earth, and right in the middle is the reflection of the sun. Let's try it on our own earth.

Figure 10-4. *Earth seen from space as it reflects the sun*

Naturally we are going to have to write our own specular reflection shader (or in this case, add it to the existing daylight shader).

Swap the old vertex shader for Listing 10-14, and swap the fragment shader for the one in Listing 10-15. Here I precalculate the specular information along with normal diffuse coloring, but the two are kept separate until the fragment shader. The reason is that not all parts of the earth are reflective, so the land masses shouldn't get the specular treatment.

Listing 10-14. *Vertex Shader for the Secular Reflection*

```
attribute vec4 position;
attribute vec3 normal;
attribute vec2 texCoord;

varying vec2 v_texCoord;

varying lowp vec4 colorVarying;
varying lowp vec4 specularColorVarying;                            //1

uniform mat4 modelViewProjectionMatrix;
uniform mat3 normalMatrix;
uniform vec3 lightPosition;
uniform vec3 eyePosition;

void main()
{
    float shininess=100.0;
    float balance=.75;

    vec3 normalDirection = normalize(normalMatrix * normal);       //2
    vec3 eyeNormal = normalize(eyePosition);

    vec3 lightDirection;

    float specular=0.0;

    v_texCoord=texCoord;

    eyeNormal = normalize(normalMatrix * normal);
```

```
        vec4 diffuseColor = vec4(1.0, 1.0, 1.0, 1.0);

        lightDirection=normalize(lightPosition);

        float nDotVP = max(0.0, dot(normalDirection,lightDirection));

        float nDotVPReflection = dot(reflect(-lightDirection,normalDirection),eyeNormal);    //3

        specular = pow(max(0.0,nDotVPReflection),shininess)*.75;                             //4
        specularColorVarying=vec4(specular,specular,specular,0.0);                           //5

        colorVarying = diffuseColor * nDotVP;

        gl_Position = modelViewProjectionMatrix * position;
}
```

Here's what is going on:

- Line 1 declares a varying variable to hand the specular illumination off to the fragment shader.

- Next, in line 2, we get a normalized normal transformed by the normalmatrix (yup, still sounds funny), which is needed to get the proper specular value.

- We now need to get the dot product of the reflection of the light and the normalized normal multiplied normally by the normalmatrix in an normal fashion. See line 3. Notice the use of the reflect() method, which is another one of the niceties in the shader language. Reflect generates a reflected vector based on the negative light direction and the local normal. That is then dotted with the eyeNormal.

- In Line 4 that dot value is taken and used to generate the actual specular component. You will also see our old friend shininess, and just as in version 1 of OpenGS ES, the higher the value, the narrower the reflection.

   - Since we can consider the sun's color just to be white, the specular color in line 5 can be made to have all its components set to the same value.

Now the fragment shader can be used to refine things even further, as shown in Listing 10-15.

Listing 10-15. *The Fragment Shader That Handles the Specular Reflection*

```
precision mediump float;

varying lowp vec4 colorVarying;
varying lowp vec4 specularColorVarying;                                                      //1

uniform mat4 modelViewProjectionMatrix;
uniform mat3 normalMatrix;
uniform vec3 lightPosition;
```

```
varying vec2 v_texCoord;
uniform sampler2D s_texture;

void main()
{
    vec4 finalSpecular=vec4(0,0,0,1);
    vec4 surfaceColor;
    float halfBlue;

    surfaceColor=texture2D( s_texture, v_texCoord );

    halfBlue=0.5*surfaceColor[2];                                       //2

    if(halfBlue>1.0)                                                    //3
        halfBlue=1.0;

    if((surfaceColor[0]<halfBlue) && (surfaceColor[1]<halfBlue))        //4
        finalSpecular=specularColorVarying;

    gl_FragColor = surfaceColor*colorVarying+colorVarying*finalSpecular; //5
}
```

The main task here is to determine which fragments represent sea and which do not. It's pretty easy: the blue stuff is water (powerful wet stuff, that water!), and everything that isn't, isn't.

- First in line 1, we pick up the specularColorVarying variable.

- In line 2, we pick up the blue component and divide it by half, clamping in line 3, since no color can actually go above full intensity.

- Line 4 does the filtering. If the red and green components were both less than half that of the blue, then it's a pretty safe bet that we can draw the specular glint over the water, instead of some place like Chad.

- The specular piece is now added to the fragment color in the last line, after first multiplying it with the colorVarying, because that will modulate it with everything else.

Figure 10-5 shows the results.

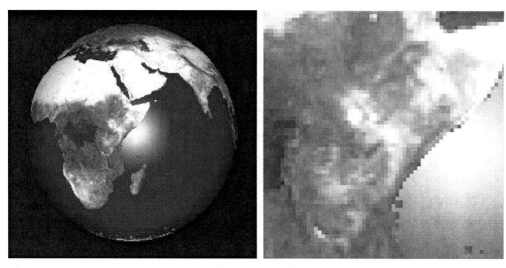

Figure 10-5. *A close-up on the right of the earth/water interface*

Bring in the Clouds

So, it certainly seems as if something else is missing. Oh, yeah. Those cloud things. Well, we're in luck because shaders can very easily manage that as well. Available in the downloadable project files I've added a cloud map of the entire earth, as shown in Figure 10-6. The land masses are a little hard to see, but in the lower right is Australia, while in the left half you can barely see South America. So, our job is to overlay it on top of the color landscape map and drop out all of the low-contrast bits.

Figure 10-6. *Full-earth cloud patterns*

Not only are we going to add clouds to our model, but we'll also see how to handle multitexturing using shaders, as in, how does one tell a shader to use more than one texture? Remember the lesson about texture units in Chapter 6? They come in really handy right now, because that is where the textures are stored, ready for the fragment shader to pick them up. Normally, for a single texture, the system defaults in a way that no additional setup is needed, save for the normal call to glBindTexture(). However, if you want to use more than one, there is some setup required. The steps are as follows:

1. Load the new texture in your main program.

2. Add a second *uniform sampler2D* to your fragment shader to support a second texture and pick it up via glGetUniformLocation().

3. Tell the system which texture unit to use with which sampler.

4. Activate and bind the desired textures to the specified TUs while in the main loop, drawInRect().

Now to a few specifics: you already know how to load textures. That is, of course, a no-brainer. So, in step 2, you will want to add something like the following to the fragment shader, the same one used for the previous couple of exercises:

```
uniform sampler2D cloud_texture;
```

And to loadShaders():

```
uniforms[UNIFORM_SAMPLER1] = glGetUniformLocation(*program, "cloud_texture");
uniforms[UNIFORM_SAMPLER0] = glGetUniformLocation(*program, "s_texture");
```

Step 3 is added in the view controller's setupGL(). The glUniform1i() call takes the "location" of the uniform in the fragment shader for the first argument and takes the actual TU number in the second. So, in this case, sampler0 is bound to texture unit 0, while sampler1 goes to texture unit 1. Since a single texture always defaults to TU0, as well as the first sampler, the setup code is not needed.

```
glUseProgram(m_DaysideProgram);
glUniform1i(uniforms[UNIFORM_SAMPLER0],0);
glUniform1i(uniforms[UNIFORM_SAMPLER1],1);

glUseProgram(m_NightsideProgram);
glUniform1i(uniforms[UNIFORM_SAMPLER0],0);
glUniform1i(uniforms[UNIFORM_SAMPLER1],1);
```

When running the main loop, in step 4, you can do the following:

```
glActiveTexture(GL_TEXTURE0);
glBindTexture(GL_TEXTURE_2D,m_EarthNightTexture.name);

glActiveTexture(GL_TEXTURE1);
glBindTexture(GL_TEXTURE_2D,m_EarthCloudTexture.name);

[self useProgram:m_NightsideProgram];
```

```
[m_Sphere setBlendMode:PLANET_BLEND_MODE_SOLID];
[m_Sphere execute:m_EarthNightTexture.name];
```

glActiveTexture() specifies what TU to use followed by a call to bind the texture. Afterward, the program can be used to the desired effect.

The cloud-luv'n fragment should now look something like Listing 10-16 to perform the actual blending.

Listing 10-16. *Blends a Second Texture with Clouds on Top of the Others*

```
precision mediump float;

varying lowp vec4 colorVarying;
varying lowp vec4 specularColorVarying;


uniform mat4 modelViewProjectionMatrix;
uniform mat3 normalMatrix;
uniform vec3 lightPosition;

varying vec2 v_texCoord;
uniform sampler2D s_texture;
uniform sampler2D cloud_texture;                                       //1

void main()
{
    vec4 finalSpecular=vec4(0,0,0,1);
    vec4 surfaceColor;
    vec4 cloudColor;

    float halfBlue;             //a value used to detect a mainly blue fragment.

    surfaceColor=texture2D( s_texture, v_texCoord );
    cloudColor=texture2D(cloud_texture, v_texCoord );                  //2

    halfBlue=0.5*surfaceColor[2];

    if(halfBlue>1.0)
        halfBlue=1.0;

    if((surfaceColor[0]<halfBlue) && (surfaceColor[1]<halfBlue))
        finalSpecular=specularColorVarying;

    if(cloudColor[0]>0.15)                                            //3
    {
        cloudColor[3]=1.0;
        gl_FragColor=(cloudColor*1.3+surfaceColor*.4)*colorVarying;
    }
    else
        gl_FragColor=(surfaceColor+finalSpecular)*colorVarying;
}
```

Here's what is happening:

- Line 1 is merely declaring the new `cloud_texture`.

- In Line 2, we pick up the cloud color from the cloud sampler object.

- The new color is filtered and merged with the earth's surface image, lines 3ff. The numbers used are quite arbitrary, but they give the best image. Naturally much of the finer detail will have to be cut out to ensure the colored land masses show through.

  Since the clouds are grayscale objects, I need to pick up only a single color to test, because the normal RGB values are identical. So, I opted to handle all texels brighter than .20. Then I ensure that the alpha channel is 1.0 and combine all three components. The `cloudColor` is given a slight boost with the 1.3 multiplier, while the underlying surface uses only .4, so as to emphasize the clouds a little more while still making them relatively opaque.

I hope you'll see something like Figure 10-7. Now it's starting to look like a real planet.

Figure 10-7. Putting it all together

This is just one very simple example of using a shader. When it comes to space themes, for example, you might generate a hazy atmosphere around a planet or 3D volumetric textures to simulate galaxies or nebula. If only I had another ten chapters....

More Fun and Games with GLKit

As mentioned previously, the introduction of the GLKit in iOS 5 was largely designed to make working in OpenGL ES a little easier. The kit supplied new functionality in four areas, three of which you already have dealt with and are very handy in either version 1 or 2:

- GLKView and GLKViewController (hiding some of the messiness when dealing with the drawing surface)
- Texture management
- Math libraries (rich and standardized math API)
- Effects (standard means to encapsulate shader-based effects)

Of the four, the latter two were specifically targeted to make working with OpenGL ES 2 a little easier. It's the final one, however, that adds a little bit of extra flash that we're going to cover now.

GLKEffects

The GLKEffects library was created as a way to manage shader-based effects. At the time of this writing, GLKit comes with two prebuilt effects classes, and I am sure we'll see more. The core to this is the GLKBaseEffects class. GLKBaseEffects incorporates, and to use Apple's term "mimics," much of what OpenGL ES 1 users had to leave behind when making the jump to 2. This includes the following:

- The basic lighting model from OpenGL ES 1, but with only three lights at a time though, vs. 8 or more under version 1.
- Materials, using the GLKEffectPropertyMaterial class
- Support for materials and all of their respective qualities
- Fog
- Multitexturing

These are the two subclasses:

- GLKReflectionMap: Turns an object into a shiny toy
- GLKSkyboxEffect: Creates a 360-degree panorama

Both the reflection and skybox are standard effects used often in games and elsewhere. The skybox is very useful in flight simulators so you can look anywhere and be immersed in the artificial world.

GLKReflectionMap

Sometimes called *environment mapping*, reflection mapping is used to make an object look like it is made out of the most polished metal or glass. Because it is cool-looking and relatively easy, it is commonly found in games and elsewhere.

The reflection effect largely comes from having a fixed texture with some geometry moving or rotating underneath. That means the texture coordinates for the reflective surfaces will vary dynamically to counteract any motion the underlying object might have.

The texture most commonly used as the "environment" typically comes in the form of what's called a *cube map*. A cube map is simply a texture that can be subdivided into six squares and then reassembled in cube form around the reflecting object. Why a cube instead of a sphere? Less fuss, mainly, unless you like fuss and want a reflected texture as pure and distortion free as possible, but creating a cube texture is easier than a full 360-degree spherical texture.

Think of what a cube made out of paper would look like unfolded, using Hedly and his pals as the subject, as shown Figure 10-8.

Figure 10-8. *Hedly and his friends. They're a quiet bunch.*

So, how is a cube map used? First, get used to adding a third component to the texture coordinates, which specifies the face of the cube to use. Cube mapping makes a number of assumptions:

- The environment in the reflection very far away, so no parallax will be visible.

- The discontinuities are largely difficult to notice unless you know what you're looking for.

- The object cannot reflect any part of itself, unless you use some special image maps to compensate.

- You have a curved surface, because cube maps don't look right in a flat surface like a mirror.

To draw an object with a reflection/cube map, OpenGL will draw a ray from your viewpoint, bounce it off the target, and figure out where it hits on the cube map. The intersection point on the object specifies what texture coordinates are to be used, and the intersection on the cube map picks out what texel to use and which of the six faces was hit.

With that in mind, let's add cube map to the earth using GLKReflectionMapEffect.

You can start again with the standard template project and then add Planet.mm to it. You will need to modify both the view controller and the planet code. First, let's handle your setupGL() method in the view controller by substituting Listing 10-17 for the template code.

Listing 10-17. *Setting Up Your Reflection Map*

```
-(NSString *)imagePath:(NSString *)image
{
    return [[NSBundle mainBundle] pathForResource:image ofType:NULL];
}

- (void)setupGL
{
    int planetSize=50;


    NSArray *images = [[NSMutableArray alloc] initWithObjects:              //1
                    [self imagePath:@"hedly1.png"],
                    [self imagePath:@"hedly2.png"],
                    [self imagePath:@"hedly3.png"],
                    [self imagePath:@"hedly4.png"],
                    [self imagePath:@"hedly5.png"],
                    [self imagePath:@"hedly6.png"],
                    nil];

[EAGLContext setCurrentContext:self.context];

    NSDictionary *options=
    [NSDictionary dictionaryWithObjectsAndKeys:
    [NSNumber numberWithBool:YES],GLKTextureLoaderOriginBottomLeft,nil];

GLKTextureInfo *info=                                                       //2
    [GLKTextureLoader cubeMapWithContentsOfFiles:images options:options error:nil];


    self.effect = [[GLKReflectionMapEffect alloc] init];                   //3
    self.effect.light0.enabled = GL_TRUE;
    self.effect.light0.diffuseColor = GLKVector4Make(1.0f, 1.0f, 1.0f, 1.0f);
    self.effect.light0.specularColor = GLKVector4Make(1.0f, 1.0f, 1.0f, 1.0f);
    self.effect.material.shininess = 15.0f;
    self.effect.lightingType = GLKLightingTypePerPixel;


    self.effect.textureCubeMap.name =info.name;

    self.effect.light0.position=GLKVector4Make(-5.0f, 5.0f, 10.0f, 1.0);

    glEnable(GL_DEPTH_TEST);
```

```
    m_Eyeposition.x=0.0;
    m_Eyeposition.y=0.0;
    m_Eyeposition.z=5.0;

    m_Earth=[[Planet alloc] init:planetSize slices:planetSize        //4
    radius:.5f squash:1.0f
    textureFile:@"earth_light.png"];

    [m_Earth setPositionX:0.0 Y:0.0 Z:-3.0];
}
```

Bet you want to know what's going on here?

▓ The six-sided cube map is specified by creating an array of the six images in lines 1ff.

▓ Line 2 generates the `GLKTextureInfo` object and uses its cube map support to fetch the six needed files.

▓ The new effects object is allocated in line 3. After that, the lighting, materials, and position info are filled in, not at all unlike good old' OpenGL ES 1.

▓ And finally, the earth is generated just like before, in line 4.

Now we need the `update()` and `drawInRect()` methods, as shown in Listing 10-18.

Listing 10-18. *Updating the Effect*

```
- (void)update
{
    GLfloat scale=2.0;
    float aspect = fabsf(self.view.bounds.size.width / self.view.bounds.size.height);//1

    GLKMatrix4 projectionMatrix =
        GLKMatrix4MakePerspective(GLKMathDegreesToRadians(65.0f), aspect, 0.1f, 100.0f);

    self.effect.transform.projectionMatrix = projectionMatrix;

    GLKMatrix4 baseModelViewMatrix = GLKMatrix4Identity;
    GLKMatrix4 modelViewMatrix = GLKMatrix4Identity;

    baseModelViewMatrix = GLKMatrix4Scale(baseModelViewMatrix,scale,scale,scale);    //2
    baseModelViewMatrix = GLKMatrix4Rotate(baseModelViewMatrix, _rotation, 0.0, 0.5,
    0.0f);
    modelViewMatrix = GLKMatrix4MakeTranslation(0.0, 0.0, -3.0);
    modelViewMatrix = GLKMatrix4Multiply(modelViewMatrix, baseModelViewMatrix);

    self.effect.transform.modelviewMatrix = modelViewMatrix;
    self.effect.matrix=GLKMatrix3Identity;                                           //3

    _rotation+=0.03;
}
```

```
- (void)glkView:(GLKView *)view drawInRect:(CGRect)rect
{
    GLfloat gray=0.2;

    glClearColor(gray,gray,gray, 1.0f);
    glClear(GL_COLOR_BUFFER_BIT | GL_DEPTH_BUFFER_BIT);

    [self.effect prepareToDraw];                                    //4
    [m_Earth execute:self.effect];
}
```

In the **update()** function, you'll see how we now need to rely on the matrixy functions from the new math library; there's no glRotatef() or glTranslatef(), glPushMatrix(), or glPopMatrix() in this universe.

▨ Lines 1ff specify the projection matrix, what would normally be given over to glFrustum() in the alternate universe of version 1.

▨ Line 2 and those following create the matrices we need for the transformations, ultimately assigning the final modelViewMatrix object to the transform field of the effect's own GLKEffectPropertyTransform object. GLKEffectPropertyTransform contains both the Modelview and normal matrix.

▨ Not only does the "effect" have its own transformation matrix, it can also have an additional matrix to handle specific components of that effect. In this case, line 3 highlights this extra matrix. The Modelview matrix is for the geometry of the effect, just like it is in version 1, but this new one can be used to transform other things. In this case, it could be used to rotate the cube map. Setting it to the identity keeps the cube map static, letting just the earth model rotate.

▨ When ready, call the prepareToDraw() method of the effect's class, and it will apply the new settings, after which you may render the object itself, with the results shown in Figure 10-9.

Figure 10-9. *Reflection mapping the earth*

For complicated objects such as the earth model, you would be better off using a more simple cube map. The most basic ones typically would show a horizon, ground, and sky, usually produced by different gradients.

Summary

In this final chapter, you learned a little about OpenGL ES 2, the programmable pipeline version of ES; learned how and where shaders fit it in; and used them to add some extra detail to the earth. (For extra credit, try porting the rest of the simulator to version 2.) The final exercise used the OpenGL ES 2–exclusive GLKit effects objects to create a cube map and a shiny earth, rounding out the GLKit introduction. I advise watching the superb presentation of the GLKit by Apple from the 2011-WWDC . iTunes has all of the talks online.

Throughout this book, you've learned basic 3D theory, both in the math involved and in the overall principles. I'd like to think it's given you a basic understanding of the topic, even knowing that the book could be many times larger, considering that we've barely touched 3D graphics.

The Khronos Group, the keepers of all things officially OpenGL, has published several extensive books on the subject. Affectionately known by the color of their covers, there's the Red Book (the official programming guide), the Blue Book, (tutorials and reference), the Orange Book (shading language), the Green Book (Open GL on the Mac), and the Sort-of-Purplish Book (OpenGL ES 2). There are also numerous other third-party books that get much deeper than I've been able to go. Likewise, there are many web sites dedicated to OpenGL tutorials; `nehe.gamedev.net` is by far one of the best with nearly 50 different tutorials as of this writing.

And as you're going over the work of other authors, be it from other books or on the web, just remember that this book is the one that gave you the sun, the earth, and the stars. Not many others can claim that.

Index

Numbers and Special Characters

CPSIA information can be obtained at www.ICGtesting.com
Printed in the USA
LVOW051207221211

260635LV00011B/4/P